Gerard Manley Hopkins

Twayne's English Authors Series

Herbert Sussman, Editor

Northeastern University

TEAS 332

GERARD MANLEY HOPKINS
(Credit: Humanities Research Center, The University of Texas at Austin)

Gerard Manley Hopkins

By Jerome Bump

University of Texas at Austin

Twayne Publishers • *Boston*

Gerard Manley Hopkins

Jerome Bump

Copyright © 1982 by G. K. Hall & Company
Published by Twayne Publishers
A Division of G. K. Hall & Company
70 Lincoln Street
Boston, Massachusetts 02111

Book production by Marne B. Sultz

Book design by Barbara Anderson

Printed on permanent/durable acid-free
paper and bound in The United States
of America.

Library of Congress Cataloging in Publication Data

Bump, Jerome.
   Gerard Manley Hopkins.

   (Twayne's English authors series: TEAS 332)
   Bibliography: p. 210
   Includes index.
   1. Hopkins, Gerard Manley, 1844–1889—Criticism and
interpretation.   I. Title.   II. Series.
PR4803.H44Z597   821'.8   81–20067
ISBN 0–8057–6819–X   AACR2

For Barbara

Contents

About the Author

Jerome Bump's essays on Hopkins have appeared in *ELH*, *Bucknell Review*, *Thought*, *Georgia Review*, *Renascence*, *Victorian Poetry*, *Texas Quarterly*, *Library Chronicle*, *Victorian Newsletter*, *Hopkins Quarterly*, *Cahiers Victoriens et Edouardiens*, and two anthologies. He is also the author of the Hopkins entry in the Victorian Poets volume of the *Dictionary of Literary Biography*. He has delivered papers on Hopkins at meetings of the Modern Language Association, the American Academy of Religion, the Philological Association of the Pacific Coast, the Northeast Modern Language Association, the College Conference of Teachers of English, the Sixth International Patristic, Medieval, and Renaissance Conference, and the South Central Modern Language Association. He has also reviewed books on Hopkins for *JEGP*, *Comparative Literature*, *Hopkins Quarterly*, and *Western Humanities Review*.

Jerome Bump was born near Pine River, Minnesota. He graduated *summa cum laude* from the University of Minnesota, and received his graduate degrees from the University of California at Berkeley, where he was a Woodrow Wilson Fellow. He has taught at the University of Texas at Austin since 1970, with the exception of 1974–1975 which he spent at Oxford researching Hopkins with the assistance of a Fellowship from the National Endowment for the Humanities. He is a member of the advisory board of the *Hopkins Quarterly*, the editorial board of *Texas Studies in Language and Literature* and of the Board of Scholars of the International Hopkins Association. He is also the author of the annual review of Hopkins scholarship in *Victorian Poetry*.

Preface

This is primarily an introduction to Gerard Manley Hopkins's contribution to our civilization. Thus room for original scholarship is limited, but I attempt, whenever possible, at least to suggest new materials, emphases, and approaches which could advance our understanding of Hopkins's life and art.

I have tried specifically to include as many unpublished or relatively inaccessible primary sources as possible. The book opens with a virtually unknown photograph of Hopkins at age thirty, for instance, and includes two of his drawings rarely seen before. I have also incorporated accounts of two recently discovered letters, one from Hopkins to his brother Everard in 1885 (cited in chapter 4) and another to his sister Grace in 1883 (examined in chapter 5). These materials are samples of what is available in the Harry Ransom Humanities Research Center of the University of Texas. I also refer to various unpublished manuscripts at Campion Hall and Pusey House, Oxford, as well as to rare books in the British Library such as *Pietas Metrica* and *The Teaching of the Types*.

In order both to provide a broad survey of Hopkins's art and thought and suggest a new emphasis in Hopkins scholarship, I ask the reader to consider Robert Lowell's description of Hopkins as "probably the finest of English poets of nature."[1] Nature is obviously one of the two or three dominant themes of his poetry, yet not one of the forty books on Hopkins to date has focused on this aspect of his achievement. Therefore, I survey Hopkins's response to nature throughout his career, and I include both an account of *The Wreck of the Deutschland* as a response to the "sublime" and a long chapter on Hopkins's famous 1877 sonnets on nature.

Another important but relatively neglected aspect of Hopkins's art is his use of metaphors and verbal echoes to create an "underthought" of allusion in his poems. This is of special significance because of the general Victorian fascination with biblical "types," only now being recognized in scholarship. The typological approach is in fact particularly appropriate for an introduction such as this. The four levels of medieval biblical criticism help us to organize and assimilate the extraordinarily varied critical responses to "The Windhover," for instance. Typological readings can also revive interest in neglected poems such as "Rosa Mystica" and Hopkins's spy soliloquy.

Hopkins's love of typology is only one expression of his medievalism, moreover. This essential but relatively unexplored dimension of his poetry illuminates his famous late sonnets of desolation, as well as such forgotten poems as "Easter Communion" and "For a Picture of St. Dorothea." Focusing on the medieval origins of Hopkins's thought and art enables us to perceive his poetry of the 1860s and 1880s as unified by a recurrent focus on the temptation of *acedia,* one of the seven deadly sins. *Acedia* is characterized by the same syndrome of emotions found in the sonnets of desolation: sorrow, impotence, exile, estrangement, despair, the death wish, and, finally, wrestling with thoughts of suicide. Because of Petrarch's secularization of *acedia,* moreover, a poem such as Hopkins's "No worst, there is none" may also be read as an expression of that *melancholia* of modern humanism (so obvious in our literature of *ennui* and estrangement) which has led so many modern writers to suicide. This is but one of many important contemporary issues addressed by the dialectic between the modern and the medieval in Hopkins's poetry.

A variety of other approaches to Hopkins which open up his art to students and deserve more attention are also suggested, however briefly, such as his revolt against dualism; his concept of providence; the metaphysical significance of his word-music; the genre of his journals; the relationship between his poetry and science; his affinities with continental romanticism; the complexity of his relationship with Pater; and the influences on him of Dante, Savonarola, Keats, his father, his brother Arthur, John Keble, E. B. Pusey, and Christina Rossetti. More topics which introduce important aspects of Hopkins's achievement came to mind but had to be neglected in what remains, after all, only a brief introduction to one of the most fascinating masters of our language.

Hopkins's life, it must be admitted, is on the surface not as spectacular as his art, however. His was essentially a "world without event," as he put it in "St. Alphonsus Rodriguez." Virtually unknown in his day, even within the Society of Jesus, his audience consisted primarily of his own family and three other writers: Robert Bridges, Richard Watson Dixon, and Coventry Patmore. Because the great dramas of his life were internal, his art remains the best biography of his "war within." Thus, after a detailed chronology of the basic facts and turning points in his life and an initial chapter on his family and childhood, I incorporate the rest of the biographical information in the discussion of the relevant poems, primarily in chapters 3, 6, and 7.

Jerome Bump

University of Texas at Austin

Acknowledgments

I would like to acknowledge the assistance of all who made this book possible, including all the students and scholars with whom I discussed Hopkins, as well as my predecessors in the world of Hopkins and Victorian scholarship generally whose works inspired this one. The number and range of my debts to my contemporaries and precursors are only suggested by those explicitly cited in the notes. I would like to thank especially those who have read various sections and early versions of this book and offered their comments and advice, particularly my teachers, Avrom Fleishman, Alex Zwerdling, Hugh Richmond, and U. C. Knoepflmacher; my colleagues at the University of Texas, David DeLaura, R. J. Kaufmann, Clarence Cline, John P. Farrell, Walter Reed, William Scheick, James Wimsatt, Charles Rossman, and Juan Lopez-Morillas; and my colleagues elsewhere, J. Hillis Miller, Wendell Stacy Johnson, James Finn Cotter, Alison Sulloway, R. K. R. Thornton, Robert Boyle, Thomas M. Harwell, George Landow, Howard Fulweiler, and Herbert Sussman.

In addition, I want to express my gratitude to the National Endowment for the Humanities, the University of Texas at Austin, and the University of California at Berkeley for fellowships which facilitated the research upon which this book is based. I also want to thank the English Province of the Society of Jesus not only for granting permission to quote Hopkins's writing and reproduce his drawings but for their unfailing assistance and cooperation, especially at St. Bueno's College, Wales, and Campion Hall, Oxford. I am also grateful to Oxford University for its hospitality, paticularly that of Bernard Richards of Brasenose, Peter Levi of Campion Hall, Dennis Burden of Trinity, and Larzer Ziff of Exeter. And of course I have relied on the assistance of the staffs of the libraries where I worked, especially those at Campion Hall, Balliol College, Pusey House, and the Bodleian in Oxford; the British Library; and the

Harry Ransom Humanities Research Center of the University of Texas.

I need to acknowledge as well the assistance of the editors of the journals and anthologies where more detailed accounts of portions of this book first appeared. An earlier version of part of chapter 1 was published in the anthology, *All My Eyes See* (1975). Parts of chapter 2 appeared in the *Texas Quarterly* 16 (1973) and *Victorian Poetry* 12 (1974). Portions of chapter 3 were published in *Thought* 50 (1975) and the *Victorian Newsletter,* no. 50 (1976) and no. 57 (1980). Some of chapter 4 appeared in the "Literature, Arts, and Religion" issue of the *Bucknell Review* (1981), the *Victorian Newsletter,* no. 59 (1981), and *Victorian Poetry* 15 (1977). Parts of chapter 5 appeared in *ELH* 41 (1974), the *Hopkins Quarterly* 4 (1977), and *Renascence* 31 (1979). Portions of chapter 6 appeared in the *Georgia Review* 28 (1974), *Cahiers Victoriens et Edouardiens,* no. 7 (1978), and in the collection, *Studies in Relevance* (1973).

Finally, I would like to thank Herbert Sussman for inviting me to contribute to this series, and my wife and daughters for making it possible for me to do so.

Chronology

1844   Gerard Manley Hopkins born July 28, in Stratford, Essex.

1852   Family moves to Hampstead, a northern London suburb.

1854   Boarder at Cholmeley Grammar School, Highgate, north of London.

1862   Writes "A Vision of the Mermaids" and "Il Mystico."

1863   February 14, "Winter with the Gulf Stream" published in *Once a Week*. April, attends Balliol College, Oxford, on a Classical Exhibition scholarship.

1864   Meets Christina Rossetti. Writes "Heaven-Haven" and "A Voice from the World."

1865   "Barnfloor and Winepress" published in *The Union Review*. Writes "Easter Communion," "The Alchemist in the City," and "See how Spring opens." Begins correspondence with Robert Bridges, his classmate at Oxford.

1866   January, writes "The Habit of Perfection." July, decides to become a Catholic; September, visits Newman in Birmingham; October, received by Newman into the Catholic Church.

1867   June, graduates from Oxford with a Double-First in "Greats." September, begins teaching classics at Newman's Oratory in Birmingham.

1868   May, resolves to become a priest, burns his poems, and writes only two occasional poems in the next seven years. September, begins his Novitiate in the Society of Jesus at Manresa House, Roehampton.

1870   Begins his Philosophical Studies at St. Mary's Hall, Stonyhurst.

1872   Discovers Duns Scotus.

1873   Begins year-long appointment as teacher of "Rhetoric" at Roehampton.

1874   Begins Theological Studies at St. Beuno's College, Wales.

1875   Begins *The Wreck of the Deutschland.*

1876   *The Wreck of the Deutschland* is rejected by *The Month.*

1877   Writes his great nature sonnets. September, ordained a priest; October, begins duties as subminister and teacher at Mount St. Mary's College, Chesterfield.

1878   April, begins teaching classics at Stonyhurst College; June, initiates correspondence with Richard Watson Dixon, his teacher at Highgate; July, begins as curate at the Jesuit church in Mount Street, London; December, begins as curate at St. Aloysius's Church, Oxford; writes "The May Magnificat."

1879   Writes "Binsey Poplars," "Duns Scotus's Oxford," and "Henry Purcell." October, on temporary staff as curate at St. Joseph's, Bedford Leigh; December, begins as select preacher at St. Francis Xavier's, Liverpool.

1880   Writes "Felix Randal."

1881   Writes "Spring and Fall"; April, sends three sonnets to Hall Caine, a friend of Rossetti's, for publication in a sonnet anthology but all are rejected. September, on temporary staff at St. Joseph's, Glasgow. October, begins Long Retreat (Third Year Novitiate) at Roehampton.

1882   September, begins as teacher of classics at Stonyhurst College. Writes "Ribblesdale" and "The Leaden Echo and the Golden Echo."

1883   Writes "The Blessed Virgin compared to the Air we Breathe." Meets and begins correspondence with the famous Catholic poet, Coventry Patmore.

1884   Begins as Fellow in Classics at the Royal University of Ireland and Professor of Greek at University College, Dublin. Writes "Spelt from Sibyl's Leaves."

1885   Writes "Carrion Comfort," "No worst, there is none," and other sonnets of desolation.

1887   Writes "Harry Ploughman" and "Tom's Garland."

1888   Writes "That Nature is a Heraclitean Fire" and "St. Alphonsus Rodriguez."

1889   Writes "Thou art indeed just," "The shepherd's brow," and "To R.B." June 8, dies of typhoid fever; buried in the Jesuit plot at Glasnevin cemetery, Dublin.

1918   The first edition of his *Poems*, edited by Robert Bridges, is published.

Chapter One

The Impressionable Years

The highly idiosyncratic style which made it difficult for Hopkins's contemporaries to accept his poetry continues to baffle biographers attempting to account for his radical creativity, partly because the same forces of romanticism that encouraged Hopkins to de-emphasize his debts to other writers led theorists to represent creativity as a private, unique, almost miraculous inspiration of a very individualistic person, usually a rebel against society.

However, one of Hopkins's scientific contemporaries, Francis Galton, believed that human creativity could be explained genetically. Focusing on poets and other eminent people in his famous book, *Hereditary Genius*, he researched relationships among generations, families, and other "social agencies," including literary "schools" and rivalries.[1] Most scientists now recognize that his basic assumption was wrong: the rise of man has been due not so much to genetic as to exogenetic, that is, cultural evolution. Nevertheless, if we expand his approach to include the interpersonal influences represented by certain "social agencies" and "schools," we can begin to shed some light on human creativity, even that of a poet so original that Galton and his contemporaries could not comprehend him.

The primary "social agencies" for Hopkins's artistic creativity were his family (especially his father and his brother Arthur), Highgate school (particularly Richard Watson Dixon), Oxford (Walter Pater, Robert Bridges, E. B. Pusey, H. P. Liddon, etc.), friends of the family such as Christina and Maria Rossetti, and the "school" of Keats and Dante in Victorian poetry known as the Pre-Raphaelites, the school which produced mentors and rivals for Hopkins ranging from Christina Rossetti to A. C. Swinburne.

Hopkins's Family

As figure 1 reveals, Hopkins's extended family constituted a social environment that made the commitment of an eldest son to religion, language, and art not only possible, but highly probable. His mother, Kate Smith Hopkins (1821–1920), was a devout High Church Anglican who brought up her children to be religious. Hopkins read from the New Testament daily at school, for instance, to fulfill a promise he made to her. The daughter of a London physician, she was better educated than most Victorian women, and was particularly fond of music and of reading, especially German philosophy and literature, the novels of Dickens, and eventually her eldest son's poetry.

Her sister Maria taught drawing to Gerard. As her grandson, Launcelot Sieveking, describes it: "she and her nephew often sat side by side sketching in the woods and lanes around Epsom and Croydon," and he adds that some of her sketches "are quite startlingly like those of Gerard Manley that have survived."[2] Drawings originally executed as headings on letters from her home, Blunt House, Croydon, to Hopkins's mother and father reveal the kind of precise, detailed drawing that Gerard was taught. The influence of Maria (Smith) Giberne on her nephew can be seen by comparing these letter headings with Hopkins's sketch, *Dandelion, Hemlock, and Ivy,* which he made at Blunt House, Croydon.[3] The focus on precision and detail in these sketches was no doubt also influenced by the new invention of photography: Maria's husband, George Giberne (1797–1876), was an excellent sketcher who took up photography in 1849, making his own camera and plates. His photographs of medieval architecture fascinated his nephew, and a number of his photographs of Gerard survive to this day.

Another of Gerard's maternal uncles, Edward Smith (1833–1900), sustained this emphasis on the visual arts. He began as a lawyer but soon made painting his profession. In addition, Richard James Lane (1800–1872), Gerard's great uncle on his mother's side, was an engraver and lithographer who exhibited at the Royal Academy. His daughters Clara and Eliza (or Emily) were also artists and they exhibited at the Society of Female Artists. Galton would have made much of the fact, moreover, that Lane's mother was Gainsborough's

FIGURE 1

Some of Gerard Manley Hopkins' Relations
noted for their Artistic, Literary, or Religious Sensibilities

1. On His Mother's Side

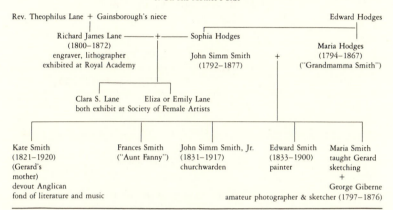

2. On His Father's Side

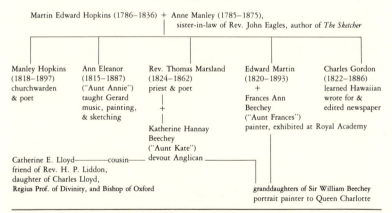

3. Gerard's Brothers & Sisters

Gerard	Cyril	Arthur	Milicent	Lionel	Kate	Grace	Everard
(1844–1889)	(1846–1932)	(1847–1930)	(1849–1946)	(1854–1952)	(1856–1933)	(1857–1945)	(1860–1928)
priest & poet		illustrator, painter, exhibited at Royal Academy	Anglican nun	expert on languages	devout Anglican & sketcher	devout Anglican & musician	illustrator, painter

niece. If Lane and Edward Smith contributed to Gerard's artistic heritage, another maternal uncle, John Simm Smith Jr. (1831–1917), sustained the religious tradition which Gerard's mother passed on to him: he was a churchwarden at St. Peter's, Croydon, known for forty years for his strength, consistency, and unfailing charity.

Hopkins's father, Manley, was also surrounded by artistic and religious relations. At the Grove, Stratford, Essex, where Gerard was born, he provided a home not only for his own family but also for his mother, his sister Anne Eleanor, and, for a while, for his brothers Charles and Thomas. Anne Eleanor (1815–87), called "Aunt Annie" by her nephew Gerard, was a good sketcher and painter who tutored her nephew in those arts as well as history and music. G. F. Lahey describes the result of her coaching in music: Gerard's "correct ear and clear, sweet voice made him an easy and graceful master of the traditional English, Jacobean, and Irish airs. This love for music never left him, and years afterwards, in the Society of Jesus, he used often to appear at their musical entertainments to sing, like William Blake, the songs he had composed and put to music. All his life he was composing songs and melodies, and until he studied musical theory under Dr. R. P. Stewart in Dublin, he used to bring them home for his sister, Grace, to harmonize for him."[4]

Manley's brother, Thomas Marsland Hopkins (1824–62), on the other hand, represented that fusion of literature and religion that Manley himself was to pass on to his son. Thomas was perpetual curate at St. Saviour's, Paddington, and coauthor with Manley of *Pietas Metrica; Or, Nature Suggestive of God and Godliness* (1849), "By the Brothers Theophilus and Theophylact." The preface states, "Of the authorship of the present volume suffice it to say, that one of the writers ministers in the Temple; the other had admittance to the outer courts only. It is dedicated to the Church . . . By Two of Her Sons."[5] Thomas Marsland Hopkins's *Sermons* was published posthumously in 1864, but his *Pietas Metrica* provides the most important context for Gerard's poetry, as we shall see.

He was married to Katherine Beechey, called "Aunt Katie" by her nephew Gerard. Galton would have emphasized that she was the granddaughter of Sir William Beechey, portrait painter to Queen

Charlotte, but she was more important to Gerard as a representative of the religious tradition of his family. She was "very High Church," as they say.[6] Gerard saw her in Oxford in 1879 along with her cousin, Catherine E. Lloyd, a friend of Gerard's former confessor, H. P. Liddon. Catherine Lloyd helped Liddon with his biography of E. W. B. Pusey, another of the men Gerard admired at Oxford in his undergraduate days. She was the daughter of Charles Lloyd, Regius Professor of Divinity and bishop of Oxford (1827–29), who was an important influence on the High Church Tractarian movement which originally included not only Pusey and Liddon but also John Henry Newman, who later received Gerard into the Catholic Church.

Aunt Katie's sister, Frances Ann Beechey, referred to as "Aunt Frances" by her nephew Gerard, married his paternal uncle and godfather, Edward Martin Hopkins (1820–93). If her sister upheld the religious traditions of the Hopkins family, Aunt Frances sustained the artistic. She was a good painter famous in North America especially for her documentary paintings of the Canadian voyageurs. She was the only woman allowed on the "Red River Expedition" from Lake Superior to Winnipeg and four of her paintings of the expedition now hang in Archives Hall in Ottawa. Gerard saw her in London as early as 1865, and after 1870, when Edward Hopkins retired from the Hudson's Bay Company, she exhibited at the Royal Academy.

Manley Hopkins's other brother, Charles Gordon (1822–86), traveled even farther from home, emigrating to Hawaii where he held a number of government posts. Inheriting the Hopkins's gift for languages and literature, he learned Hawaiian and edited and contributed to the official government paper, the *Polynesian*. In 1856 he helped his brother Manley become consul-general for Hawaii in London, and Manley in turn helped establish an Anglican bishop and mission in Honolulu.

In 1844, the year of Gerard's birth, Manley Hopkins (1818–97) founded a marine insurance firm, now known as Manley Hopkins, Son and Cookes. It is no accident that shipwreck, one of their perennial concerns, was also the subject of Gerard's most ambitious poem, *The Wreck of the Deutschland* (1875). Nor can the emphasis on religion in that poem be attributed solely to the mother's influence. Manley was a devout High Church Anglican and churchwarden of St. John's in Hampstead, where he taught Sunday school.

He also loved music and literature, passing on his fondness for puns and wordplay to his sons Gerard and Lionel and his love for poetry to Gerard especially. In 1843 he published *A Philosopher's Stone and Other Poems*; in 1849, *Pietas Metrica*; in 1857, *A Handbook of Average,* which became a classic in its field; in 1862, *Hawaii: an historical account of the Sandwich Islands*, with a preface by Samuel Wilberforce, bishop of Oxford; in 1867, *A Manual of Marine Insurance*; in 1873, *The Port of Refuge, or advice and instructions to the Master-Mariner in situations of doubt, difficulty, and danger*; in 1887 *The Cardinal Numbers* which included a contribution by his son Gerard; and in 1892, *Spicilegium Poeticum, A Gathering of Verses by Manley Hopkins.* He also reviewed poetry for the *Times*, contributed to the *Polynesian,* and wrote a novel and an essay on Longfellow (both unpublished).

Given the backgrounds of their father and mother, aunts and uncles, it is hardly surprising that most of the Hopkins children were, like Gerard, also interested in art, language, and religion. Gerard's sister Milicent (1849–1946), for instance, was preoccupied with music at first but eventually became an "out-sister" of All Saints' Home, an Anglican sisterhood founded in London in 1851. The label Gerard later used to describe her—"given to Puseyism"[7]— could have as easily been applied to himself in his early Oxford years. All Saints kept Milicent and the Hopkins family in touch with Maria Rossetti who became a full member of the sisterhood in 1873. Like Gerard, Milicent herself finally became a religious. She took the sister's habit in 1878, and eventually died at All Saints Convent in St. Albans.

Like Milicent and their mother, both of Hopkins's other sisters, Kate and Grace, remained devout High Church Anglicans. Kate (1856–1933) shared Gerard's love of language, humor, and sketching; she was the one who helped Robert Bridges publish the first edition of Gerard's poems in 1918. His youngest sister, Grace (1857–1945), set some of Gerard's poems to music and composed accompaniments for some of his melodies for poems by Robert Bridges and Richard Watson Dixon.

Love of language was most evident in Gerard's brother Lionel (1854–1952) who was top of the senior division of Modern School at Winchester where he earned a reputation for "thoughtful and thorough" work in French and German (*J,* 309). He became an interpreter in the British Consular Service in China and eventually consul-general in Tientsin. He was also a world-famous expert on the archaic scripts of the Chinese language and on colloquial Chinese. Like his father and his brother Gerard he loved puns, jokes, parodies, and all kinds of wordplay.

Gerard's brother Arthur (1847–1930), on the other hand, was an excellent sketcher who became a professional illustrator and artist. He illustrated Hardy's *Return of the Native,* for instance, was a member of the Royal Water-Colour Society, and exhibited at the Royal Academy. The youngest brother, Everard (1860–1928), followed in his footsteps. He held the Slade Scholarship for his entire time at the Slade School of Art and he too became a professional illustrator and cartoonist for many newspapers and periodicals. He also exhibited watercolors and pastels in London. Both Everard and Arthur were regular contributors to *Punch* and shared Gerard's admiration for the paintings of John Everett Millais, the most "photographic" of the Pre-Raphaelite painters. A comparison of Gerard's sketches with Arthur's and his poems with his father's poetry will suggest the contributions made by his family to Gerard's creativity.

Father and Son

Gerard transcribed eleven of the poems from his father's first volume, *A Philosopher's Stone,* into his Oxford notebooks. One of his father's favorite subjects, nature, soon became his as well. In "Sonnet," for instance, the father expressed a Keatsian dismay over science's threat to a magical or imaginative response to nature:

> We ask away the poesy of flowers,
> And steal by science from skies, rocks, and birds,
> The magic that once pleased our simple sires,—
> And to light wisdom's light, we oft quench fancy's fires.[8]

Manley Hopkins's desire to preserve a Wordsworthian love of nature in his children is still more evident in his "To a Beautiful Child":

> . . . *thy* book
> Is cliff, and wood, and foaming waterfall;
> Thy playmates—the wild sheep and birds that call
> Hoarse to the storm;—thy sport is with the storm
> To wrestle;—and thy piety to stand
> Musing on things create, and their Creator's hand!

This was a remarkably prophetic poem for Manley Hopkins's first "beautiful child," born only a year after this poem was published. The phrase, "And birds that call / Hoarse to the storm," invites comparison with the son's images of the windhover rebuffing the big wind in "The Windhover" (1877) and the great stormfowl at the conclusion of "Henry Purcell" (1879). The father's prophecy, "thy sport is with the storm / To wrestle" is certainly fulfilled in Gerard's poems, *The Wreck of The Deutschland* and "The Loss of the *Eurydice*" (1878). These two shipwreck poems, replete with spiritual instruction for those in doubt and danger, also became the son's poetic and religious counterparts to his father's volume, *The Port of Refuge, or advice and instructions to the Master-Mariner in situations of doubt, difficulty, and danger.*

The son's awareness of the gentle beauty of a singing bird, on the other hand, was increased by a poem such as "A Bird Singing in a Narrow Street," one of the eleven poems from *The Philosopher's Stone* he copied into his notebook:

> Bold-hearted captive! who thy song canst trill
> So blithely in thy darksome cage,—and fill
>   The throbbing air around
>   With such mellifluous sound,
> Making our bosoms to thy cadence thrill!
>   Hast thou forgot
> All thou hast lost?—the fields, the open sky,
> The rising sun, the moon's pale majesty;—
> The leafy bower, where thy airy nest
> Was hung; and her, thy mate, once so caressed!

This theme of the bird confined recurs most obviously in the son's "The Caged Skylark" (1877), but may be detected even in his comments on the imprisoning narrowness of urban civilization in his letters. The son also responded to his father's image of a bird filling the "throbbing air" with sound and "making our bosoms to thy cadence thrill" in "The Nightingale" (1866):

> For he began at once and shook
> My head to hear. He might have strung
> A row of ripples in the brook,
>   So forcibly he sung,
> The mist upon the leaves have strewed,
> And danced the balls of dew that stood
> In acres all above the wood.

This particular note is heard again in Gerard's "Spring" (1877): "and thrush / Through the echoing timber does so rinse and wring / The ear, it strikes like lightnings to hear him sing." The father's attempt to represent a bird's experience of "the fields, the open sky, / The rising sun, the moon's pale majesty;— / The leafy bower, where the airy nest is hung" was also one of the inspirations of the son's lengthy account of a lark's gliding beneath clouds, its aerial view of the fields below, and its proximity to a rainbow in "Il Mystico" (1862) as well as the son's attempt actually to enter into a lark's existence and express its essence mimically in "The Wood-lark" (1876).

The father continued to influence his son's response to nature even long after Gerard left home to take his place in the world. In 1879, for instance, Hopkins wrote to Bridges, "I enclose some lines by my father called forth by the proposal to fell the trees in Well Walk (where Keats and other interesting people lived) and printed in some local paper."[9] Surely it is no coincidence that it was only two months later that Gerard composed "Binsey Poplars" to commemorate the felling of a grove of trees near Oxford.

In addition to specific inspirations and rivalries such as these, the father communicated to his son a sense of nature as a book written by God which leads its readers to thoughtful contemplation of Him, a theme particularly evident in Manley's next book of poems, *Pietas*

Metrica. Consequently, Gerard went on to write poems which were some of the best expressions not only of the romantic approach to nature but also the older tradition of explicitly religious nature poetry.

Pietas Metrica is clearly devoted to that particular marriage of nature and religion so characteristic of Gerard's poetry. It is also valuable as a model of the norm of contemporary religious nature poetry which Hopkins was trying both to sustain and surpass. The aims of the authors, his father and uncle, became his own: "It was the design of the writers of this volume to blend together two of man's best things, Religion and Poetry. They aimed at binding with another tie the feeling of piety with external nature and our daily thoughts. The books of Nature and Revelation have been laid side by side and read together."[10]

The most joyous synchronic reading of the Bible and the Book of Nature was the hymn of creation, a traditional genre inspired by Psalm 148. Poems of Gerard's such as "God's Grandeur" (1877), "Pied Beauty" (1877), "Hurrahing in Harvest" (1877), and "Easter" (1866) derive from this genre. Many critics would ascribe a conventional line such as "Flowers do ope their heavenward eyes" in "Easter," for instance, to Hopkins's love for the poetry of George Herbert but the representation of a flower "breathing up to heaven / The incense of her prayer" like a "natural altar" in "The Fraxinella" in *Pietas Metrica* reveals that it is just as appropriate to look to contemporary poetry for a context for Hopkins's poems as it is to look back to the metaphysical poets. Indeed, in some cases, it may be more appropriate. Though Herbert's "The Flower" is a famous example of a flower straining toward heaven, Herbert employs no satellite imagery of opening eyes; in fact he only twice used the word "ope" in all of his poems, neither time referring to flowers, and he never used the adjective "heavenward."

The personification of Earth in Hopkins's "Easter," moreover— "Earth throws Winter's robes way. / Decks herself for Easter Day"— recalls the personification of Nature evident in "Catholic Truth" in *Pietas Metrica:*

> "Earth, sea, and sky proclaim the holy tuth,
> The universe, a temple open wide,
> Where nature, priestess sacred, from her youth
> For ever sings the song beatified.

A reader of Hopkins's poetry familiar with contemporary creation hymns like this would expect, moreover, the song rhythm in which Hopkins's version of these ideas is expressed in the third stanza of his "Easter" because in this genre nature is usually represented as more faithfully singing God's praise than mankind. Hopkins extends the rhythm to include man in the fourth stanza of "Easter" because ultimately mankind joins in the song in related hymns in this genre such as Christina Rossetti's "And there was no more Sea" in which all possible voices are united "in oneness of contentment offering praise."

Contemporary readers of poems like "Easter" also knew that although man and nature are ultimately bound by Love in one hymn of creation, nature is traditionally represented not only as more consistently heeding the commandment to song which concludes Hopkins's "Easter," but also as best fulfilling the demand of his first stanza for a plenitude of offerings. "Where are the Nine?" in *Pietas Metrica* develops this concept of nature's unstinted offering and points the traditional contrast between man and nature implicit in the first stanza of "Easter":

> And is it so that Nature stints her praise,
> With niggard thanks makes offering to her God?
> . . . .
> No, Nature is not backward, she declares
> Each blessing as it comes, and owns her Lord,
> She is no miser of her thanks, she spares
> No praise, due to Heaven, beloved adored.

For Hopkins as for his immediate precursors man seemed "backward" in comparison with nature, especially in "God's Grandeur," "Spring," "In the Valley of the Elwy" (1877), "The Sea and the Skylark" (1877), "Binsey Poplars," "Duns Scotus's Oxford" (1879), and "Ribblesdale" (1882). Hopkins also discovered to his despair the truth of the final complaint of "Where are the Nine?":

>   Alas for man! day after day may rise,
>   Night after night, may shade his thankless head,
>   He sees no God in the bright, morning skies
>   He sings no praises from his guarded bed.

This use of the hymn of creation to teach a moral lesson is one of the traditional sources of that didacticism which pervades Hopkins's later nature poetry. Unlike the romantics, many Victorians thought of Nature as another book of Revelation to be used for the same practical ends as the Bible: to inculcate lessons in the religious life. As the statement in its preface about placing the books of Nature and Revelation side by side suggests, *Pietas Metrica* is an excellent illustration of his tradition. While the Wordsworthian influence in the volume is occasionally implicit in poems like "Love," the sermonical aim is almost always explicit, as in the title, "Autumnal Lessons."

Flowers were especially popular for purposes of instruction, their function in Hopkins's "Easter." The flowers in "Catholic Truth," for example, are "All telling the same truth; their simple creed," and the author of "The Fraxinella" sighs, with the exclamation so characteristic of Hopkins, "Ah! could our hearts / Read thoughtful lessons from thy modest leaves." When we place Hopkins's nature poetry in this tradition we not only perceive the contemporary precedents for the homilies which conclude so many of his nature poems, we also begin to discern some of the distinguishing features of his didacticism. Hopkins's commands strike us as more direct and imperative, and we discover that his religious poetry was unusually proselytical before he became a Catholic, and long before he became a Jesuit.

This moral response to nature was not the only literary theme the father passed on to his son. Romantic love of childhood as well as nature is evident in Manley's "To a Beautiful Child" and "The Nursery Window," and this Wordsworthian theme of childhood innocence is also stressed by his son in "Spring," "The Handsome Heart" (1879), and "The Bugler's First Communion" (1879). The father also composed straightforward religious poems such as his long poem on John the Baptist in *The Philosopher's Stone,* and his son soon surpassed his father in this category as well. Gerard's many poems about martyrs also recall his father's preoccupation with physical suffering in poems such as "The Grave-Digger" and "The Child's Dream."

The son's obsession with mortality in poems such as "Spring and Death" (no date), "Spring and Fall" (1880), and "The Leaden Echo" (1882) can also be linked to poems of his father's such as the sonnet, "All things grow old—grow old, decay and change," and "A Philosopher's Stone" which warns that "The withered crown will soon slide down / A skull all bleached and blent" and concludes in that didactic mode typical of a number of his son's religious poems:

> The Alchymists rare, are they who prepare
> For death ere life be done;
> And by study hard WITHIN THE CHURCHYARD
> IS FOUND THE PHILOSOPHER'S STONE.

Gerard also wrote a poem about an alchemist, "The Alchemist in the City" (1865), but this tone is captured best in the eleventh stanza of *The Wreck of the Deutschland.*

It was no doubt partly to escape contemplation of some of the more morbid details of his marine insurance business that Manley Hopkins cultivated a Wordsworthian love of nature. The example of Wordsworth's youth in nature, and the contrasting example of Coleridge's youth in the city, "Debarr'd from Nature's living images, / Compelled to be a life unto itself,"[11] encouraged Manley Hopkins to live in Hampstead rather than in London proper where he worked. He moved his family to Hampstead in 1852 and Gerard and his brother Cyril (1846–1932), the son who was to enter his father's business, were sent to live with relatives in the Hainault Forest where they spent the summer exploring and studying nature. When he returned to his family, Gerard found himself living near groves of lime and elm, many fine views, the garden where Keats composed his "Ode to a Nightingale" under a mulberry tree, and the heath celebrated in painting after painting by Constable. Hopkins obviously enjoyed living there: Cyril recalled that he was a fearless climber of trees, especially the lofty elm which stood in their garden.

At the age of ten, Gerard left the garden and his family home for Robert Cholmeley's boarding school at Highgate, a northern height of London less populous and more forested than Hampstead. Like Hampstead, it commanded a good view of the surrounding area and was associated with the memories of artists, including Marvell, Lamb, Keats, and De Quincey; the tomb, even the coffin, of Coleridge could be seen near the chapel when Hopkins was there. One of Hopkins's friends at Highgate was Coleridge's grandson, E. H. Coleridge, who became a biographer of Byron and named one of his sons after his friend, Gerard. Hopkins's affinity with him is suggested by "The Escorial" (1860), the earliest Hopkins poem extant. The description of the destruction of the Escorial by the sweeping rain and sobbing wind recalls Byron, but the allusions to Raphael, Titian, Velasquez, Rubens, and Claude, as well as to various styles of architecture, reveal Hopkins's desire to combine his love of poetry with his love of the visual arts.

Hopkins's own expertise in the visual arts was evident in the sketches of Bavarian peasants he produced when his father took him to southern Germany in 1860. Hopkins's sketches were a contribution to the family drawing exercises, which were usually devoted to nature. Their aim was generally what is known as the education of a gentleman or a lady. One of the key texts was the sixteenth-century *Book of the Courtier* by Castiglione, which emphasizes drawing as much as "writynge rhyme" and recommends it first of all as an exercise in natural theology: the "engine of the worlde" with its "Hylles, Dales, and Rivers" is "so decked with suche diverse trees, beawtifull flowres and herbes, a man maye saye it to be a noble and a great peincting, drawen with the hande of nature and of God: the whych, whoso can folow in myne opinion he is woorthye much commendacion."[12] The importance of drawing as a spiritual discipline in Hopkins's family is suggested by Hopkins's comments on some magazine illustrations by his brother Arthur: "my brother's pictures, as you say, are careless and do not aim high. . . . But, strange to say—and I shd. never even have suspected it if he had not quite simply told me—he has somehow in painting his pictures, though nothing that the pictures express, a high and quite religious aim" (*B*, 51).

The Book of the Courtier suggests other aims of the Hopkins family drawing exercises as well. Castiglione recommends drawing also because it requires "knowledge of manye thinges" and endows even the amateur with a new pleasure in realistic art and in reality itself. Indeed, Castiglione's emphasis on the human body reveals why Hopkins decided that professional painting was too "passionate" for one with a religious vocation, but Hopkins did not sacrifice drawings of nature after he became a Jesuit, presumably because that focus on miraculous detail which characterizes the Hopkins family sketches had a specifically religious sanction. Peacham's seventeenth-century *Compleat Gentleman* reinforced this emphasis: "the imitation of the surface of nature, by it as in a book of golden and rare-limned letters, the chief end of it, we read a continual lecture of the wisdom of the almighty Creator by beholding even in the feather of a peacock a miracle."[13] As we have seen, Hopkins's father, also an amateur sketcher, and his uncle Thomas, used similar language in the preface to their book of nature poetry, *Pietas Metrica*.

The Hopkins family drawings in fact embody most of the features that amateur drawing acquired over the years. In addition to a religious preoccupation with detail, Peacham recommends drawing to record sights seen in travels, obviously another motivation for sketching in the Hopkins family, as evidenced by Gerard's sketches of Bavarian peasants. While traveling, amateur sketchers often sought picturesque landscapes as well. Under the influence of French tutors, and later William Gilpin and George Beaumont, a decorative version of "picturesque" and "sublime" scenes or "prospects" became the goal of amateurs. This ideal was preserved in the Hopkins family circle by John Eagles's *The Sketcher*, the only drawing manual in their library as far as we know. The Reverend Eagles, who was Manley Hopkins's maternal uncle (*J*, 313), recommends the classical idealism of Gaspard Poussin and an elegant, expressive mode of pastoral. However, the fourth volume of John Ruskin's *Modern Painters* was published the same year as *The Sketcher*, and it promulgated important modifications of Eagles's ideal of amateur drawing. Ruskin's emphasis on objective, detailed truth to nature soon became evident in the sketches of the Hopkins family.

As we have seen, many aunts and uncles taught this kind of drawing to the Hopkins children, especially Ann Eleanor Hopkins who lived with them and tutored Gerard in drawing until he was twelve, and Maria and George Giberne. The children's first response to their training is exemplified in the headings of Gerard's boyhood letters to his brothers and sisters. The love of drawing at an early age recalls Ruskin, but the free play of fancy suggests other and happier influences, for Ruskin's own childhood was too isolated and disciplined for him to produce or enjoy this sort of thing. Gerard's letter to Milicent showing a beetle driving a locomotive reflects the influence of J. J. Grandville's illustrations for *Fables de la Fontaine* which, like *The Sketcher*, was to be found in the Hopkins library. The drawings in this book, like the headings of Gerard's letters to his brother Arthur, consist of elaborations of first letters of initial words. Gerard's letterheads also reveal affinities with Fred Walker's illustrations of the initial letters of words for Thackeray's *The Adventures of Philip* and with *The Bountiful Beetle* and other combinations of fanciful drawing and word play in Edward Lear's illustrated nonsense.

Two Brothers

Ruskinese representations of nature soon became the dominant genre of the children as well as the adults, however. The resemblance between the children's "Ruskinese" drawings is often quite striking. Take, for instance, the sketches produced on the family vacation of 1863 at Shanklin on the Isle of Wight. Gerard's study of a rock formation in the sea, *The Needles in the evening sun. July 23,* is matched by *The Needles (From the downs above, in an evening sun) July 23* apparently by his brother Arthur. Both sketches are of the same object at the same time from identical perspectives. The central representations of the rock formation are so alike they are almost facsimiles of each other; the only differences are in incidentals like the wave patterns and the addition of a few gulls in Gerard's drawing and a ship in Arthur's. Similarly, Gerard's *Shanklin. Manor Farm. July 19. Buds of the white lily* and Arthur's flower study, *July 21 1863* were drawn two days apart but focus on the same species and perhaps the same individual plant. Arthur waited until some of the buds had bloomed, however, and thus accepted the challenge of flowers as well as buds. The effect of these two sketches together is like time-lapse photography, with the focus and level of detail almost identical in each frame. Similarly, Gerard's *Longstone. Mottistone. July 23. 1863* is complemented by a sketch by his brother Arthur with the same title; both focus on the same stone but see it from different angles.

These drawings reveal that Gerard was in many respects no better at drawing than younger members of the same household who shared his goals and training. Indeed, it could be argued that in some ways he showed less promise. Arthur's *Shanklin Chine. August 4 1863*, for instance, is more fully and consistently detailed than Gerard's *Head of Shanklin Chine. August 4* and, because of its tondo circumscription, Arthur's gives an impression of greater plenitude, completeness, and unity. A comparison of Gerard's *In Lord Yarborough's Place. S. Lawrence. Undercliff. July 22* with Arthur's *Elm Tree in Lord Yarborough's Place St. Lawrence. Isle of Wight. July 22nd 1863* leads to the same conclusion. Again Gerard takes on a larger scene and fails to complete his sketch, while his brother selects a single tree and produces a more convincingly detailed and satisfying unity.

Hence it is difficult to accept as probable "fact" the idea that Gerard "may indeed have had more talent than his brother."[14] On the contrary, the differences between Gerard's sketches and Arthur's suggest a need to revise the accepted opinion that Gerard's "success was so great that had his career not been shaped by other incidents he would undoubtedly have adopted painting for his profession, as a future-drawing master strongly advised him to do."[15] Rather, it would appear that just as Lope de Vega's success in drama induced Cervantes to develop an alternative genre, Arthur Hopkins's superior sketching abilities encouraged his older brother to concentrate his energies on literary and religious creativity instead.

Although some of Gerard's drawings suggest that he could have achieved more detail if he had tried, it is apparent that, while he shared the motivations of his family for drawing, he soon developed specific aims and interests which differed significantly. In the case of the Shanklin Chine and Yarborough sketches Gerard apparently became less interested in a finished picture than in noting certain effects of shading and perspective in ravines. His letter from Shanklin to his friend, A. W. M. Baillie, of July 10, 1863, confirms that he soon developed special interests which he did not feel his family shared: "I venture to hope you will approve of some of the sketches in a Ruskinese point of view:—if you do not, who will, my sole congenial thinker on art? . . . I think I have told you that I have particular periods of admiration for particular things in Nature; for a certain time I am astonished at the beauty of a tree, shape, effect, etc., then when the passion, so to speak, has subsided, it is consigned to my treasury of explored beauty and acknowledged with admiration and interest ever after, while something new takes its place in my enthusiasm" (*F*, 202).

We will focus on how his sketches contributed to his artistic development in the next chapter, but some of the differences between his aims and those of his brother, Arthur, are fairly evident in the results of their sketching from the cliff in Freshwater Bay on the Isle of Wight in 1863. Focusing on an unusual, bridgelike rock formation in the sea, Arthur produced a memorable subject for a picturesque travel record: *Arched Rock. Freshwater Bay. (from the cliff) July 23. 1863.* Gerard, on the other hand, tried to reproduce the pattern made by the waves below; he wrote, "Note: the waves of the returning waves overlap, the angular space between is smooth but covered with a network of foam. The advancing wave already broken, and now only a mass of foam, upon the point of encountering the reflux of the former. Study from the cliff above. Freshwater Gate. July 23." Gerard's aims clearly diverged from Arthur's in at least two important ways: he became more interested in drawing as a means of visual research and more willing to supplement his visual art with verbal art.

In *Arched Rock* Arthur sought the single object which impresses itself on the memory of the traveler, while Gerard used his sketch to help him perceive, if not represent, a larger unity. These two sketches thus illustrate the meaning of "inscape," that conundrum of Hopkins's readers. A common misconception of the word is that it signifies simply a love of the unique particular, the unusual feature, the singular appearance, but that meaning fits *Arched Rock* better than Gerard's note on waves. Gerard lost interest in what was merely unique; as in the wave study he usually sought the distinctively *unifying* design, the "returning" or recurrent pattern, the *in*ternal "network" of structural relationships which clearly and unmistakably integrates or *scapes* an object or set of objects, and thus reveals the presence of integrating laws throughout nature and a divine unifying force or "stress" in this world. The suggestion of metaphysical significance is clearer in an 1874 note on waves: "The laps of running foam striking the sea-wall double on themselves and return in nearly the same order and shape in which they came. This is mechanical reflection and is the same as optical: indeed all nature is mechanical, but then it is not seen that mechanics contain that which is beyond mechanics" (*J*, 252).

Like his brother, Arthur was fascinated by waves and produced some excellent sketches of them, especially *1st September, '75, Breaking Waves, Whitby* and *Study of the back of a breaking wave seen from above and behind. Whitby. 30 Aug. '75*. These sketches are clearly superior to any of Gerard's drawings of waves in detail, finish, delicacy of shading, and illusion of motion. Likewise, Arthur's *Study of 'The Armed Knight' a reef at the Land's End. 4 Sept. '79* easily surpasses Gerard's 1863 sketches of rock formations as well as his own both in truth of detail and aesthetic development, and his *At Whitnash. Warwickshire 8 Sept. '77* reproduces more subtle and delicate effects of light and shade than Gerard ever achieved in his sketches of groves of trees.

Gerard did not even try to sketch the majesty and sublimity of an ocean wave as Arthur did, however. Characteristically, in his *Study from the cliff above* Gerard conveyed the motion of the waves with words. Phrases like "the advancing wave already broken, and now only a mass of foam" supply a scenario, a succession of events in time, to complement the spatial representation. Gerard was no doubt aware that Eagles recommended not only sea-pieces in *The Sketcher* but even shipwrecks. Eventually this advice, along with similar recommendations from Ruskin, and the family preoccupation with danger at sea, inspired Gerard's attempt to represent a shipwreck. Besides his father's publication of *Port of Refuge* in 1873, another factor may well have been Arthur's wave studies of August 30 and September 1, 1875. Only a few months later Gerard began his own response to the sea in the medium which was to make him famous: not painting, but poetry. If he had insisted on competing directly with his brother, he might well have gone on to become a draughtsman less well known than him. Adapting to the situation, however, his response to the sea, *The Wreck of the Deutschland,* was an even better fulfillment of the suggestion of his great-uncle, the Reverend John Eagles, that those who appreciate the sublime acquire "greater notions of the power and majesty of Him who maketh the clouds his chariot, and walketh upon the wings of the wind."[16]

Gerard's greater tendency to use words to supplement, translate, or replace visual impressions was also encouraged by Eagles, who placed great stress on the union of poetry and drawing. *The Sketcher* brought to a head that intimate collaboration of visual and verbal art which had become a tradition of amateur drawing, and Gerard obviously surpassed the other sketchers in his family in that tradition. Like Ruskin, he profited greatly from the Water-Colour Society's customary amalgamation of drawing and nature poetry—they exhibited works accompanied by poetic quotations and critics often described the "poetic" associations of their watercolors as well.

Hence if "the visual image, the vision of the painter, is everywhere predominant" in Hopkins's journal,[17] the essence of his creativity was verbal rather than visual, as the following account of a glacier reveals:

There are round one of the heights of the Jungfrau two ends or falls of a glacier. If you took the skin of a white tiger or the deep fell of some other animal and swung it tossing high in the air and then cast it out before you it would fall and so clasp and lap around anything in this way just as this glacier does and the fleece would part in the same rifts: you must suppose a lazuli under-flix to appear. The spraying out of one end I tried to catch but it would have taken hours: it is this which first made me think of a tiger-skin, and it ends in tongues and points like the tail and claws: indeed the ends of the glaciers are knotted like talons. (*J,* 174)

Hopkins had tried to "catch" the spraying out of one end of the glacier in three sketches inscribed *July 15, '68; July 15;* and *July 15, Little Scheidegg,* but he soon realized that he had relatively little talent for sketching. He could "have taken hours" and persisted, but instead he let his visual impression stimulate his linguistic creativity, specifically his extraordinary capacity for metaphor. His frustration in one genre only stimulated him to be truly creative in another, putting into practice that transference implied by the doctrine of *ut pictura poesis* which he so often defended in his early years. [18]

One of his earliest applications of that doctrine is "A Vision of the Mermaids" (1862), a pen-and-ink drawing followed by a poem, both apparently inspired by the poetic vision of the mermaids in *The Sketcher*. Eagles's comment, "how difficult it would be, by any sketch, to convey the subject! . . . The *most* faithful representation of such a spot would be the ideal," [19] reveals why Hopkins followed his drawing with words and in general why he felt language was a better vehicle for expression of the ideal than visual art.

Teacher and Student

His particular choice of words to accompany his drawing of the mermaids was influenced by one of his teachers at Highgate, Richard Watson Dixon. Sitting opposite Dixon in the classroom, Hopkins was face to face with a man who had been involved in the vanguard of much that seemed exciting in the art of the time. Dixon had been taught painting by Dante Gabriel Rossetti and received a commendatory letter from Ruskin for his review of *Modern Painters*. Dixon had also helped Rossetti and William Morris paint the Oxford Union mural and was a friend of Edward Burne-Jones from boyhood. More importantly, he was a poet whose poems were praised by Rossetti.

Dixon's *Christ's Company and Other Poems* (1861) appeared the year he arrived at Highgate. His poems featured Rossetti's decorative, sensuous beauty and remote dreamworlds, a Gothic delight in gruesome situations, and a typically Victorian love of word-painting. Yet Dixon's title emphasized the fact that his longer poems were High Church hagiographical verses, and his religious commitment is equally evident in the focus on the doctrine of the Incarnation in his poems.

Dixon had been attracted to the Oxford Pre-Raphaelites, especially Morris and Burne-Jones, by their Ruskinese stress on Christian art and by the original pietism of the group itself. Almost every member of the group had initially intended to take Holy Orders, but most of them were deflected from their purpose by their desire to be artists. Dixon also at one point had given up his religious commitment to become a Pre-Raphaelite painter, but, unlike the other members of the group, he finally did take Holy Orders and thus set an important example for Hopkins.

Dixon's example consisted of his art as well as his life: Hopkins praised and respected his poetry and even copied out favorite stanzas when he entered the Jesuit novitiate. The affinities between Dixon's poems and Hopkins's early poetry is evident when we compare the descriptions of the sunsets in "The Sicilian Vespers," Dixon's boyhood prize poem, and in "A Vision of the Mermaids," thought by some to be one of Hopkins's prize poems at Highgate. Both teacher and student focus on an isle breaking the sunset's tide of light and both reveal a preference for iambic pentameter couplets and the adjectival compounds, long sentences, and colorful pictorial images characteristic of Victorian word-painting. In short, Dixon introduced Hopkins to "the school of Keats" in Victorian poetry.

Chapter Two

Early Poetry, Prose, and Drawings

Keatsian Aestheticism 1860–1863

As Hopkins recalled, Dixon would "praise Keats by the hour—which might well be: Keats' genius was so astonishing, unequalled at his age and scarcely surpassed at any, that one may surmise whether if he had lived he would not have rivalled Shakespere" (*D*, 6). The effect of Dixon's praise of Keats is particularly obvious in "A Vision of the Mermaids" which reproduces the archaic diction, literary and mythological allusiveness, precious neologisms, luxurious sensuality, subjective dreaminess, and amoral, otherworldly aestheticism of Keats's early poems. "A Vision of the Mermaids" reveals that Hopkins's early poetry was in fact more indebted to Keats than that of almost any other Victorian poet.

Yet most of these traits disappeared in Hopkins's mature poetry, a process of maturation typical of Victorian poets.[1] Hopkins soon realized that there was something excessive in his version of the Keatsian love of sensations. As he put it in another early poem, "Spring and Death," there is "A little sickness in the air / From too much fragrance everywhere."

One of the consequences of this intemperate love of sensations was a limited, superficial vision of nature. Whatever was not pleasant was simply to be ignored. As Keats suggested in "Sleep and Poetry," "they shall be accounted poet kings / Who simply tell the most heart-easing things" (ll. 267–68). With this perspective Keats was, as Hopkins discovered, "without any noble motive, felt at firsthand, impelling him to look below its surface" (*F*, 387). The same criticism could be made of Hopkins's own "A Vision of the Mermaids," however, which seems, as Matthew Arnold said of Alfred Tennyson's Keatsian landscapes, to be merely "dawdling with the painted shell" of the universe.[2] If we compare it with Hopkins's first mature poem, *The Wreck of the Deutschland,* we can see why Hopkins had to develop an alternative—as Tennyson, Arnold, A. C. Swinburne, William Morris, and George Meredith had—to Keats's response to nature.

Hopkins's attraction to the self-indulgent love of luxury in Keats's early poetry also explains the lack of concentration, construction, or unity in "A Vision of the Mermaids." Keats's example in *Endymion*—"I must make 4,000 lines of one bare circumstance and fill them up with Poetry"—had a deleterious effect on many of his successors. Hopkins conceded that "of construction [Keats] knew nothing to the last" (*F,* 387), but again he could have illustrated his point with his own early poems. "The Escorial," "Il Mystico," and "A Vision of the Mermaids" show how hard he had to struggle against his own Keatsian love of beauty in order, in Matthew Arnold's phrase, "not to be prevailed over by the world's multitudinousness,"[3] in order to attain that sense of concentration that makes his mature poems often seem so un-Victorian.

Hopkins's comment about Keats's choice of subjects also applies to "A Vision of the Mermaids": "His contemporaries . . . still concerned themselves with great causes [such] as liberty and religion, but he lived in mythology and fairyland the life of a dreamer" (*F,* 386). The mermaids' song of plaintive "piteous siren sweetness" in Hopkins's poem, the Keatsian temptation for him and the other Victorian poets, was a recurrent siren song in English literature, one of the traditional charms of the mythical "bowre of bliss" in Spenser's *Faerie Queene,* for instance. Lured by the lush aestheticism of a purely subjective fantasy world peopled by mythical creatures and clothed in fantastic beauty, the temptation is to live alone in a world of private visions where the reality of the impersonal world may be freely altered according to personal desire.

Hopkins could resist that temptation even in his early poetry, however. For all their archaic diction, precious neologisms, and secondhand allusions, Hopkins's early poems reveal at times how their author would go on to create such poems as "The Windhover." Once again what Hopkins said about Keats applies as well to his own early poems: "even when he is misconstructing one can remark certain instinctive turns of construction in his style, shewing his latent power" (*F*, 387).

The most significant "instinctive turn" in Hopkins's early poetry occurs in "Il Mystico," which replaces his Keatsian dream visions with older, more traditional religious ideals. Though the two brands of otherworldliness tended to blend, especially in Hopkins's Oxford poems, "Il Mystico" anticipates that general move that Hopkins, like Tennyson, made from the imitation of Keats to a more explicitly Christian romanticism. This conversion enabled him to fulfill his own prophecy for Keats: "What he did not want to live by would have asserted itself presently and perhaps have been as much more powerful than that of his contemporaries as his sensibility or impressionableness, by which he did want to live, was keener and richer than theirs" (*F*, 386).

Another "instinctive turn" was taken by Hopkins in "Il Mystico," moreover. The poem begins as an imitation of Milton's "Il Penseroso," but its development embodies in embryo the general movement in Hopkins's early art from representations of purely ideal worlds to representations of this world which culminated in his famous 1877 poems on nature. His initial attempt to attain a spiritual vision is fragmented until the speaker finds that his best expression of his aspiration for some other, more perfect realm is an objective correlative in nature, the ascent of the lark, which translates that desire into action.

"Ruskinese" Realism in Hopkins's Drawings, 1862–1868

Hopkins's drawings and journals helped him find such objective correlatives. They were inspired in part by the example of the great Victorian art critic, John Ruskin. Ruskin recalled that

one day on the road to Norwood, I noticed a bit of ivy round a thorn stem, which seemed, even to my critical judgment, not ill "composed": and proceeded to make a light and shade pencil study of it in my gray paper book, carefully, as if it had been a bit of sculpture, liking it more and more, as I drew. When it was done, I saw that I had virtually lost all my time since I was 12 years old, because no one had ever told me to draw what was really there! . . . it ended my chrysalid days. Thenceforward my advance was steady, however slow.[4]

If this was a key incident in Ruskin's development, still more important was his subsequent drawing of an ordinary aspen tree. He felt the lines of the tree " 'composed' themselves by finer laws than any known of men . . . more than Gothic tracery, more than Greek vase-imagery, more than the daintiest embroiderers of the East could embroider, or the artfullest painters of the West could limn,—this was indeed an end to all former thoughts with me. . . . I returned along the wood-road feeling that it had led me far;—farther than ever fancy had reached . . ." (35:314–15).

Hopkins's "sketches in a Ruskinese point of view," as he called them (*F*, 202), played a similar role in his development. They helped bring him also out of his chrysalid days of adolescent aestheticism. He discovered that what was really there in nature was more beautiful than the farthest flights of fancy embodied in his own early Keatsian poetry, more beautiful than even the imagery on the Grecian urn that Keats himself had immortalized.

Hopkins's light and shade pencil sketches without watercolors— "outline drawings" Ruskin called them—are excellent examples of what Ruskin meant by "truth to nature" (22:28). Ruskin tended to associate color with the distraction of imagined beauty and plain form with truth itself (1:470), precisely the emphasis that Hopkins, as a poet of nature, needed to balance that propensity toward sensuous but purely imaginary beauty so evident in such early poems as "A Vision of the Mermaids."

The ultimate purpose of "outline drawings" was to reconcile art with science. In Ruskin's *The Elements of Drawing* (1857) "every excercise in the book has the ulterior object of fixing in the student's mind some piece of accurate knowledge, either in geology, botany, or the natural history of animals" (15:440). Outline drawings of scenes were so successful in this regard that Ruskin defined them as an entirely new scientific process (35:624).

The influence of science in Hopkins's sketches "in a Ruskinese point of view" is evident in their objectivity and their minute fidelity to detail. Hopkins preferred to sketch nature not in terms of conventional types of beauty but in all its ragged asymmetry, in Ruskin's

words "frankly, unconstrained by artistical laws." This approach—
empirical observation relatively free from *a priori* rules and conventions—is basically the initial response to nature of both revolutions
which dominate our time, romanticism and science. In 1864, for
instance, Hopkins wrote in his journal, "Saw one day dead (water—
?) rat floating down Isis. The head was downward, hind legs on
surface, thus." Hopkins added a small drawing of the dead rat (*J*,
24) which illustrates Ruskin's assertion that outline drawing "entirely refuses emotion. The work must be done with the patience
of an accountant, and records only the realities of the scene—not
the effects of them" (35:624).

In addition to their objectivity, the accuracy of detail in Hopkins's
drawings reflects the rise of science. Consider, for instance, Hopkins's *Shanklin. Sept. 12* (figure 2). To understand Victorian drawings
like this, however, we need to remember that their inspiration was
as much religious as it was scientific. As Henry Ladd has observed,
in the Victorian era "the 'Nature' of the romantic poets was probed

Figure 2

and exploited by a group of university men who considered themselves scientific rather than inspirational. They described and classified the phenomena of the external world with valuable precision,
but induced conclusions that amounted to a revival of the 'natural
religion' of the sixteenth and seventeenth centuries. . . . Science
was performing the romantic functions of the earlier poets; it was
literally demonstrating heaven in wild flowers."[5] Hopkins's "Ruskinese" drawings, therefore, reflect not only science and romanticism, but also a Victorian version of natural theology which
encouraged a sacramental attitude toward nature. The richness of
detail in Hopkins's drawings, journals, and poems is an expression
of that ancient principle of plenitude which reappeared in the art
of Victorian England.[6] They reveal his feeling that this world is
filled to bursting with the grandeur of God; like the olive oil as the
olives are pressed, "it gathers to a greatness" ("God's Grandeur").

The Victorian obsession with detail was also indebted to technology, especially the invention of photography. As we have seen,
Hopkins's uncle, George Giberne, acquainted his nephew Gerard
with this new invention and no doubt it set the standard for the
detail in Hopkins's sketches. Ruskin preferred drawings to photographs, however, because no matter how great their literal realism,
drawings more clearly confess their human fallibility, their inability
to fully substitute for nature itself: "It is precisely in its expression
of this inferiority, that the drawing itself becomes valuable"
(15:353). Most of Hopkins's drawings clearly condemn themselves
in their incompleteness, in those blank spaces which suggest that
what was being imitated was ultimately beyond the powers of art.

Drawings possessed the further advantage, Ruskin argued, of
cultivating certain special powers: "a power of the eye and a power
of the mind wholly different from that known to any other discipline,
and which could only be known by the experienced student—he
only could know how the eye gained physical power by the attention
to details . . . things and causes which it could not otherwise
trace. . . . A person who had learned to draw well found something
to interest him in the least thing and the farthest-off things; in the
lowest thing and the humblest things" (16:440).

Hopkins's *Shanklin. Sept. 10.* (figure 3) suggests what "least things" and what "farthest-off things" Hopkins's eyes tended to focus on: plants in the immediate foreground and clouds on the horizon. With his seemingly more powerful eyes, trained by sketching the details of plants, Hopkins was able to discover a whole new world of detail in clouds. In 1866, for instance, he discovered "a very slim-textured pale causeway of mare's tail cloud . . . with the set of the hair in threads at right angles, and this on looking closer seen to be in jointed sprigs" (*J*, 142). This tendency for the "microscopic" eye for detail to become also "telescopic," as it were, is evident in other Victorian sketchers as well. Of William Holman Hunt, for instance, it was said that he "could see the moons of Jupiter with his naked eye."[7]

In addition to these remarkable powers of the eye certain habits of mind were cultivated by detailed drawing such as patience, discipline, earnestness, and a love of work for its own sake. Perhaps the most important was a remarkable ability to concentrate. Ruskin concentrated so hard on some flowers on one occasion, for instance,

that he complained that they had undergone too many changes in half-an-hour to be drawn properly, while the painter Thomas Seddon was said to have remarked that "three months was insufficient time to draw properly the branch of a tree."[8]

This kind of concentration is essential for a sense of the unity of things, according to Ruskin: "no human capacity ever yet saw the whole of a thing; but we may see more and more of it the longer we look" (6:368). In 1868 Hopkins defined this "long looking" as an activity "in which the mind is absorbed (as far as that may be), taken up by, dwells upon, enjoys a single thought: we may call it contemplation" (*J*, 126). The same year Hopkins joined the Jesuit order and began to practice the Spiritual Exercises of Saint Ignatius. These exercises, with their extraordinary emphasis on vividly and sympathetically imagining religious scenes and objects, reinforced the habit of concentration cultivated by Hopkins's "Ruskinese" drawing habits.

The importance of this power of the mind should not be underestimated. Ruskin felt that "it is like a new faculty, a sixth sense. . . . in fact, the enjoyment of the sketcher from the contemplation of nature is a thing which to another is almost incomprehensible. If a person who had no taste for drawing were at once to be endowed with both the taste and the power, he would feel, on looking out upon nature, almost like a blind man who had just received his sight" (1:283, 285).

This new vision was clearly a step beyond Hopkins's early Keatsian sense of nature as a beautiful surface. "Long looking" revealed the "whole of a new thing," the deeply penetrating form, the unity within (*J*, 126). Many of Hopkins's sketches of individual trees, for instance, seem to be attempts to discover what Ruskin called the "fountain-like impulse" in them according to which "each terminates all its minor branches at its outer extremity so as to form a great outer curve, whose character and proportion are peculiar for each species." The aim was to discover " 'organic unity,' the law, whether of radiation or parallelism, or concurrent action, which rules the masses of herbs and trees" (15:92, 116). This search for unity as well as for individual detail in nature is even more conspicuous in Hopkins's journals.

"Ruskinese" Realism in Hopkins's Journals, 1863–1874

Hopkins emerged from his chrysalid days of adolescent aestheticism by using his journals as well as his drawings as realistic, almost scientific counterpoises to his Keatsian, otherworldly idealism. In his journals, composed about the same time as his early poems, Hopkins initiated that synthesis of the ideal and the real, the infinite and the finite which eventually culminated in "The Windhover" and other poems. This synthesis was required when the concept of the "type" of the species emerged as a rival to realism in Hopkins's portrayal of nature in his journals. The result was his paradoxical concept of "inscape" reconciling his attractions to particular detail and to transcendent unity. His journals also reveal his discovery in 1872 of a religious sanction for this synthesis in the writings of John Duns Scotus. Hopkins's journals thus provide us with an overview of those developments in his thought which made possible his mature poems of the 1870s and 1880s, especially his nature sonnets of 1877.

Strikingly different from his early Keatsian poetry, with their notes on birds, plants, and the weather similar to those of many scientists of the day, Hopkins's journals clearly belong to a special genre of English and American literature which flourished from 1770 to 1880: "the treatment of natural history as a branch of literature." The writers in this tradition share certain basic assumptions, namely, "that the study of nature is intellectually rewarding; that it is spiritually edifying; and that it is aesthetically gratifying."[9]

Hopkins's distinguishing features emerge when we compare his journals with others in this genre. Particularly striking by comparison are his diction, his particular painterly sensibility, his focus on minute detail, his impersonal tone, his love of plenitude, his attraction to spectacles of light and color, his distinctive musical organization of color, and his pre-occupation with unity, regularity, "types," and "inscapes." Hopkins's journals, in short, reveal the genesis of a new voice in English letters.

They are distinguished especially by their highly idiosyncratic diction. Hopkins often prefers archaic, regional, and dialectical words, for instance, because of their direct etymological or phonic relation to the object they name. In addition, he employs a wide variety of geometric terms and applications to specify exact sizes, shapes, and positions of flowers, trees, clouds, and even flowing water. Hopkins's desire to be precise also leads him to resurrect long-forgotten, etymologically derived meanings of more familiar words, to invent unusual metaphorical senses to try out new shades of meaning in them, and on occasion to create entirely new words such as "inscape," "instress," and "outscape."

His prose is distinguished as well by metaphors remarkable for their precision, range, yoking of disparate elements, and the multiplicity of vehicles used to convey the likeness of a single subject. Nor did Hopkins limit his experimentation to individual words and metaphors. He also knitted together distinctive syntactic units with hyphens, for instance, such as "up-blown fleece-of-wool flat-topped dangerous-looking pieces" (J, 142).

The particular vision conveyed by this kind of word-painting in his journals is more original and professional than that of his predecessors in its focus on color, shadow, outline, depth, projection, texture, and tone. In June, 1868, for instance, he wrote: "sky painted and with faint curdling vapour rolling over, distances dim blue, and yet, near, the edges all sharpened, every grain in the sky-line of Caen wood and all the slant cards of the Dugmores' limes being crisply given: on such days the body there is in the air gives depth and projection to the landscape; sheet, moistness, and bloom to the shadows; sobriety at once and richness to the colours; and especially as I saw with one ricked oak in the foreground of Caen wood an opaque, solid, gummy tone to the dark oak crests" (J, 168).

Instead of seeking to delineate certain conventional combinations of forms in nature called the "picturesque," as others had done before him, Hopkins sought to portray nature with the special sensitivity to crisp detail, sharp edges, brightness, and rich colors that characterized a school of painters revolting against the drab ugliness of industrial England: the Pre-Raphaelites. Inspired by Ruskin's admiration for art before Raphael, that is, medieval and early-Renaissance art, and led by Dante Gabriel Rossetti, John Everett Millais, and William Holman Hunt, they generally expressed their realism through an almost photographic precision of detail and their idealism through preternaturally brilliant color and light.

Hopkins's journals and sketches usually illustrate what Ruskin said about "Pre-Raphaelitism," that it "has but one truth in all that it does, obtained by working everything, down to the most minute detail, from nature and from nature only" (12:157). Like Pre-Raphaelite paintings, Hopkins's journals as well as his sketches were an attempt to surpass even photography in "truth to nature." The result is often a closer, more detailed vision than even the accounts of Victorian naturalists who actually used magnifying glasses. [10]

In July, 1866, for instance, Hopkins discovered that "Carnations if you look close have their tongue-shaped petals powdered with spankled red-glister, which no doubt gives them their brilliancy" (*J*, 143). Encouraged by his training in "Ruskinese" sketches, Hopkins began to "look close" more often and saw many aspects of nature he had been blind to before. Whole worlds of nature that most people have never seen became familiar to him, the world of frost and garden mold, for instance: "the garden mould very crisp and meshed over with a lacework of needles leaving (they seemed) three-cornered openings . . . the smaller crumbs and clods were lifted fairly up from the ground on upright ice-pillars, whether they had dropped these from themselves or drawn them into the soil: it was like a little Stonehenge" (*J*, 201). Hopkins discovered this "little Stonehenge" not only by bringing himself closer to it physically but also by somehow training or teaching his eyes to look more closely, to search out detail and scrutinize it. In addition, his eyes had "been trained to look severely at things apart from their associations, *innocently* or *purely* as painters say" (*J*, 77). The objectivity that Hopkins's outline drawings taught him is evident throughout his journals. Indeed, despite their basically personal and literary motivation, they are characterized by a more impersonal and detached tone than the prose of even the most scientifically inclined naturalists of the day. [11]

In addition to this scientific emphasis on objective, detailed "truth to nature," another feature of Pre-Raphaelitism evident in Hopkins's journals is his love of sunsets, rainbows, and clear-cut outlines of light and shade. In 1869, for instance, Hopkins noted,

A few days before Sept. 24 a fine sunrise seen from no. 1, the upstairs bedroom—: long skeins of meshy grey cloud a little ruddled underneath, not quite level but aslant, rising from left to right, and down on the left one more solid balk or bolt than the rest with a high-blown crest of flix or fleece above it.

About the same time a fine sunset, which, looked at also from the upstairs windows, cut out all the yews all down the approach to the house in flat pieces like wings in a theatre (as once before I noticed at sunrise from Magdalen tower), each shaped by its own sharp-cut shadow falling on the yew-tree next behind it, since they run E. and W. Westward under the sun the heights and groves in Richmond Park looked like dusty velvet being flushed into a piece by the thick-hoary golden light which slanted towards me over them. (*J*, 192)

Hopkins's journal is also distinguished by his meticulous representation of fine shades of color; his notations on problematical perceptions of colors; and his distinctive musical organization of color into octaves, scales, medleys, keynotes, chords, modulations, flats, and sharps.

In addition, the feature that led the Impressionists beyond Pre-Raphaelite realism—the play of light—also led Hopkins beyond mere abundance of detail. Many Victorians were susceptible to excited, melodramatic, even deeply religious reactions to brilliant spectacles of light in nature,[12] but none more so than Hopkins. Sun and leaves often became actors in his highly dramatized representations of light, not only in a poem such as "Binsey Poplars" but also in his journals. In 1873, for instance, he noted, "July 18— Bright, with a high wind blowing the crests of the trees before the sun and fetching in the blaze and dousing it again. In particular there was one light raft of beech which the wind footed and strained on, ruffling the leaves which came out in their triplets threaded round with a bright brim like an edge of white ice, the sun sitting at one end of the branch in a pash of soap-sud-coloured gummy bim-beams rowing over the leaves but sometimes flaring out so as to let a blue crust or platter from quite the quick of the orb sail in the eye" (*J*, 233).

Type and Inscape in the Journals, 1865–1874

Yet it is Hopkins's special consciousness of the significance of unifying forms in nature in his journals which, though originally inspired by Ruskin,[13] most clearly differentiates him from most of his Pre-Raphaelite contemporaries as well as most previous nature writers. Hopkins felt he had to reconcile his irrepressible sensory awareness of the multitudinous variety of the world, his love of all the distinctive individual objects and details of nature, with his commitment to a transcendent unity, God. His search for the patterns which unified single objects or sets of objects, and for more general laws of aesthetic organization in nature was a quest for the evidence of the divine force responsible for unity on earth as well as in heaven.

The essence of the idea of form for Hopkins was regularity; "regular" and "regularly" are normative words throughout his journals. His habit of comparing two or more things together resulted in numerous perceptions of structural attributes repeated in many different objects and thus an increasing sense of unity pervading all of nature. Each time one of his favorite patterns of the web, the loom, or the spine-and-ribs reappeared, Hopkins's faith in the ultimate order and regularity of nature increased, and he reaffirmed his vision of the world in which everything is related by common patterns, "nothing at random" (*J*, 201), a vision as scientific as it is religious.

His immediate goal was the discovery of the common pattern or "type" of a species, the form which characterized and represented the entire class. The type can only be discerned in the details of the individual, however, the uniqueness of which, in turn, can only be defined in contrast to the type—one invariably implies the other. But we usually stress one aspect more than the other, and Hopkins began to shift his emphasis from the individual toward the type as early as 1865 when he read the essays of Walter Bagehot and J. C. Shairp rejecting distracting detail in favor of the portrayal of the type of a scene or species.[14] The shift from love of detail to love of types is most striking in Hopkins's devaluation of the paintings of Millais in 1874.[15]

"Type" became an increasingly important word in Hopkins's journals because a type discovered again and again led to the perception
of visible law, "character," beauty, and the "composition" or unifying order of the whole (*J*, 139). The word "type" also had a special
religious meaning which we will discuss in chapter 4. Ultimately,
for Hopkins the sense of unity conveyed by the discovery of types
was evidence of God's presence, a metaphysical discovery which
could challenge the increasing relativism of Darwinian science. As
early as 1867 Hopkins argued that "It will always be possible to
show how science is atomic, not to be grasped and held together,
'scopeless,' without metaphysics: this alone gives meaning to laws
and sequences and causes and developments" (*J*, 118). Increasingly
aware of the importance of "metaphysics" or religion as the ultimate
source of unity, Hopkins began to be more critical of mere love of
detail, "that kind of thought which runs upon the concrete and the
particular, which disintegrates and drops towards atomism in some
shape or other" (*J*, 119).

He was particularly critical of some of the implications of Darwin's
Origin of Species: "one sees that the ideas so rife now of a continuity
without fixed points, not to say *saltus* or breaks, of development in
one chain of necessity, of species having no absolute types and only
accidentally fixed, all this is a philosophy of flux" (*J*, 120). He
began to consider ways to "challenge the prevalent philosophy of
flux. The first is that of type or species . . . there are certain forms
which have a great hold on the mind and are always reappearing
and seem imperishable, such as the designs of Greek vases and lyres
. . . and these things are inexplicable in a theory of pure chromaticism or continuity—the forms have in some sense or other an
absolute existence" (*J*, 120).

The great event which separates this essay of 1867 from Hopkins's
1864 essay defending the concrete and the particular (*J*, 74–79)
was his conversion to Catholicism, a spiritual system which could
ultimately grasp and hold together his own atomistic journal notes.
Consequently, the biblical concept of the type rather than the Platonic ideal of pure form eventually became Hopkins's dominant
paradigm. As we shall see, the biblical "type" reconciled Hopkins's
attraction to historical particulars with his desire for universal sig-

nificance. Hopkins clearly never conceived of "ideal" forms in nature as a strict Platonist would; that is, he did not see the forms in nature as but imperfect imitations of some perfect, supernatural abstractions. Rather, as Wordsworth, Ruskin, Bagehot, and Shairp recommended, he sought the type in nature, and thus in his prose he often sought to portray it in its fullest substantiation of detail.

Hopkins created the word "inscape" to embody this paradoxical balance of the ideal and the real inspired by the Hebrew idea of "the type," especially as exemplified in the Incarnation. His first recorded use of the word was in his 1868 notes on Parmenides where it is described as the proportion of the mixture in the phenomenal world of particular oneness or Being and the differentiating force of matter or Not-Being. In other words, inscape is the mark of the unifying force of Being on the phenomenal world. Hopkins conceives of this mark or pattern made by the unifying force (which he sometimes identifies as "instress") as manifest in an object's surface or "outline," and as pervading it and holding it fast (*J*, 127–30).

Thus when Hopkins uses the term "inscape" in his journals he is almost always referring to the pattern, structure, form, or shape of an object. When a number of objects are compared this meaning coalesces with his sense of the type as a pattern which governs the behavior of each object. "Outscape," "offscape," "make," "scape," and "idiom" are used to distinguish various interesting, but less important aspects of form from the special typifying or unifying pattern which he calls "inscape." In any case, whether he uses the term "inscape" to describe a recurring pattern which integrates a group of objects or only a pattern which unifies a single object, the primary denotations of the word remain unity and regularity: "All the world is full of inscapes and chance left free to act falls into an order as well as purpose: looking out of my window I caught it in the random clods and broken heaps of snow made by the cast of a broom" (*J*, 230).

As we have seen, this kind of observation enabled Hopkins to look past his early Keatsian vision of nature as a beautiful surface and glimpse the deeply penetrating form, the unity within. "The further in anything . . . the organization is carried out, the deeper the form penetrates" and the more "contemplation" is required to perceive it (*J*, 216). By concentrating on even such an amorphous object as running water he was able to discover some of its deeper, recurrent formations: "by watching hard the banks begin to sail upstream, the scaping unfolded" (*J*, 200).

The phrase "watching hard" recalls a phrase such as "on looking closer" which characterizes Hopkins's almost microscopic eye for detail (*J*, 142). Both his perception of inscapes and his eye for detail rely on prolonged concentration and seem to magnify some aspect of the perceived object. The difference is that the "microscopic eye" magnifies the finest single details whereas the "penetrating eye," if we may call it that after Ruskin's "imagination penetrative" (1:92), seeks to bring into strong relief that recurring regularity in the overall form of the object which distinctively unifies it.

An increasing sense of inscape in nature and art made Hopkins more and more aware of "instress," the unifying force behind such designs in the world. Hopkins first used the term in his 1868 notes on Parmenides to mean basically the force of Being, the inner flushness of an object, which draws it together. In the journals it usually means the effect on the mind of a force of Being which unifies and upholds an object or set of objects in such a way as to unmistakeably distinguish or individualize them. In 1871 he noted, "But such a lovely damasking in the sky today I never felt before. The blue was charged with simple instress" (*J*, 207). It is not accidental that he used "charged" in much the same way as he would later in his famous line, "The world is charged with the grandeur of God."

Duns Scotus

A year later, in 1872, Hopkins wrote, "I had first begun to get hold of the copy of Scotus on the *Sentences* in the Baddley library and was flush with a new stroke of enthusiasm. It may come to nothing or it may be a mercy from God but just then when I took in any inscape of the sky or sea I thought of Scotus" (*J*, 221). John Duns Scotus, the medieval philosopher and doctor of the church, provided exactly what Hopkins required: a theological sanction for his love of nature's inscapes, a way of relating them to the grandeur of God. In Scotus's view an object in nature was a composite of an individuating principle and its "specific common nature"—the sum total of those qualities by which it belongs to a species or a genus and therefore the physical basis for universal statements. Scotus maintained, in opposition to Plato and Thomas Aquinas, that knowledge begins with the individual sense-object and proceeds to the universal rather than the reverse.[16]

Yet, like other medieval philosophers, Scotus was ultimately interested in the most universal aspect of things; he wanted to know and love not just particular objects but Being in its totality, which he identified closely with God:

when it is argued that God by reason of His unique singularity cannot be known through some concept univocally common to Himself and creatures, the consequence is invalid. . . . the singularity of a thing is no impediment to the abstraction of a common concept. . . . what we know of God is known through the intelligible species of creatures. . . . Thus it is that creatures which impress their own proper species on the intellect can also impress the species of the transcendentals which are common to themselves and to God. . . . God is conceived not only in a concept analogous to the concept of a creature, that is, one which is wholly other than that which is predicated of creatures, but even in some concept univocal to Himself and to a creature.[17]

Scotus's doctrine of the univocity of Being, which provided Hopkins with a Catholic sanction for perceiving nature as somehow participating in the Being of God, was supported, moreover, by Scotus's view of the Incarnation. His assertion that Christ was predestined to become man even before Adam's fall made the Incarnation more than an atonement. The Incarnation was the fundamental expression of God's participation in the being of nature, the act by which Christ became the head of a great chain of univocal Being which included all of nature as well as man: "had there been no sin of angels or men, the coming of Christ would have been the efflorescence or natural consummation of the creative strain; men's minds and wills would have risen spontaneously and harmoniously from creatures to God."[18] The Incarnation is thus perceived as the act which emphasizes Christ's role as the head of all of nature—elemental, vegetative, and sensitive—as well as the human race (*S*, 351).

It is easy to see why Hopkins was excited about Scotus's idea that "it is within God's power to make the Body of Christ really present *universaliter,* anywhere and everywhere in the universe" (*S*, 113). Christ's presence after the Resurrection is necessarily mysterious and mystical, however, consisting of his continued life in the members of his church. The metaphor of the Body of Christ derives of course from Paul: those who have been baptized are the members (1 Cor. 12:12–27). As the head of the Body, Christ redeems all of nature as well as mankind, however, according to Scotus. As in Hopkins's "God's Grandeur" the Holy Spirit is thus the soul and redeemer of the mystical Body not only in mankind but also in nature. Nature and mankind are united in the Body of God.

This anagogical sense of nature as part of the mystical Body of Christ is discussed in more detail in Chapter 6. Suffice it to say at this point that it is not to be confused with pantheism, either materialist pantheism which reduces God to the world and thereby effectively denies his existence, or spiritualist pantheism, which defines the universe as spirit and thus reduces matter to an illusion. Hopkins accepts neither of these tenets, nor their various corollaries which deny the possibility of existence apart from God or of genuine individual freedom. Hopkins maintains his belief in God's capacity for separateness and his belief in the Trinity, including the transcendence of the Father and a personal relationship with Christ. As John Keating puts it, "pantheism is an outlook inconceivable for one of Hopkins' creed and training; the Scholastic theodicy so prominent in the *Deutschland* requires the careful distinction between the finite being and the Infinite. Yet the poet recognizes that the God who infinitely transcends the physical world is everywhere immanent in it. Nature is sacramental. . . ."[19]

Hopkins received a Catholic sanction for a poetic interpretation of sacramental nature from Scotus's idea that the particular concrete object was known not only by the senses but also intuitively by the mind. Jesuit theology and philosophy in Hopkins's day were quite rationalistic,[20] but Scotus argued that the mind could have an intuitive insight into the individual object. Knowing a thing intuitively could then lead to a conception of it in terms of its genus and species and thus its precise place and meaning in the manifold of reality—each individual was but one note in the grand symphony of creation.[21] Therefore, aesthetic knowledge of the individual creature led to knowledge of the greatest universal, God.

Such knowledge was clearly the ultimate aim of Hopkins's journals as well as his poetry. In 1869 he wrote, "I do not think I have ever seen anything more beautiful than the bluebell I have been looking at. I know the beauty of our Lord by it" (*J*, 199). A few months later, watching the Aurora Borealis he noted, "this busy working of nature wholly independent of the earth and seeming to go on in a strain of time not reckoned by our reckoning of days and years but simpler and as if correcting the preoccupation of the world by being preoccupied with and appealing to and dated to the day of judgment was like a new witness of God and filled me with delightful fear" (*J*, 200). Hopkins's next entry in the journal begins with the words, "Laus Deo," directly relating the observation of nature which follows to the "praise of God." Throughout the rest of the journals, Hopkins avoided explicit connections between nature and God much as Ruskin did in his more impersonal prose, but one of the last entries strikes the keynote again: "As we drove home the stars came out thick: I leant back to look at them and my heart opening more than usual praised our Lord to and in whom all beauty comes home" (*J*, 254).

Effect of the Journals on the Poems

This sacramental response is not fully realized in Hopkins's poetry until the late seventies, however. The word-painting which dominates his journals had a more immediate impact on many poems of the 1860s. It is evident in such painterly diction as "you traced," "were drawn," and "duly touch'd," for instance, in "Richard" (1864). Hopkins's extended, hyphenated, adjectival phrases, moreover, such as "soft vermilion leather just-budded leaves" and "those multitudinous up-and-down crispy sparkling chains" (*J*, 142–43), also reappear in his poetry, most conspicuously in the opening sentence of "The Windhover." Word-painting pervades other poems in the 1870s as well, such as "The Woodlark," and is the dominant aim of even such a late poem as "Harry Ploughman" (1887).

The titles of Hopkins's poems, from the juvenile "The Escorial" to the late "On the Portrait of Two Beautiful Young People" (1886), testify to the extent to which his poetry, like his prose, reflects the influence of the visual arts. The painter's fascination with changing light and color evident in his journals, for instance, is found as well in such Oxford poems as "Richard," "The wind that passes by so fleet" (1863), and "The Peacock's Eye" (1864). Similarly, the Pre-Raphaelite love of sunsets and rainbows is also evident in such poems as "The Alchemist in the City" and "It was a hard thing" (1864).

The sense of plenitude of detail expressed visually in Hopkins's drawings and in many passages of his journals recurs in his Oxford poetry (1864–66) in such lines as "jostling thick, the bluebell sheaves / The peacock'd copse were known to fill" ("A Voice from the World," 1864), "as thick as fast, / The crystal-ended hyacinths blow" (J, 55), "such flood / Of flowers that counting closes" (J, 58), and "The stars were packed so close that night / They seemed to press and stare" (J, 72), as well as in later poems such as "God's Grandeur." The love of individual detail which dominates Hopkins's sketches and journals is also quite striking in Hopkins's Oxford poetry, especially his "Richard," "Io" (1864), and poems such as "The Nightingale" and "The Elopement" (1868) which demonstrate how emotional crises heighten awareness of precise detail. The precision of the detailed comparisons of Hopkins's journals recurs in a metaphor such as "like shining from shook foil" in "God's Grandeur," of which Hopkins said, "I mean foil in the sense of leaf or tinsel, and no other word whatever will give the effect I want" (B, 169).

Even the special fusion of metaphor and music so characteristic of "God's Grandeur" and other poems which followed was first discovered in Hopkins's journals. Listen to Hopkins's description of "the water-ivy bush," for instance: "the plucked and dapper cobweb of glassy grey down, swung slack and jaunty on the inshore water" (J, 235). As we have seen, the most direct and obvious examples of the influence of such passages are to be found in Hopkins's Oxford poems, however, which were not only written at the same time but often initially composed in the journals themselves.

Chapter Three
Oxford Poetry

In 1863, with some of his journals, drawings, and his early Keatsian poetry in hand, Hopkins arrived at Oxford, "steeped in sentiment as she lies, spreading her gardens to the moonlight and whispering from her towers the last enchantments of the Middle Ages."[1] Here he became more fully aware of the religious implications of the medievalism of Ruskin and the Pre-Raphaelites. Inspired by Christina Rossetti, by the awakened interest in Savonarola in the 1860s, and by the doctrine of the Real Presence, he eventually embraced Ruskin's definition of "Medievalism" as a "confession of Christ" opposed to both "Classicalism" ("Pagan Faith") and "Modernism" (the "denial of Christ") (12:139). Most of the Pre-Raphaelites were originally attracted to this aspect of medievalism and their early religious commitments explain much of Hopkins's desire to be a Pre-Raphaelite painter and poet.[2]

Christina Rossetti

That desire was reinforced especially by the striking example of Christina Rossetti, who along with Richard Watson Dixon, was one of the few Pre-Raphaelites to sustain the original religious impulse. By carrying the spiritual dimension of Pre-Raphaelitism so evident throughout her poetry to its logical conclusion, Hopkins moved beyond the Keatsian art-for-art's sake poetics promulgated by her brother, Dante Gabriel Rossetti, and beyond the "Ruskinese" realism of the other two founders of Pre-Raphaelitism, John Everett Millais and William Holman Hunt.

Christina Rossetti revealed to Hopkins the need to replace Keats with a more spiritual literary master: Dante. She published articles on Dante, his influence pervades her poetry, and many aspects of her person and character suited her to play the role of Beatrice in the imaginations of Hopkins, Swinburne, and other poets.[3] Dante's focus on Beatrice was in fact the key to much of his influence in English literature. Many of the preferences for Dante over Milton in nineteenth-century English letters are based on the contrast between Milton's antifeminism and the exalted role of woman in Dante's texts. Dante obviously more effectively evoked what Carl Jung called "the anima," the "eternal feminine" guide to and mediator of the world within, provider of access to the unconscious and to love.

Attraction to this aspect of Dante may be traced all the way back to Chaucer. The *Invocatio ad Mariam* in his second nun's prologue, for instance, was inspired primarily by canto 33 of the *Paradiso*. If Chaucer's "mother / maiden" oxymorons anticipate those of Hopkins's "Ad Mariam," Chaucer's Dantesque representation of St. Cecilia in the second nun's tale was a prototype for Hopkins's St. Dorothea poems: both heroines are martyrs identified iconographically with lilies, stars, and great luminscence and both convert doubting males by sending angels with flowers out of season from paradise. These and other variations of the Beatrice anima became particularly popular in the nineteenth century. Johann Tieck, for instance, emphasized that both Novalis and Dante loved women who died at early ages and both men found consolation in poetry.

The relationship between Hopkins and Christina Rossetti was more like the Victorian interpretation of Shelley's response to Emilia Viviani, however: Shelley's "relations with her were similar to those of Dante with Beatrice; he knew her but little, saw her rarely, and his love for her was purely Platonic, ideal, vague, symbolical. . . . she was a creature of imagination, in whom he idealized love with all its intensity of passion. He himself calls 'Epipsychidion' a mystery; 'as to real flesh and blood, you know that I do not deal in those articles.' It seems altogether probable that the figure of Beatrice was before him as he wrote the poem."[4]

It seems altogether probable that the figure of Beatrice was before Hopkins as well when he wrote "A Voice from the World," his response to Christina Rossetti's "The Convent Threshold." In one of her articles on Dante she insisted that "not a hint remains that

Beatrice even guessed her boy-friend's secret. He sought her company, and felt the ennobling influence of her presence—so noble an influence that love (he avers) rules him not contrary to the dictates of reason." Christina Rossetti went on to speak of the *Vita Nuova* as a "tribute of praise from his lowliness to her loftiness," an apt description not only of "A Voice from the World" but many of Hopkins's other responses to the anima as well, including "Margaret Clitheroe" (no date), his two poems on St. Thecla, his three poems on St. Dorothea, his four poems on St. Winefred, his explicitly Marian poems—"Ad Mariam" (no date), "Rosa Mystica" (no date), "The Blessed Virgin compared to the Air we Breathe" (1883), "Ad Matrem Virginem" (no date), and "May Lines" (no date)—and his representation of nuns in "Heaven-Haven" (1864) and *The Wreck of the Deutschland*. In her article, Christina Rossetti also recalled the story that in his "period of bereavement, Dante donned the Franciscan habit as a novice in the monastery of San Benedetto in Alpe among the Apennines,"[5] a story not entirely irrelevant to Hopkins, who also donned the habit of a religious order and entered a monastery in the hills, in his case St. Beuno's in Wales.

Thus if we consider Hopkins's comment on literary "schools" in one of his letters to Dixon it is not difficult to determine which "school" he was himself associated with:

I must hold that you and Morris belong to one school, and though you should neither of you have read a line of the other's. I suppose the same models, the same masters, the same tastes, the same keepings, above all, make the same school. It will always be possible to find differences, marked differences between original minds; it will be necessarily so. So the species in nature are essentially distinct. Nevertheless, they are grouped into genera: they have one form in common, mounted on that they have a form that differences them. I used to call it the school of Rossetti; it is in literature the school of the Pre-Raphaelites. (*D*, 98)

Theories about "schools" are unusual in the English poetic tradition, and poets of striking originality like Hopkins are almost by definition excluded from them, but if species of poets, despite "marked differences between original minds," can be grouped into genera, the question arises, to what group did Hopkins himself belong?

In certain respects he too must be affiliated with the Pre-Raphaelites and their circle or, as he called them elsewhere, "the school
of Keats." Keats was obviously his early master and Hopkins shared
many of the same tastes and keepings with this school of Victorian
poetry. Indeed, as we have seen, because his early poems were even
more full of imitations of Keats's sensuousness, stasis, precious diction, and dreamy otherworldliness than those of most of his contemporaries, Hopkins proceeded to remove these influences even
more eagerly than they did. Similarly, because his debt to the "school
of Keats" was all too obvious, especially to Christina Rossetti and
to Swinburne, Hopkins made a great effort to remove the more
obvious signs of their tastes and keepings as well.

Hopkins's letter to Dixon forces us to ask a question, however:
what "one form" does Hopkins have in common with the Pre-
Raphaelites, on which he constructed that "form that differences"
him? Geoffrey Hartman was clearly on the right track when he
suggested that "Hopkins seems to develop his lyric structures out
of the Pre-Raphaelite dream vision. In his early 'A Vision of the
Mermaids' and 'St. Dorothea' he may be struggling with such poems
as Christina Rossetti's 'The Convent Threshold' and Dante Gabriel
Rossetti's 'The Blessed Damozel,' poems in which the poet stands
at a lower level than the vision, or is irrevocably, pathetically dis-
tanced."[6] Such poems were the essence of medievalism in poetry
according to William Morris, who felt that Keats's contribution to
this genre, "La Belle Dame Sans Merci," was the germ from which
all Pre-Raphaelite poetry sprang.[7] Standing beyond Keats, however,
the primary source of this genre, as Christina Rossetti made clear,
was Dante.

Beatrice's appeal to Dante is recalled by Christina Rossetti in
"The Convent Threshold":

> I choose the stairs that mount above,
> Stair after golden skyward stair,
>
> . . . .
> Lo, stairs are meant to lift us higher:
> Mount with me, mount the kindled stair.
>   Your eyes look earthward, mine look up.
> . . . .

> How should I rest in Paradise,
> Or sit on steps of heaven alone?
> . . . .
> Oh save me from a pang in heaven.
> By all the gifts we took and gave,
> Repent, repent, and be forgiven:
> (ll. 4–5, 15–17, 69–70, 77–79)

Hopkins read "The Convent Threshold" at a crucial moment in his career, when he was actually considering renouncing his own powerful attraction to this world for a life beyond the cloister threshold. He translated portions of her poem into Latin elegaics and devoted much of his poetic creativity in 1864 to his own response to it, which he called at first "A Voice from the World" (later "Beyond the Cloister") and subtitled, "An Answer to Miss Rossetti's *Convent Threshold*." The surviving fragments express the speaker's sense of spiritual inferiority and his admiration for the decision of Christina Rossetti's heroine to join the convent. Hopkins's title identifies his persona as the one whose eyes "look earthward" but he is willing to lift them up:

> At last I hear the voice well known;
> . . . .
> You see but with a holier mind—
> You hear and, alter'd, do not hear
> Being a stoled apparel'd star.
> . . . .
> Teach me the paces that you went
> I can send up an Esau's cry;
> Tune it to words of good intent.
> This ice, this lead, this steel, this stone,
> This heart is warm to you alone;
> Make it to God. I am not spent
> . . . .
> Steel may be melted and rock rent.
> Penance shall clothe me to the bone.
> Teach me the way: I will repent.
> (ll. 1, 40–42, 125–30, 134–36)

Hopkins may have had little personal contact with the woman who was to inspire some of his best art in the 1860s—we know of only one meeting between them (in 1864)—but Christina Rossetti in Hopkins's poetry, like Beatrice in Dante's, represents the lady who is spiritually more advanced, superior in holiness. Much as Beatrice intervened to save Dante in Hell, the example of Christina apparently interrupted Hopkins's more worldly poetic endeavors and called upon him to pursue higher ideals.

The basic approach to life exemplified by Christina Rossetti in "The Convent Threshold" eventually became Hopkins's and the pattern of his career followed hers: an outwardly drab, plodding life of submission quietly bursting into splendor in holiness and poetry. They shared a commitment to holiness above all else: whenever religious renunciation and self-expression were felt to be at odds, as they often were, self-expression was to be sacrificed. Some poetry of nature was allowed, but it had to be subordinated to religion.

With this attitude, Christina's representation of nature was necessarily almost as different from that of the other Pre-Raphaelites as her ascetic religion was. Less interested in a reductionist amalgamation of the visual and verbal arts, in literally imitating the stasis of the plastic arts, she discovered that her genre was the song of heaven rather than the picture of earth. It is true that she shared their feeling for the plenitude of glorious sensations in this world, but she usually fought harder against that attraction than they did. Less overwhelmed by it, she provided Hopkins with examples of simple, unified songs which helped free him from some of the excesses of his early word-painting. She showed him how to trade the prolix word-painting of "Il Mystico" and "A Vision of the Mermaids," for instance, for the unity and concentration of "Pied Beauty" and "Spring."

Christina Rossetti's subordination of art to religion quickly became a key feature of Hopkins's aesthetic as well. About a year after he met Christina he responded to Lessing's attack on the religious functions of Greek statues, for instance, with an essay titled "On the true idea and excellence of sculpture" in which he argued that "art is made vigorous and more efficient by being, not its own mistress, but the helpmate of religion."[8]

As we have seen, an obvious example of nature poetry as the "helpmate of religion" is that joyous, synchronic reading of the Bible and the Book of Nature known as the hymn of creation. This traditional genre includes Christina's "All Thy Works Praise Thee, O Lord" and "What Purpose is This Waste," as well as Hopkins's "Easter" and his great nature sonnets of the 1870s. Hopkins's "Pied Beauty," for instance, like Christina's "All Thy Works," shows how heavens, fish, birds, and men reveal God's glory and inspire worship of him. Hopkins's ending—"He fathers forth whose beauty is past change / Praise him"—is simply a more concise expression of her song of "Winter and Summer." In this song she addresses God, "Before whose changelessness we alternate," and concludes: "Praise God, praise God, praise God." Similarly, Hopkins's suggestion in "God's Grandeur" that the grandeur "will flame out, like shining from shook foil" is analogous to her representation of "Lightning and Thunder" which "flash forth His Fame"; indeed, different versions of "God's Grandeur" have "flash out" for "flame out" and "lightning" for "shining."[9] The next line of "God's Grandeur"— "It gathers to a greatness, like the ooze of oil"—also taps this tradition. Christina's "Easter Carol," for instance, includes oil in its account of creation's plenitude, and there is a strong sense of a gathering to a greatness, a filling to overflowing and still swelling, in her passage on the plenitude of creation in "And there was no more Sea."

Generally, however, she restricts herself to merely suggesting analogies between God and nature. Even when nature is the immediate or ostensible subject of one of her poems it is seldom considered in its own right: the aim is to use it to represent some other, clearly superior order of reality. To this end she produced many allegories, parables, emblems, fables, and correspondences between God and nature.

Hopkins's "The May Magnificat" (1878) begins as an exercise in this tradition of correspondences, though it finally turns into more of a hymn of creation in which nature plays a larger role than it would in a merely emblematic approach. His "The Blessed Virgin compared to the Air we Breathe" is more clearly in the vein of Christina Rossetti's ingenious correspondences in prose, and reminds us of their shared interest in the metaphysical as well as medieval poets. In this poem Hopkins's speaker finds that air "Minds me in many ways" of Mary, and he develops the analogy at great length. As in most of Christina's poems the emphasis is placed more on the spiritual than on the material reality.

Christina's increasingly severe asceticism in fact relied less and less on the representation of nature itself, until ultimately only metaphorical meanings were to be entertained. Her basic idea was that God is not in nature but above, and therefore we must ascend the heavenward stair invoked in her "A Shadow of Dorothea," "The Convent Threshold," and other poems. A similar transition from the natural to the supernatural in Hopkins's early poetry is evident in both his version of this legend, "For a Picture of St. Dorothea" (undated, discussed in Chapter 4), and in his "Heaven-Haven."

Influences as various as Homer, the Psalms, St. Paul, Thomas More, George Herbert, Wordsworth, Keats, and Tennyson are apparent in "Heaven-Haven," but the original titles, "Rest" and " 'Fair Havens' or the Convent," are redolent of the most pervasive of those influences: Victorian medievalism, especially such images as the convent cemetery scene in Millais's *The Vale of Rest* and the nun amid the lilies in Charles Collins's painting, *Convent Thoughts.*[10]

Like most of Christina Rossetti's poems, "Heaven-Haven" is a short, simple lyric, composed in conventional, general diction, more of a song than a picture. Hopkins's original title, "Rest," points directly to her poetry—indeed, "rest" is such a normative word in her poetry that her brother William made it a separate topic in the table of contents of his edition of her poems. Almost as pervasive in that edition is her dream of the garden of heaven. That dream, for Christina and Hopkins, as for the seventeenth-century metaphysical, Henry Vaughan, and countless other predecessors, was a vision of a quiet, beautiful landscape of springs and flowers protected from the storms and mutability of the temporal world.

This sense of the unreliability and instability of this world evident in "Heaven-Haven" and many of Hopkins's other poems of the 1860s led almost inevitably to a desire to transcend it, in order to discover some other, better world less subject to the triumph of time. Hence, of the two paths to holiness—the inner and the outer—

by far the most common is the one Christina usually took: withdrawal from the external world in order to turn inward, plumb the secret depths of one's own soul, and prepare oneself for the world to come. Hopkins followed her, but never really gave up the search for unity in the external world, and thus almost constantly experienced not only the tension between idealism and realism in his representation of nature, but the larger strains of the related dialectic between the inner and outer paths to holiness. However, because the inner way was clearly the usual path for the novice who needs to be sure of his own election and therefore must concentrate at least initially on purifying himself before he returns to the outside world, from 1865 to 1868 Hopkins turned increasingly inward.

This is a regular stage in the conversion pattern of many, as Christina's "Three Stages" suggests. Her speaker, like Hopkins's in "The Habit of Perfection" (1866), finds all knowledge of "things that seem" untrustworthy, and resolves to "shut" herself "and dwell alone" in silence and darkness, "Though I may see no more the poppied wheat / Or sunny soaring lark." Her "Three Nuns" begins with the same decision.

Hopkins's "The Habit of Perfection" is a response to this recurrent call of desert Christianity. As he put it, "This ruck and reel which you remark / Coils, keeps, and teases simple sight," that is, the external world is an unstable flux which can never be known. It is a Heraclitean "stream of alteration," a Cyrenaic "string of sensations," leading to Plato's "despair at the multiplicity of phenomena," to use phrases from Hopkins's own essays.[11] As in Christina's "The Convent Threshold," *Goblin Market,* and other poems, this Heraclitean flux is represented in "The Habit of Perfection" as a distraction, a temptation, a trap, or a snare. Hopkins invokes the older meaning of "coil"—to enfold in a coil, to ensnare—and "keep"— to seize, snatch, catch. The beauty of this world is thus seen as "dangerous" in the sense in which the word is later used in "To what serves Mortal Beauty" (1885) and "The Leaden Echo and the Golden Echo" (1882). These connotations of *natura maligna,* like those in the opening of "Il Mystico," in "Spelt from Sibyl's Leaves" (1885), and in Christina's "The World," are reinforced by the biblical undercurrent of "The Habit of Perfection" invoked in the final lines: "Lay not up for ourselves treasures upon the earth, where moth and rust doth corrupt" (Matt. 6:19). Hence Hopkins's commitment is to the inner world: "Elected Silence. . . . Pipe me to pastures still."

Unfortunately, Hopkins's withdrawal from the world was often accompanied by ennui. His contemplation of sin in "Myself unholy" (1865) shows how his sense of impurity in others as well as himself made him yield "to the sultry siege of melancholy." In the opening stanzas of his "The Alchemist in the City" the external world of change and motion is contrasted with the persona's still, stagnant inner world where, like many of Christina's personae, he broods over his consciousness of the triumph of time, his own impotence, his own inability to participate in the world of motion and change. He wishes to retreat to nature to merely gaze at "the yellow waxen light" of the sunset "With free long looking, until I die."

The sonnet, "See how Spring opens with disabling cold" (1865), summarizes this melancholy, to which Hopkins was "subject all [his] life" (F, 11) but especially in the sixties and eighties, and his attendant feelings of coldness, impotence, and loneliness. The whole syndrome may best be defined as *acedia*. We will discuss it in detail in Chapter 7 on the poetry of the eighties, but it is also a feature of Hopkins's Oxford poetry. It too is closely associated with Christina Rossetti: "if one of the Seven Deadly sins found harbourage in the soul of this mid-Victorian Virgin Saint it was *Accidia* . . . usually mistranslated 'sloth,' but . . . 'a form or at least a corruption of Melancholy.' "[12]

One of the most famous definitions of *Accidia* or *acedia* in English is the Parson's in Chaucer's *Canterbury Tales*: "Thanne cometh a manere cooldnesse, that freseth al the herte of man" (l. 722). In addition to the "disabling cold" of "See how Spring opens," in most of Hopkins's poems of the sixties the imagery of "ice" and "winds impenitent," "This outer cold" represents what in "Pilate" (1864) Hopkins called this "exile from old / From God and man." The cold furnace in "The Alchemist in the City" foreshadows the poetic impotence of Hopkins's late sonnet, "To R. B." (1889), but it is primarily the Lenten exile from the resurrected God that is embodied in "the draught of thin and pursuant cold" in "Easter Communion"

(1865), while the "ice" in the speaker's heart in "A Voice from the World" is as much a sign of his distance from God as from his loved one.

Chaucer's Parson notes that one of the features of this freezing "Accidie" is "that a man is enoyed and encumbered for to doon any goodnesse" (l. 687), an image which anticipates Hopkins's metaphor of a threshold encumbered with obstruction in "See how Spring." Chaucer's concept of failing to "doon any goodnesse" also evoked the biblical undercurrent of Hopkins's "Trees by their yield" (1865): "by their fruits ye shall know them" (Matt. 9:20; 12:33–55). Two of the fruits Hopkins was painfully conscious of failing to bring forth at Oxford were making his conversion official and entering the religious life: "Thanne cometh the synne that men clepen *tarditas*, as when a man is to laterede or tariyinge, en he wole turne to God." Such a man relies on "excusasioun" (l. 680), much as Hopkins's speaker does in his allusions to Rimmon and Bela in "A Voice from the World" (ll. 137–53).

Thus, according to Chaucer's Parson this *acedia* is the opposite of "strengthe" (l. 728); that is, it is a disabling impotence, making the soul "fieble" (l. 730). A similar feeling of impotence is evident in the representation of the "disabling" cold in "See how Spring" and characterizes many of Hopkins's darker poems of the sixties and the eighties. It is the predicament of both the alchemist and the persona of "Earth and heaven, so little known" (1866), both isolated from the planning, building, and achieving they see around them in nature and in society. The alchemist is not only "incapable," he is "more powerless than the blind or lame," with "no promise of success." In the eighties the "waste done in unreticent youth" of "See how Spring" becomes "ruins of wrecked past purpose" ("Patience, hard thing!" 1885), and Hopkins again uses plant imagery to convey his sense of infertility in "Thou art indeed just, Lord" (1889). In this sonnet the speaker's isolation from the changes and building of the world around him also recalls the impotent alchemist.

Sensations of impotent paralysis such as these were evident in the intellectual and emotional crises of many Victorians. "In the sixties," moreover, as Walter Houghton has shown, "the situation, if anything, was worse."[13] The situation was worst of all at Oxford in the sixties according to Mrs. Humphry Ward. In her novel, *Robert Elsemere,* an Oxford don named Langham—a character apparently inspired by Hopkins's own tutor, Walter Pater—suffers most from this paralysis.

That form of worldliness associated with Pater, with its foundation in classical literature and philosophy, is apparently the obstruction that paralyzes, blocking the way to the field of good soil in Hopkins's "See how Spring." This Epicurean worldliness in Hopkins's view apparently became the thorn which in the parable so choked the seed—the "word of the kingdom of God" (Luke 8:4–15)—with the cares and pleasures of this life that it brought no fruit to perfection. The result in Hopkins's view was the "waste" of his youth, the "waste" of meted hours lamented in "The Alchemist in the City," time spent in the "waste" woods of early love poetry in "A Voice from the World," as well as the hours given to backsliding temptations represented by the "wasteful" Nile in "A Soliloquy of One of the Spies Left in the Wilderness" (1864).

While the "chilling remembrance of days of old" in "See how Spring" is a recollection of adolescent worldliness generally, the focus on the "waste done in unreticent youth" places special emphasis on writing poems, those "songs among the secret trees" that Christina Rossetti urged her reader to sacrifice in "The Convent Threshold." Hopkins responded with a sense of remorse for his early Keatsian poetry, a feeling which no doubt encouraged his admiration for vows of silence in "The Habit of Perfection" and the actual burning of his poems in 1868.

As a contrast to *acedia*—the sin of waste and spiritual sloth—in the *Purgatorio* Dante cites the example of Mary who "went into the hill country with haste," and Dante's terms echo throughout the poetry of Christina Rossetti and Hopkins, especially the early poems he wrote under her influence: "Haste, haste, lest time be lost for little love . . . that zeal in well-doing may make grace come green again." Dante warns the reader specifically against the "negligence and delay that you have shown by lukewarmness in well-doing" (18:100–08). He then compares those who succumb to *acedia* to the Hebrews who passed over the Red Sea (132–35) but suffered sadness in the desert and nostalgia for their stable life in Egypt. Their sadness led them at times to abhor even the manna and thus led to the punishment of being deprived of the Promised Land (Num. 14).

Savonarola and Asceticism

Hopkins's "A Soliloquy of One of the Spies Left in the Wilderness" is obviously a version of this common "type" of *acedia*. It appears, moreover, to be based directly on an account Hopkins read of the great reformer, Savonarola, the famous burner of profane art in Renaissance Italy. Savonarola was "the only person in history (except perhaps Origen) about whom" Hopkins had "real feeling" because for Hopkins Savonarola was "the prophet of Christian art" (*F*, 17–18). One of the books Hopkins read about Savonarola, by Alexis Rio, stated that "among the seven plagues of Egypt there were at least three to which the imagination of Savonarola found means to attach analogous significations; the Jews, who loathed the manna in the wilderness, and sighed after the fleshpots of Egypt, prefigured Christians, who, having the word of God at their command, neglected it, in order to devote themselves to profane studies."[14] The spy in Hopkins's poem represents the sort of man Hopkins feared he would become if he neglected the Bible for his Greek studies and became too attached to their pagan worldliness.

Savonarola's example reinforced Christina Rossetti's in this way and encouraged Hopkins to move beyond not only his Greek studies but also the imitation of nature that characterized his early art, and ultimately inspired him to give up nature, beauty, and art altogether in 1868. Savonarola's attack on naturalism made it difficult for Hopkins to maintain his allegiance to the "Ruskinese" doctrine of truth to nature which Hopkins embodied in his drawings and defended in his 1864 essay on the arts. Hence Hopkins soon followed the example set by Savonarola's and Christina Rossetti's sacrifice of beauty and returned to the inner way, to the ashes, "the garb of woe, and the sad footsteps slow" he had discarded in "Easter," to the physical mortification of "Easter Communion," and to the ascetic deprivation of "The Habit of Perfection."

As early as November of 1865 he wrote, "On this day by God's grace I resolved to give up all beauty until I had His leave for it"

(*J*, 71). Two months later, in "The Habit of Perfection," as we have seen, he concluded that he must sacrifice not only beauty but virtually all external sensations in preparation for a retreat from the external world of nature to the internal world of the self. Like Christina Rossetti's poetry, Savonarola's sermons encouraged this resolution, for they too emphasized an internal worship, a turning inward, away from the untrustworthy senses.

Savonarola's example also inspired the next stage of Hopkins's asceticism in the 1860s, the sacrifice of his art, not merely his songs of nature, but even attempts to express the beauty of asceticism such as "Easter Communion" and "The Habit of Perfection." This self-destroying tendency is an ever-present possibility in English otherworldly art which, like a moth to a flame, so often flirts with that Puritan fear of art which Savonarola articulated so well. As Pater put it, "the sensuous expression of conceptions which unresevedly discredit the world of sense is the delicate problem which Christian art" must face.[15]

A week after he composed "The Habit of Perfection" Hopkins was considering what he should give up for Lent and he singled out his poetry (*J*, 72). Later that year Hopkins apparently offered to give up his "profane" studies altogether, but John Henry Newman, the exemplar for Hopkins's conversion, urged him not to (*F*, 405). In February of 1868 he wrote to A. W. M. Baillie, "You know I once wanted to be a painter. But even if I could I wd. not I think, now, for the fact is that the higher and more attractive parts of the art put a strain upon the passions which I should think it unsafe to encounter" (*F*, 231). This was the same justification Rio ascribed to Savonarola's sacrifice of art: "From his first entrance into monastic life, he imposed upon himself the obligation of surrendering everything which might excite his affection too strongly."[16] The sacrifice of painting was in fact common among artists who followed Savonarola. Praising the willingness of artists to give up their art as signs of their commitment to Savonarola, Rio points to Botticelli's sacrifice of painting and resolution to die of hunger rather than return to it, to Fra Bartolommeo who, like Hopkins, gave up painting because it was a distraction to his monastic pursuit of the ascetic ideal, and to Monte di Giovanni whose seven-year renunciation of painting set the example for Hopkins's seven-year renunciation of poetry from 1868 to 1875.

On May 5, 1868, Hopkins firmly "resolved to be a religious" (*J*, 165). Less than a week later, apparently still inspired by Savonarola, he made a bonfire of his own poems and gave up poetry almost entirely for seven years. He burned even his religious poems because he "saw they wd. interfere with my state and vocation" (*B*, 24), though his phrase "slaughter of the innocents" (*J*, 165) implies that he realized that these poems were not guilty of the same worldliness as the pagan books and paintings Savonarola burned. All poetry was "profane study," however, according to Savonarola and it was because of profane studies that those who heard the word of God neglected it and sighed after the fleshpots of Egypt. Finally, in the fall of 1868 Hopkins joined a "serged fellowship" like the one he admired in "Easter Communion," a commitment foreshadowed in his emphasis on vows of "Silence" and "Poverty" in "The Habit of Perfection."

The stress in that poem on increased pleasure in feasting after fasting, however, as well as on relishing incense, on "feel-of-primrose hands," and on feet "that want the yield of plushy sward," suggests the complexity of the relation between Hopkins's art and his asceticism. Pater's explanation of the effect of abstinence on the senses of the medieval ascetic, for instance, reveals a relation between Hopkins's asceticism and the extreme sensitivity and violence of sensation in his poetry: "a passion of which the outlets are sealed, begets a tension of nerve, in which the sensible world comes to one with a reinforced brilliance and relief—all redness is turned into blood, all water into tears."[17] In fact, similar imagery recurs in Hopkins's simile, "it is as if the blissful agony or stress of selving in God had forced out drops of sweat or blood, which drops were the world" (*S*, 197).

Natural desires are suppressed to conquer the self and to imitate Christ but, as "The Habit of Perfection" reveals, the result is almost inevitably heightened sensations in this life as well as the next. This reflexive aspect of asceticism is conveyed perfectly by the word-music of "Easter Communion." Words whose meanings relate them to the pain of Lent are rhymed by short *e* assonance—"Lenten," "breathtaking," "chequers," "ever-fretting," "punishment"—while words whose meanings are associated with the joy of Easter are rhymed by long *e* assonance—"feast," "Easter," "sweetness." From the striking rhyme of "fasted" and "feast" in the first line, alliteration and assonance stress the connection between these apparently antithetical sensations. The cold East wind associated with famine in Gen. 41 also prepares us to hear the rhyming of opposites in "feast" and "east," "Easter" and "East," while less obtrusive assonance links "sackcloth" and "gladness," "weary" and "myrrhy."

Revolt Against Dualism

Victorian writers loved these paradoxical similarities as well as the sharp contrasts between opposites. Theirs was not only the era of "the divided self," of Christina Rossetti and the popularity of Savonarola, but also of the reconciliation of opposites, a movement led by the Pre-Raphaelites. In his essay on Dante Rossetti, Pater summarized the Pre-Raphaelite rejection of such dualisms as "the Manichean opposition of spirit and matter": "Spirit and matter, indeed, have been for the most part opposed, with a false contrast or antagonism by schoolmen, whose artificial creations those abstractions really are. In our actual concrete experience, the two trains of phenomena which the words *matter* and *spirit* do but roughly distinguish, play inextricably into each other."[18]

One of the features that attracted many critics to Hopkins's mature poetry initially was precisely this rejection of simplistic dichotomies, which they saw in Hopkins's ambiguities, paradoxes, and metaphysical conceits. This revolt against dualism became one of the chief values not only of Hopkins's poetry but of modern poetry generally.[19]

Hopkins's most important revolt, his rejection of the antithesis of spirit and matter, was supported by Catholicism as well as Pre-Raphaelitism. In his essay on Dante Gabriel Rossetti, Pater stressed that "practically, the church of the Middle Age by its aesthetic worship, its sacramentalism, its real faith in the resurrection of the flesh, had set itself against that Manichean opposition of spirit and matter, and its results in men's way of taking life; and in this, Dante is the central representative of its spirit."[20] Ironically, among the

Victorians, Hopkins, rather than the Rossettis, became the central representative of this spirit.

After his initial withdrawal into himself, Hopkins learned a great deal from the Pre-Raphaelite revolt against dualism, especially from their attempts to create symbols for the larger whole which contains and transcends such oppositions as ideal versus real and spirit versus matter. Yet, while they tended to be either too specific, producing allegory rather than symbolism, or too general, choosing images with only vague, imprecise connotations of an ideal, invisible world, Hopkins eventually discovered that with centuries of Catholic iconography at his disposal he could create a truly sacramental symbolism in which the real genuinely participates in the ideal. The result is that a poem such as "The Windhover" can transmit their ultimate perception of unity in duality to some readers for whom the Pre-Raphaelites have become a lost chapter in the history of nineteenth-century art.

Hopkins's conversion to Catholicism was also part of his revolt against dualism. He converted to Catholicism not to be more ascetic, for asceticism was as Protestant as it was Catholic, but to be able to embrace the Catholic doctrine of the Real Presence of God in the Eucharist, the "Half-Way House" of God in this world, as Hopkins called it in his poem of that name (1864).

This explanation was not enough to satisfy his family, however. Hopkins's letter to them came as a great shock. He wrote to Newman: "I have been up at Oxford just long enough to have heard fr. my father and mother in return for my letter announcing my conversion. Their answers are terrible: I cannot read them twice" (*F*, 29). Meanwhile, Manley Hopkins was writing to Gerard's Anglican confessor, H. P. Liddon: "The blow is so deadly and great that we have not yet recovered from the first shock of it. We had observed a growing love for asceticism and high ritual, and . . . we believed he had lately resolved on taking orders in the English Church. . . . save him from throwing a pure life and a somewhat unusual intellect away in the cold limbo which Rome assigns to her English converts. The deepness of our distress, the shattering of our hopes and the foreseen estrangement which must happen, are my excuse for writing to you so freely" (*F*, 434–35). After receiving Liddon's reply, Manley wrote to him again, accusing Gerard of speaking "with perfect coldness of any possible estrangement from us, who have loved him with an unchanging love. His mother's heart is almost broken by this, and by his desertion from our Church, her belief in, and devotion to, [*sic*] which are woven in with her very being" (*F*, 435). Manley used similar terms in his letter to his son: "the manner in which you seem to repel and throw us off cuts us to the heart. . . . O Gerard my darling boy are you indeed gone from me?" (*F*, 97). These are the last words we know of between father and son from 1866 to 1871.

When Gerard converted to Catholicism he felt he had actually forfeited his rightful place in the family home; he did not even know if his father would let him in the house again. His letter reveals that his father consented to his presence there on one condition: "You are so kind as not to forbid me your house, to which I have no claim, on condition, if I understand, that I promise not to try to convert my brothers and sisters." This was not an easy condition for him to accept, however: "Before I can promise this I must get permission, wh. I have no doubt will be given. Of course this promise will not apply after they come of age. Whether after my reception you will still speak as you do now I cannot tell" (*F*, 94).

Despite these differences, Gerard did spend his Christmas holidays with his family in 1866 and 1867, but what his father called "the foreseen estrangement which must happen" necessarily increased when Hopkins became a Jesuit in 1868. He spent Christmas away from his family from 1868 to 1871. He returned to the family hearth for Christmas in the following years, but in 1885 his Dublin poems still testified to the lonely isolation and anticipation of death characteristic of many Victorian orphans:

> To seem the stranger lies my lot, my life
> Among strangers. Father and mother dear,
> Brothers and sisters are in Christ not near
>
> . . . .
> I am in Ireland now; now I am at a third
> Remove. Not but in all removes I can
> Kind love both give and get. . . .

When, aged only forty-four, he was finally close to the farthest remove, death, another reconciliation was attempted, but it was too late. His was a painful and poignant tragedy all too typical of Victorian families.

His father had written, "by study hard WITHIN THE CHURCH YARD / IS FOUND THE PHILOSOPHER'S STONE." Ironically, it was by following this advice that father and son became estranged. The son did study hard within the churchyard and he found that the Incarnation and especially the Catholic concept of the Real Presence was his philosopher's stone. The Catholic doctrine of Transubstantiation became for him the mystical catalyst which could transmute into gold, redeem and regenerate, all that is base—what Hopkins called the "triviality of this life" (*F*, 19), "the *sordidness* of things" (*F*, 226). In his letter to his father, Hopkins stated:

This belief once got is the life of the soul and when I doubted it I shd. become an atheist the next day. But, as Monsignor Eyre says, it is a gross superstition unless guaranteed by infallibility. I cannot hold this doctrine confessedly except as a Tractarian or as a Catholic: the Tractarian ground I have seen broken to pieces under my feet. What end then can be served by a delay in wh. I shd. go on believing this doctrine as long as I believed in God and shd. be by the fact of my belief drawn by a lasting strain towards the Catholic Church? (*F*, 92)

Contrary to his father's assertions, these were not last minute thoughts. Hopkins had long been attracted to the idea of the Incarnation, especially as epitomized in the doctrine of the Real Presence. It was an idea which could radically change his poetic as well as his religious temperament. In January of 1866 he had written to E. H. Coleridge:

It is incredible and intolerable if there is nothing wh. is the reverse of trivial and will correct and avenge the triviality of this life. To myself all this trivialness is one of the strongest reasons for the opposite belief and is always in action more or less . . . I think that the trivialness of life is, and personally to each one, ought to be seen to be, done away with by the Incarnation. (*F*, 19)

In September of 1865 Hopkins wrote his friend A. W. M. Baillie
about

the difference the apprehension of the Catholic truths one after the other
makes in one's views of everything, beyond all others those of course of
the blessed sacrament of the altar. You will no doubt understand what I
mean by saying that the *sordidness* of things, wh. one is compelled per-
petually to feel, is perhaps, . . . the most unmixedly painful thing one
knows of: and this is (objectively) intensified and (subjectively) destroyed
by Catholicism. If people cd. all know this, to take no higher ground, no
other inducement wd. to very many minds be needed to lead them to
Catholicism and no opposite inducement cd. dissuade them fr. it.   (F,
226–27)

As early as June of 1864 Hopkins wrote to E. H. Coleridge: "The
great aid to belief and object of belief is the doctrine of the Real
Presence in the Blessed Sacrament of the Altar. Religion without
that is sombre, dangerous, illogical, with that it is—not to speak
of its grand consistency and certainty—loveable. Hold that and you
will gain all Catholic truth" (F, 17). Ironically, as we have seen,
"Catholic Truth" was the title of one of the poems in his father's
volume, *Pietas Metrica*.

The next month Hopkins wrote to Baillie, "I have written three
religious poems which however you would not at all enter into, they
being of a very Catholic character" (F, 213). The first of these poems
was apparently "Barnfloor and Winepress," published the next year
in the *Union Review* (1865). This poem, inspired by the doctrine of
the Real Presence, foreshadowed the poetry of nature Hopkins was
to compose in the late 1870s. It reveals how Hopkins could in his
imagination extend the idea of the mystical Body of Christ in the
communion bread and wine to the rest of nature. In this poem, the
wheat and grapes are not mere raw materials for Transubstantiation,
but rather are represented metaphorically as if they were already
participating in the Being of God. One of the attractions of the
doctrine of the Real Presence for Hopkins was that it was in this
way the central instance of a metaphor participating in the reality
it represents, the archetype for a sacramental poetry of nature.

"New Readings" (1864), the spring complement to this harvest poem, also reverses the imagery of the spy soliloquy: grapes and wheat are associated not with pagan Egypt but with Christ. Arid asceticism is repudiated by the water imagery of the first four lines of the poem, and by the last two lines of the poem which emphasize Christ's refusal to use a version of the heavenward stair to escape from this earth.

Admittedly, as we have seen, these poems were followed by more explicitly ascetic poems which stressed the inner rather than the outer way. Moreover, Hopkins did not discover Scotus until 1872, and "The Windhover" was not composed until 1877. Nevertheless, the seeds had been planted and the growth of a new style can be discerned even in the few exceptions Hopkins allowed in his seven-year renunciation of poetry: "Rosa Mystica," "Ad Mariam," and his revisions of "For a Picture of St. Dorothea."

Chapter Four

A New Style

Hopkins's new style was developed in response to his question, "If the best prose and the best poetry use the same language . . . why not use unfettered prose?" (*J*, 84). He answered, "It is plain that metre, rhythm, rhyme, and all the structure which is called verse both necessitate and engender a difference in diction and in thought." The first difference is "concentration and all which is implied by this. This does not mean terseness nor rejection of what is collateral nor emphasis nor even definiteness (*J*, 84). Indeed, though Hopkins achieved a conciseness and concentration unusual among Victorian poets, he did so not by rejecting but by inviting collateral meanings of words, that is, not by an exclusiveness but by an inclusiveness of meaning. For him a word was not limited to one of its meanings: "every word may be considered as the contraction or coinciding-point of its definitions" (*J*, 125). Thus, if the first principle of his new poetics is concentration, the second is multiple levels of meaning or, to borrow a term from science, multivalence.

Poetry differs from prose by a greater concentration not only of meaning, moreover, but also of word-music and imagery, according to Hopkins. Inspired by the pervasiveness of parallelism throughout the Bible, Hopkins reduced these third and fourth features of his poetry to his principle of parallelism or recurrence in the sounds and thought in a poem:

The artificial part of poetry, perhaps we shall be right to say all artifice, reduces itself to the principle of parallelism . . . in rhythm, the recurrence of a certain sequence of syllables, in meter, the recurrence of a certain sequence or rhythm, in alliteration, in assonance and in rhyme. Now the force of this recurrence is to beget a recurrence or parallelism answering to it in the words or thought and, speaking roughly and rather for the tendency than the invariable result, the more marked parallelism in structure whether of elaboration or of emphasis begets more marked parallelism in the words and sense. And moreover parallelism in expression tends to beget or passes into parallelism in thought . . . metaphor, simile, parable, and so on, where the effect is sought in likeness of things, and antithesis, contrast, and so on, where it is sought in unlikeness. (*J*, 84–85)

Such a definition of poetry supplies the broad parameters within which Hopkins developed the style that made him a great English poet, a style developed primarily between 1868 and 1875, seven years during which, paradoxically, he composed very few poems. The birth of the new style is apparent, however, in revisions of his earlier Pre-Raphaelite poems, especially "For a Picture of St. Dorothea," and in the only new poems of this period, "Ad Mariam" and "Rosa Mystica." These initial attempts to discover his "authentic cadence"[1] illustrate the practical effects of his definition of poetry and, relatively simple in their own right, they show us how to approach the more difficult poems which followed.

Hopkins's revisions of "For a Picture of St. Dorothea," for example, demonstrate concisely how his definition of poetry as parallelism in sound led to his conception of poetry as speech, music, dramatic performance, and sacrament. "Rosa Mystica," on the other hand, illustrates clearly the answering parallelism in the thought in a poem, especially that special kind of recurrence described by such terms as "type," "antitype," and "archetype" which imply a multiplicity of "vertical" parallels and movements between God and the world as well as a sense of mystery and, at times, even obscurity of meaning. "Rosa Mystica" also epitomizes Hopkins's conception of poetry as discourse on a higher level of generality than prose and illustrates how Hopkins's conventional imagery restricts his originality primarily to his parallelism in sound, that is, his word-music.

Parallelism in Sound

Confronted with the example of Christina Rossetti's songs of heaven, Hopkins began to consider which of the senses is most important in our response to words: seeing or hearing. Ever since the invention of the alphabet, the initial visualization of language in the Western world, there has been a propensity to regard literature as essentially a visual art. "Oral Literature" is in fact a contradiction in terms, for "literature" means "letters." Hopkins eventually became aware, however, of the danger of this overemphasis on the role of the eye in communication and began to modify the visual models of language he had inherited from Keats, Ruskin, and the Pre-Raphaelites in order to place more emphasis on the role of the ear.

Ironically it was his revision of "For a Picture of St. Dorothea" that generated much of his distinctive auditory poetics, including his first use of sprung rhythm, his first dramatic monologue,[2] and his special use of word-music to "beget" metaphor. Though the title, "For a Picture of St. Dorothea," proclaims the poem's genre as the verbal imitation of the visual arts, Hopkins's revisions invoke the conventions of rival genres appealing to the ear more than the eye, that is, appealing more to the Victorians' fondness for reading aloud than to their love of word-painting, thus emphasizing the poem as speech, drama, and music.

Hopkins's aim was to revitalize the medieval legend of St. Dorothea. Just before her martyrdom, a lawyer named Theophilus jeeringly asked Dorothea to send him some fruits and flowers from the heavenly garden she believed awaited her. He converted when an angel delivered them. This legend became a favorite of the Pre-Raphaelites: Dante and Christina Rossetti, William Morris, Edward Burne-Jones, and A. C. Swinburne had all represented St. Dorothea in their art before Hopkins took her up in 1864.[3] When a subject such as this was represented in a Pre-Raphaelite painting, moreover, they frequently accompanied it with a poem for the painting in Dante Rossetti's manner, often inscribed in the frame of the painting itself.

Hopkins's title reminds us that he originally wanted to be a painter and a poet after the fashion of Dante Rossetti and the Pre-Raphaelites.[4] They obviously inspired both his subject and his choice of the genre of poems-for-pictures. Hopkins differed from them by substituting lilies, larkspurs, and a quince for the roses and apples in the legend, and by developing the exchange between Theophilus and Dorothea and/or her angel. His special emphasis on the role of speech and music, however, two auditory effects as likely to compete with visual sensations as to complement them, most clearly distinguished him from the Pre-Raphaelites.

Hopkins soon perceived that the ancient definition of poetry as a speaking picture is intrinsically dialectical, a contradiction in terms. His decision to stress speech made his poem-for-a-picture not merely independent of an imaginable picture but distinctively different from any picture. As he put it, "the sensations of the eye are given in space, those of the ear in time."[5] Speech, being invisible, with no existence in space, tended to force the imaginary picture of his title back into that world of time from which the spatial arts seem to escape.

Hopkins thus discovered how language has its own intrinsic generic propensities, especially a tendency to generate drama. In his first revision Hopkins's subtitle stressed the presence of two different speakers in the poem, and in his second he actually broke the poem up into five separate speeches. This incipient attraction to drama is more obvious in his plays—*Floris in Italy, Castara Victrix,* and *St. Winefred's Well*—but they, along with his more dramatic versions of "For a Picture of St. Dorothea," remain unfinished. His theatrical tendencies, like those of many Victorian poets, blossomed instead in his lyrics, in the interpolated "oh's," "ah's," and exclamation marks which, like the outbursts of the narrator in Dickens's novels or the histrionic gestures of Victorian melodrama, emphasize climactic moments. In "The Windhover" and "The Starlight Night" (1877), for instance, his interjections dramatize his excited discoveries of unusually felicitous sacramental symbols.

This love of drama led to the invention of "sprung rhythm" and the sacrifice of many of the painterly effects in "For a Picture of St. Dorothea" (I). Seeking the more dramatic conciseness and directness of the sense-stress rhythms of Renaissance verse drama, Hopkins replaced regular rhythms in the poems such as "I am so light, I am so fair" and "And at the basket that I bear," with the more concise "sprung" rhythms, "I am so light and fair" and "With the basket I bear" (II). A comparison of the original lines with their revisions reveals the most striking feature of sprung rhythm: the freedom to vary the number of unaccented syllables, allowing more conciseness, and a more dramatic stress on the accented syllables. It is a rhythm, as Hopkins said of his use of it in "Harry Ploughman," "which is altogether for recital, not for perusal (as by nature verse should be)" (B, 263).

This realization of the dramatic potential of language encouraged the idea that poetry should not be merely word-painting, but also, as Wordsworth put it, "man speaking to men." This archaic sense of literature as "speaking," and thus reading as "reading aloud," the common usage in ancient and medieval cultures, was revived in the nineteenth century, apparently as a response to the accelerating mechanization of printing. Even novels were read aloud to families and large audiences. Philip Collins reminds us that a hundred years ago "much current literature was apprehended in this way—was indeed written with such a reception in mind," and thus "many people met contemporary literature as a group or communal, rather than an individual experience."[6]

Hopkins in particular must have been conscious of the many parallels between the communal experiences of literature and religious ritual. At the time he was revising his Dorothea poem he was agonizing about his religious vocation and no doubt was aware that some of the most popular Victorian public readers were clergymen— indeed, two of the most successful were Anglican priests who had gone over to Rome. Moving in the same direction himself, Hopkins was in fact experiencing two simultaneous and related conversions; he felt the necessity of restoring not only the medieval religion but also some of the oral traditions with which it was identified.

Hence in his version of the legend of St. Dorothea Hopkins concentrated on the speeches that led to the conversion of Theophilus and, in the process, developed his theory of sprung rhythm. As he explained to his brother Everard in 1885,[7] sprung rhythm

gives back to poetry its true soul and self. As poetry is emphatically speech, speech purged of dross like gold in the furnace, so it must have emphatically the essential elements of speech. Now emphasis itself, stress, is one of these: sprung rhythm makes verse stressy; it purges it to an emphasis as much brighter, livelier, more lustrous than the regular but commonplace emphasis of common rhythm as poetry in general is brighter than common speech.

In his revisions of the Dorothea poem, Hopkins uses sprung rhythm to stress the "parley," the debate between Dorothea and Theophilus, which ironically had the effect of the delivery of a "writ" to the pagan Theophilus, himself the Protonotary, writer of writs, now converted by the spoken rather than the written word.

Hopkins's representation of the "parley" making its "market here as well," moreover, increases our sense of a discussion with an audience, both inside and outside the poem, which is to be persuaded to strike a bargain, "to make market," to trade, to buy. This dramatization of the role of the audience led to the explicit exhortations and question and answer technique in the sequel to the Dorothea poem, "The Starlight Night": "It is all a purchase, all is a prize. / Buy then! Bid then!—What?—Prayer, patience, alms, vows."

In many of Hopkins's subsequent poems the performance of the poem, the "parley" between the poem's speaker and the audience, is clearly intended to be the delivery of a "writ" for the audience's conversion. In other words, Hopkins replaced the modern axiom of the autonomy of the artistic imagination with the older idea of poetry as rhetoric. It can be argued that most of Hopkins's poetic techniques were developed to serve this clearly proselytical purpose. His most "modern" innovation, sprung rhythm, was obviously developed primarily for its rhetorical and oratorical potential: "Why do I employ sprung rhythm at all," Hopkins wrote to Bridges, "Because it is . . . the native and natural rhythm of speech, the least forced, the most rhetorical. . . . My verse is less to be read than heard, as I have told you before; it is oratorical, that is the rhythm is so" (*B*, 46). Along with the rhythm, the highly mnemonic sound structure of Hopkins's poems and their commonplace themes all suggest deep roots in the ancient tradition which defined poetry as a special kind of rhetoric, a tradition large enough to embrace even poems-for-pictures, for it prized *enargeia* (pictorial vividness) and *ecphrasis* (giving speech to an art object).[8]

As his commitment to medievalism in religion and art increased in the 1860s, Hopkins conceived of poetry not only as speech and drama but also as music. Music, the least representational, the most spiritual of the arts, generally replaced painting as the sister of poetry in the Middle Age. Thomas Aquinas's hymn, "Adoro Te

Supplex," for instance, which Hopkins translated, asserts of God: "Seeing, touching, tasting are in thee deceived; / How says trusty hearing? that shall be believed" ("S. Thomae Aquinatis Rhythmus," undated). Aquinas's emphasis on the ear was reinforced in the eighteenth century by Edmund Burke and Gotthold Lessing, who reaffirmed Aristotle's assertion that poetry belongs with music as an art of temporal movement. This thesis was also supported by the German critics most important to Hopkins, those who promulgated romanticism as a medievalist movement animated by Christian spiritualism: Johann Herder, W. H. Wackenroder, Novalis, and the Schlegels. They praised music as the nonmimetic, expressive art to which lyric poetry should aspire.

The English romantics adapted their musical analogy, often in Aeolian harp imagery, and John Keble consecrated it for the Victorians.[9] Thus, while Keats's "Ode on a Grecian Urn" epitomizes the romantic attraction to the visual arts, many other nineteenth-century poems emphasize affinities between poetry and music—so many, in fact, that romanticism has been defined as the shift from *ut pictura poesis* to *ut musica poesis*.[10] In his revisions of his Dorothea poem, Hopkins was reconstructing this basic pardigm of romanticism.

He unified his own poem-for-a-painting through word-music rather than word-painting. Recognizing that we need to integrate a poem (which we usually apprehend first in discrete units) more than a painting (which we first perceive in one glance), Hopkins unified his poems with what he called "verbal parallelisms." Recurrent patterns of consonance and assonance, along with the audible rhythms of structural parallelism which he called "the figure of grammar," replace the Pre-Raphaelite painters' unifying techniques of ornamental designs and color harmonies. Perhaps the most obvious examples are the initial images of "a basket lined with grass" (I–III), in which "basket" and "grass" are audibly linked by *a* assonance and *s* consonance, and the later image of a "quince in hand" (I) which is integrated by *i* assonance and *n* consonance. Similarly, it is the audible rhythm of structural parallelism ("the figure of grammar") that narrows the focus from St. Dorothea's basket of flowers to her lilies: "flowers I carry . . . Lilies I shew" (I). In addition to this kind of fugal iteration of structure, Hopkins also repeats sounds like "nor" to unify his picture, or in this case its disappearance: "We see nor fruit, nor flowers, nor Dorothy" (I).

The result is that although in fact we never see her, when the poem is read aloud we hear her music and that becomes the "message" of the poem. The impression of unity created by the word-music in "For a Picture of St. Dorothea" conveys the beauty of the final union with God in the realm in which Dorothea is "sphered": that heaven of "choice celestial music, equal to the motion of the spheres," invoked in Massinger's Renaissance drama of Dorothea, *The Virgin Martyr* (V, ii).

It was no doubt because music had such spiritual as well as formal powers that the musical analogy eventually became central to Hopkins's definition of poetry. He speculated that originally "music and verse were one" (*J*, 268) and such words as *"measure," "timbre," "melody," "air," "cadence," "rest," "modulation,"* and *"pitch"* pervade his discussions of poetry. Toward the end of his life he even preferred musical to rhetorical models for the performance of his poems: "above all remember what applies to all my verse, that it is, as a living art should be, made for performance and that its performance is not reading with the eye but loud, leisurely, poetical (not rhetorical) recitation, with long rests, long dwells on rhyme, and other marked syllables, and so on. This sonnet should be almost sung: it is most carefully timed in *tempo rubato*" (*B*, 246).

By aspiring to the condition of music, romantic poetry also sought to minimize the referential quality of language (which Victorian word-painting depended on), and thus lent itself to Hopkins's definition of poetry as "speech framed to be heard for its own sake and interest even over and above its interest of meaning. Some matter and meaning is essential to it but only as an element necessary to support and employ the shape which is contemplated for its own sake. (Poetry is in fact speech only employed to carry the inscape of speech for the inscape's sake—and therefore the inscape must be dwelt on)" (*J*, 289). In his own poetry Hopkins "dwells on" fugal repetition of the auditory inscape "to be heard for its own sake." Conventional syntax and clarity are consistently sacrificed for such musical effects, and the result in, say, "The Leaden Echo and the

Golden Echo," is an operatic performance which clearly subordinates the referential qualities of language to the musical.

This emphasis on language *qua* language and Hopkins's initial attraction to visual metaphors such as "the shape" of a poem, has naturally led us to associate his theories with modern criticism and its basic tenet of art for art's sake. The result, however, is often a misunderstanding of Hopkins's aims and methods. Many twentieth-century formalist critics, with basically spatial paradigms of language, naturally assume that language was primarily visual for Hopkins too and therefore the essence of poetry for him was writing and reading silently, alone.

Yet Hopkins said that "such verse as I do compose is oral, made away from paper, and I put it down with repugnance" (*F*, 379). Hopkins's increasing emphasis on auditory rather than spatial effects often means that his poetry, for all its apparent modernity, cannot be read the way we normally read modern literature, as Hopkins himself discovered to his surprise: "When on somebody returning me the *Eurydice*, I opened and read some lines, reading, as one commonly reads whether prose or verse, with the eyes, so to say, only, it struck me aghast with a kind of raw nakedness and un-mitigated violence I was unprepared for: but take breath and read it with the ears, as I always wish to be read, and my verse becomes all right" (*B*, 79). "The Loss of the *Eurydice*," his other shipwreck poem, was also on his mind when he wrote to Everard: "I am sweetly soothed by your saying that you could make anyone understand my poem by reciting it well. That is what I always hoped, thought, and said; it is my precise aim. And thereby hangs so considerable a tale, in fact the very thing I was going to write about Sprung Rhythm in general."

Hopkins's considerable tale concerns the relationship between poetry and music. He took liberties with traditional grammar and diction in order to transform speech into something like music. "Some matter and meaning is essential" but we are to concentrate on the musical "shape" of the words, until the music itself becomes meaningful. Encouraged by onomatopoetic etymologies of contem-porary linguists, Hopkins believed that similarity of sound in words "begets" similarity of meaning, that phonic harmony generates semantic harmony. Hopkins's choice of the word "begets," echoing the Nicene Creed's "Begotten not made, one in Being with," emphasizes not only the causal relationship, but the essential unity of sound and meaning.

This concept of the higher meaningfulness of the music of a poem had many nineteenth-century precedents. The romantics revived Pythagoras's theory of the music of the world, what Boethius called *musica mundana,* because they believed its sole aim is the Infinite.[11] Pater defined this Pythagorean and Platonic "music of the spheres in its largest sense, its completest orchestration" as "the harmonious order of the whole universe."[12] While contemporary musicologists related their studies to this music of the spheres and other mystical paradigms, Wordsworth asserted that "the roar of waters, torrents, streams / Innumerable" on top of Mt. Snowdon was "felt by the starry heavens."[13]

The Platonic emphasis on the rhetorical and ethical effects of man-made music, what Boethius called *musica humana,* also remained popular. The romantics recalled Longinus's assertion that harmonious word-music makes us receptive to sublimity, and Newman claimed that the "perfection of the Intellect" has "almost the beauty and harmony of heavenly contemplation, so intimate is it with the eternal order of things and the music of the spheres."[14] Similar ideas affected theorists both as modern as Valery, who felt that the aim of music in poetry was to produce an extraordinary harmony in the listener,[15] and as reactionary as the nineteenth-century medievalists, who resurrected many other traditional connotations of verbal harmony. Hopkins's word-music in his poem on Dorothea and her angel, for instance, may well be a response to Anna Jameson's insistence, in the book that inspired the cult of St. Dorothea, that "there is nothing more beautiful, more attractive in Art than the representation of angels" as the singers of the "music of the spheres."[16]

Hopkins's word-music was designed to "beget a recurrence or parallelism answering to it in the words or thought," moreover, ultimately a recurrence of the music of heaven. These connotations of harmony in poetry suggest how Hopkins's word-music was designed to convey that sense of the possibility of a radically different order of time and experience that is one of the goals of most religions. Hopkins's Dorothea poem shows how, from the beginning of his career, even in his most conventional, mimetic phase, Hopkins was interested in representing not only nature but that which seemed to miraculously deviate from nature. Religion encouraged Hopkins to represent this independent reality, this world unto itself, this time out of time. "For a Picture of St. Dorothea," like so many other Hopkins poems, is the music of this other word of centuries of religious traditions as well as the song of a particular self.

Ironically, while revising his poem-for-a-picture in search of new ways to tap the poetic power of these traditions, Hopkins's most important discovery was that the ear was more important than the eye. He sensed that the medieval age which his imaginary "picture" evoked was more alive than his own to the power of the spoken word, in the sacraments and in its oral traditions generally. Such traditions, as Walter Ong has shown,[17] consisting of audible rather than visualized words, make the world more personal, for spoken words invoke the presence of speakers.

It is a sign of the ability Hopkins acquired to revive those traditions that his poems written for performance often evoke a world inhabited by personified presences, a vitalistic world in which all objects are animated by powers "deep down" inside them, a world very much like that resurrected by his ultimate revision of the Dorothea poem: "The Starlight Night." In that poem as in so many others, Hopkins taps the extraordinary power of this vital oral tradition with a virtuoso auditory performance which rejuvenates and energizes the ancient metaphors. He extends their life in time in another sense as well: when the metaphors of "The Starlight Night" are spoken aloud, as they should be, they inevitably seem more successive and less simultaneous, for the tongue is much slower than the eye. But only by performing this and other poems by Hopkins aloud can a reader apprehend this aspect of his metaphors and feel the primary effect he aimed at in all his poetry: the parallelism of his sounds actually "begetting" the parallelism of his images, the integration of his word-music activating and reinforcing the unifying power of the metaphors.

Hopkins thus resurrected the original meaning of the term "sonnet"—like "sonata" it means "to be sounded or played." That his poems are based on a theory of poetry as performance was the rest of that "considerable tale" he adumbrated in his letter to Everard in 1885:

Every art then and every work of art has its own play or performance . . . books play, perform, or are played and performed when they are read; and ordinarily by one reader, alone, to himself, with the eyes only. . . . Poetry was originally meant for either singing or reciting; a record was kept of it; the record could be, was, read, and that in time by one reader, alone, to himself, with his eyes only. This reacted on the art: what was to be performed under these conditions for these conditions ought to be and was composed and calculated. Sound-effects were intended, wonderful combinations even; but they bear the marks of having been meant for the whispered, not even whispered, merely mental performance of the closet, the study and so on. . . . This is not the true nature of poetry . . . *till it is spoken it is not performed,* it does not perform, it is not itself. . . .

Hopkins's use of the word "perform" here is full of echoes of the King James Bible familiar to most Victorians. These echoes include that sense of fulfilment of prophecy so basic to the typological imagination: "For I am the LORD; I will speak, and the word that I shall speak shall come to pass . . . in your days . . . will I say the word, and will perform it" (Ezek. 12:25).

But the biblical "perform" is not limited to this typological meaning; it conveys all the connotations of speech as act: "I am the LORD that . . . confirmeth the word of his servant, and performeth the counsel of his messengers; that saith to Jerusalem, Thou shalt be inhabited; and to the cities of Judah, ye shall be built, . . . That saith to the deep, Be dry, and I will dry up thy rivers; That saith of Cyrus, He is my shepherd, and shall perform all my pleasure; even saying unto Jerusalem, Thou shalt be built, and to the temple, Thy foundation shall be laid" (Isa. 44:24–28). One of the reasons that the Bible is *the* book of Western civilization is that it is the one most in tune with those original oral traditions which endow our language with great power. The source of the ultimate performatives in our language, the Bible is the drama of word as event, speech as act, from the creation ("And God said, Let there be light: and there was light") to the New Testament: "In the beginning was the Word, and the Word was with God, and the Word was God." Biblical words are clearly kinetic, dynamic—they make things happen.

The emphasis is of course on speech, not writing, for the Hebrew tradition is oriented to the ears, not the eyes. The God of the ten commandments is heard, not seen: "And the LORD spake unto you out of the midst of the fire; ye hear the voice of the words, but saw no similitude; only ye heard a voice: And he declared unto his covenant, which he commanded you to perform" (Deut. 4:12–13). Other echoes of the word "perform" also stress the effect of the voice of the invisible God on the ear: "And the LORD said to Samuel; Behold, I will do a thing in Israel, at which both the ears of everyone that heareth it shall tingle. In that day I will perform" (Isa. 3:11–12).

To move closer to Hopkins's own situation, much of this sense of the power of the word is transferred to the poet when the word of the Lord comes to him and he accepts the role of the prophet with his "Amen" ("So be it"): "The word that came to Jeremiah from the LORD, saying, Hear ye the words of this covenant, and speak unto the men of Judah, and to the inhabitants of Jerusalem; And say unto them, Thus saith the LORD God of Israel; cursed be the man that obeyeth not the words of this covenant . . . Obey my voice, and do them, according to all which I command you; so shall ye be my people, and I will be your God: That I may perform the oath that I have sworn unto your fathers, to give them a land flowing with milk and honey, as it is this day. Then answered I, and said, So be it, O LORD" (Jer. 11:1–5).

So far we may seem to have stayed within the oral tradition, though the Bible is its visual transcription, but the biblical echoes of the word "perform" include explicit instructions on how to perform a written text: "And the king stood by a pillar, and made a covenant before the Lord, to walk after the Lord, and to keep his commandments and his testimonies and his statutes with all their heart and all their soul, to perform the words of this covenant that were written in this book" (2 Kings 23:3). In this model of reading, the performance of the words of a text demands the complete participation of the reader; his heart and soul are to embrace the heart and soul of the text: "I have inclined my heart to perform thy statutes alway, even unto the end" (Ps. 119:112). It is not enough to read the text, or even to speak it aloud; one must pour one's whole being into the performance of it: "That which has gone out of thy lips thou shalt keep and perform" (Deut. 23:23); "Now therefore perform the doing of it; that as there was a readiness to will, so there may be a performance also out of that which ye have" (2 Cor. 8:11).

This sense of the text as the script for a performance is clearly at the other end of the spectrum from the idea of the text as merely a visual object. Hopkins soon discovered that to read with the eyes only is to be deaf and dumb, to have one's organs closed to the magical or miraculous power of words in performance. In his sermon, "Cure of the Deaf and Dumb Man; Ephphetha," for instance, Hopkins recalls that "having made the organs ready to hear and speak he looked up to heaven and groaned. . . . *And said Ephphetha, Be opened*—The evangelist tells us the very word which had this magical or rather miraculous effect. . . . Much more should we admire what Christ has done for us—made us deaf hear, if we will hear . . . made us dumb speak" (*S*, 17–18).

Hopkins's literary goal was a new genre of spoken lyric emphasizing poetry's affinities with speech and drama rather than the visual arts. Anticipating H. Marshall McLuhan and Walter Ong, he suggested how the phonograph, which had been invented only seven years before, could help restore the human voice to literature:

I look on this as an infinite field and very little worked. It has this great difficulty, that the art depends entirely on living tradition. The phonograph may give us one, but hitherto there could be no record of fine spoken utterance. . . . the natural performance and delivery belonging properly to lyric poetry, which is speech, has not been enough cultivated, and should be. When performers were trained to do it (it needs the rarest gifts) and audiences to appreciate it it would be, I am persuaded, a lovely art. . . . With the aid of the phonograph each phrase could be fixed and learned by heart like a song.

As I have suggested elsewhere, the poetics expressed in this letter suggest our need to reevaluate how we teach literature and how we communicate generally.[18]

Parallelism in Thought

Hopkins's emphasis on the performance of his auditory parallelism also affected his conception of the role of the answering parallelism in thought, especially metaphor. He "performed" his picture of St. Dorothea, for instance, primarily by prolonging the metaphoric parallels as only spoken language can, stressing the dramatic metamorphosis inherent in the idea of metaphor.

Hopkins usually rejects instantaneous parallels between two realms of experience—the reduction of a poem to an image like "her quince, the moon; her flowers, the stars"—because his aim is ultimately to dramatize the fact that the realms are not merely parallel but interpenetrating, capable not only of juxtaposition but also of mutual metamorphosis:

> Had she a quince in hand? Yet gaze:
> Rather it is a sizing moon.
> Lo, linked heavens with milky ways!
> That was her larkspur row.—So soon?
> Sphered so fast, sweet soul?—We see
> Nor fruit, nor flowers, nor Dorothy. (I)

Quince is not merely compared to moon, flowers to stars: they become them. The earth is not merely juxtaposed with heaven, rather the part of it represented by Dorothea ascends into heaven. In this and his later poems Hopkins emphasizes these dramatic vertical actions possible in metaphor. The upward motion from man to God is stressed here, but there is also evidence of the downward motion from God to man possible in metaphor, the opportunity for sacramental symbolism, the ultimate verbal synthesis.

In his revisions of this early poem Hopkins took a few steps toward his distinctive natural supernaturalism which reconciles Pre-Raphaelitism and the Oxford Movement, pictures of earth and songs of heaven, the visual and the visionary, outer and inner realities, both sight and sound. In both revisions he insisted that Dorothea's "parley was not done and there!" After she is "sphered," Theophilus turns to the luminous traces of the supernatural left behind in the natural world, hints of aspects of the Incarnation persisting even after the Ascension:

> It waned into the world of light,
> Yet made its market here as well:
> My eyes hold yet the rinds and bright
> Remainder of a miracle. (II)

We recall Henry Vaughan's "They are All Gone into the World of Light," but for Theophilus, and for Hopkins's speakers in subsequent poems, all is not "gone." The flaming sunset clouds, the moon, and the stars are perceived as rinds—verges, rims, or borders—of the world of light, revelations of the luminosity of eternity still perceptible, albeit waned, in the mortal world.

The poem itself is a rind and bright remainder of a miracle, moreover. It is a marvelous vision which, like the original vision of St. Dorothea, soon ends, but leaves some luminous traces on the reader's mind. As such it must have suggested to Hopkins the possibility of genuinely sacramental poetry, the utterance of words that bestow grace. If the purpose of Dorothea's "parley" and her sacred "writ" was to bring "grace" to Theophilus and convert him, Hopkins no doubt hoped that eventually his own speech and writing might confer grace on some of his readers, convert them, draw them closer to God, and thereby become truly sacramental. Ultimately, his poems are not only vehicles for conversion but even, in a sense, for transubstantiation, for "performative utterances" of the Word in the tradition of the Bible and the liturgy somehow share in the Being of the Word, in the Being of God, in the world. [19]

With such sacramental functions, Hopkins's parallelism in thought, his metaphors, acquire great powers of fusion. All metaphors and all literature based on them are inherently ambiguous, but Hopkins draws on the religious context of his art and life to extend and enrich the potential for unification inherent in the indeterminacy of language. Most metaphors are more alive when they can tap forces in their context—in the rest of the poem, in the poet's other poems, in his art and life as a whole, and especially in literature and language over the centuries—but the metaphors with the greatest potential for integration are undoubtedly those still the focus of a living religion, for "religious myth," as Philip Wheelwright put it, "is the large-scale authorization of poetic metaphor."[20]

Hopkins's metaphors were indeed the focus of a living religion, and thus it is essential to understand something about that religion, especially the religious context which authorized his sense of parallelism in thought, that of the conservative Oxford Movement (also known as Tractarianism) and the Catholic Revival. John Henry Newman's role in Hopkins's conversion is conspicuous, but we must also consider the impact on his art of the other two leaders of the Oxford Movement, E. B. Pusey and John Keble, both of whom remained Anglicans. Pusey was Hopkins's first confessor, Hopkins attended his lectures on Old Testament types, and even after his conversion Hopkins said he revered him "most of all men in the world."[21] Keble's *The Christian Year*, based on poetics similar to Pusey's, was the most famous Victorian prototype for Hopkins's religious nature poetry.[22]

One of the specific literary traditions they encouraged in Hopkins was that of the typical and typological representational modes of medieval art. Darwinism and allied philosophies of flux generally displaced this kind of imagery in modern poetry, but, as we have seen, Hopkins responded to Darwin's challenge. He defended the idea of the "type" by arguing that "there are certain forms which have a great hold on the mind and are always reappearing and seem imperishable . . . and these things are inexplicable on the theory of pure chromaticism or continuity—the forms have in some sense or other an absolute existence" (*J*, 120).

This concept of the "type" in Hopkins's argument is crucial to an understanding of Hopkins's sense of parallelism and his life and art generally. It has at least two related sets of meanings. First of all, as we have seen, the "type" is the general form distinguishing a particular group or class: the pattern, mold, model, or paradigm of the group or species, a sense of the word related to the idea of Platonic "forms" and to the idea of a "typical" member of a group. The second set of meanings focuses on how a "typical" member of a species represents or stands for the whole group. In this sense "type" has come to mean almost anything symbolical or emblematic.

In this second sense of the word, "type" (*tupos*) or "figure" (*figura*) has a particular meaning of special importance to Hopkins. In biblical interpretation, an Old Testament person, event, or thing which parallels, prefigures, or foreshadows a New Testament person, event, or thing is said to be a "type," and the parallel New Testament person, event, or thing is called the "antitype," a word which means not the opposite of the Old Testament type but a recurrence of it in the same mold (our word "type" derives from the Greek word for "mold"). In this way "type" has come to mean the signifier and "antitype" the signified. Thus Job's suffering is a type, and its parallel in the New Testament, Christ's passion, is its antitype. Similarly, Eden is a type of our mental state after baptism and/or our experience of heaven after death. This set of meanings of the word "type" was specially significant for Hopkins because of its focus on Jesus, for him the "archetype," the ultimate "mold" for all aspects of his life and art. Jesus' example was *the* "form" which had the greatest "hold on the mind," was "always reappearing," was "imperishable," a type which had "in some sense or other an absolute existence."

Inspired by this ultimate archetype, much of Hopkins's poetry was an attempt to fulfill Ruskin's prophecy in 1852 that "some day the language of Types will be more read and understood by us than it has been for centuries" (11:41). To that end, the language of types had been expanded beyond the familiar sense of parallels between the Old and New Testaments to include parallels of all kinds between God, man, and nature by the Pre-Raphaelites and many other Victorians ranging from Ruskin, Tennyson, and the Brownings to popular hymn writers and religious versifiers.[23]

The most important pioneers of this movement for Hopkins were Newman, Pusey, and Keble, who resurrected the typological traditions of the early church fathers. Newman, for instance, thought it "significant" that Joseph Butler began his *Analogy of Religion* (1736) with a quote from Origen, a father of the church who perceived the world pervaded by multivalent types and symbols of the invisible world.[24] Along with Savonarola, Origen became one of the two men in history for whom Hopkins had "a real feeling" (F, 17).

The result of the influence of the church fathers and their interpreters in the Oxford Movement was the revival of a special kind of parallelism described by Keble in Tract 89: "We know not how much there may be, far beyond mere metaphor and similitude, in His using the name of any of His creatures, in a translated sense, to shadow out something invisible. But thus far we may seem to understand, that the object thus spoken of by Him is so far out of the number of ordinary figures of speech, and resources of language, and partakes thenceforth of the nature of a Type."[25] The nature of a type according to the Tractarians was that it could eventually become an instrument as well as sign of the supernatural, that is, it could become a sacrament. Newman emphasized that of "the two main intellectual truths which Keble's {The Christian Year} brought home to me. . . . The first of these was what may be called, in a large sense of the word, the Sacramental system: that is, the doctrine that material phenomena are both the types and instruments of real things unseen."[26]

This doctrine is the key to Hopkins's special concept of parallelism in thought, as we shall see, but first we must recognize that his poetry exemplifies both sets of meanings of the word "type," the typical as well as the typological. Despite his apparent attraction to isolated details of nature in his journals and drawings, in his poetry Hopkins rarely depicts the unique individual, preferring to represent nature more "typically," more in the manner of the "Middle Age Art" he praised as an example of the "coexistence of realism with broad conventionalism" (J, 77).

As we have seen, Hopkins distinguished between prose and poetry in many ways. He maintained the stress of the medieval *artes poeticae* on figures of words, patterns of parallelism in sound, and on parallels in thought such as metaphor and allegory. He concluded that as a result "it is commonly supposed that poetry has tasked the highest powers of man's mind . . . as it asked for greater emphasis of thought and on a greater scale, at each stage it threw out the minds unequal to further ascent" (J, 84–85).

Hopkins's own thought in his poems is indeed on a greater scale than in his journals and consequently nature is represented more typically. Even "Pied Beauty" and "As kingfishers catch fire" (undated), poems devoted to the individual selfhood of "All things counter, original, spare, strange," illustrate Hopkins's preference for plural, collective nouns in poetry—"skies," "finches," "all trades," "kingfishers," "dragonflies," "stones"—nouns which denote not the individual but the larger unity of the class. This imagery of the species rather than the unique individual was clearly encouraged by Hopkins's medievalism, the counterpoise in his poetic to his attraction to isolated details.

His medievalism influenced his typological as well as his typical mode of artistic representation, and as a result displaced his earlier attraction to the metaphysical poetry of George Herbert and others. Instead of enumerating a number of precise and rigorous parallels between two explicitly identified objects in a one-to-one analogy, as in the seventeenth-century metaphysical conceit, medieval poets, and romantics after them, often preferred to leave one of the two terms implicit in order to suggest a whole hierarchy of meanings, meanings which tended to be more "vertical," that is, more oriented to the infinite and eternal. Such vertical parallels were not often invoked in the Renaissance because God was assumed to be in the background, as He is in Shakespeare's plays, for example. However, even when He was supposed to be in the foreground—in George Herbert's *The Temple* and John Donne's *Holy Sonnets* for instance—the most common parallels remain "horizontal" comparisons of the self to other earthly objects.

Such comparisons pervade much of romantic literature, of course, and science had clearly pushed God further into the background in the nineteenth century, but for that very reason He was more strenuously sought in symbols of the presence of the infinite and the eternal in this world. The romantics were less sure about that Presence than their medieval ancestors, however, and with less of a sense of limits of meaning for their symbols, they often allowed so many disparate and contradictory meanings that their symbols were reduced to intimations of the inexpressible. Yeats's rose imagery, for example, differs markedly in this respect from Dante's.[27]

The Oxford Movement and the Catholic Revival, however, made it possible for Hopkins's images to be more like Dante's than Yeats's. They restored to romanticism some of the medieval sense of a definitive set of meanings which could still endow a symbol with the highest possible vertical parallelism. Consequently, just as the religious poets of the Middle Ages often seem less worldly than their Renaissance counterparts, Victorian religious medievalists often appear more *meta*physical than the metaphysicals. In their imagery as in their architecture the religious medievalists consistently valued traditional vertical correspondences between this world and God higher than novel lateral correspondences between earthly objects. While Newman rejoiced in the "idea of an analogy between the separate works of God," Hopkins and Christina Rossetti delighted in multifaceted similes comparing many different objects, and Francis Thompson felt that man could not "stir a flower / Without troubling of a star," such lateral parallelism was only the epiphenomena of their explicit vertical connections, their persistent unifying symbolism of the world as "word, expression, news of God."[28] Victorian religious medievalists emphasized this hierarchical rather than lateral imagery even in such ingenious systems of correspondences as Christina Rossetti's *Called To Be Saints* or such extended "metaphysical" conceits as Hopkins's "The Blessed Virgin compared to the Air we Breathe." Hence Hopkins was more capable of resurrecting the sacramental and incarnational elements of medieval art than either the secular romantics or the metaphysicals.

His success in this respect was due partly to the revival of another essential trait of his medieval ancestors, emphasis on tradition rather than novelty and personal display. The Oxford Movement attracted Hopkins and others by offering what T. S. Eliot called the "historical sense," that sense of "the timeless and the temporal together" which makes a writer "traditional," something more than an individual talent.[29] Hopkins was obviously attracted to the metaphysical and romantic preoccupation with the individual personality, especially in his poems about God and the self, but the medievalism represented by Keble, Pusey, and Newman became for him a counterpoise to that romantic obsession with individual talent which some of his modern critics identify with his "self-regarding" preoccupation with ingenious metaphysical conceits and formal patterns.[30]

Instead of being a God-like romantic creator, however, a religious medievalist was expected merely to identify parallels he did not invent and suggest how they pointed to a reality infinitely greater than his own. As in T. S. Eliot's "Tradition and the Individual Talent" he was asked for "a continual surrender of himself as he is at the moment to something which is more valuable," a "continual self-sacrifice, a continual extinction of personality." Hopkins was trying to make this kind of sacrifice when he joined the Society of Jesus, and he often tried to surrender to the more valuable tradition in his art as well.

As the references to Eliot suggest, Hopkins's transference of allegiance from seventeenth-century metaphysical to medieval models in the 1870s foreshadows a similar shift in T. S. Eliot's career when he discovered in the 1920s that "the metaphysical poetry of Dante and of his era" represented "a civilization often superior to ours, superior also to the civilization of the world of Donne."[31] Like Eliot after him, Hopkins was seeking to identify with an age which offered a more earnest, more secure faith than Donne's could, preoccupied as the Renaissance was with the rise of the new science and those vacillations between reason and faith, skepticism and spirituality which eventually attracted so many twentieth-century artists struggling with their own rationalism and cynicism.

If Eliot's shift to the medieval model becomes apparent in "Ash Wednesday," Hopkins's becomes obvious in "Rosa Mystica," an instructive example of just how "typical," rather than particular, Hopkins's imagery can be. More in the tradition of Dante than John Donne,[32] Hopkins gives his rose no distinctive details; it is only a type of the species, rose. By evoking many parallels with an order of time and existence outside earthly reality, like a turning diamond reflecting light off many facets, Hopkins's rose metaphor unifies his poem:

> The rose in a mystery—where is it found?
> Is it anything true? Does it grow upon ground?
> It was made of earth's mould but it went from men's eyes
> And its place is a secret and shut in the skies.

Refrain—
In the gardens of God, in the daylight divine
Find me a place by thee, mother of mine.

The rose's origin, name, color, number of leaves, and scent are then discussed in seven subsequent stanzas, each employing the same question-and-answer pattern followed by a refrain. All but the last refrain begins with the same line and they all end, *"mother of mine."*

The constant focus on the rose illustrates the importance of multivalence in Hopkins's new style. In the first half of "Rosa Mystica" the rose is an abstract idea of a class of things—no particular sensory details introduce the fragmented reality of the material world. Hence, kept constantly before the reader in each stanza, it can become a pure "archetype" of the collective consciousness of Western religious tradition, a true symbol in the original sense of the word ("to throw together"), fusing the meaning and associations suggested in the phrases and rhythms of the poem. It thus demonstrates the kind of conscious synthetic activity that distinguishes the archetypes of art from those of dreams and, to use Hopkins's definition of poetry, "tasks the highest powers of man's mind."

"Rosa Mystica" also illustrates Hopkins's ability to employ the typological as well as the typical representational modes of medieval art. When Hopkins's poem was first displayed during the May celebrations of Mary at Stonyhurst College over a century ago, Hopkins's original readers no doubt recognized the term "Rosa Mystica" as a biblical type deriving from the phrase "I am the Rose of Sharon" in the Canticle of Canticles (2:1). Hence they knew that Hopkins was deliberately invoking a special tradition of types outside the "number of ordinary figures of speech and resources of language," as Keble put it. In some interpretations of the Canticle the rose was represented as a bride, as Israel, or as the church, but these associations were not sufficiently vertical for Hopkins; like his medieval predecessors he usually sought the highest possible parallels.

Hence his "Rosa Mystica" invokes all three of the higher meanings adduced from the Rose of Sharon. First of all, the Old Testament rose corresponds to the New Testament image of the mystical Body of Christ: "I am the vine, ye are the branches" (John 15). Hopkins first invoked this representation of the communion of the saints in the vine imagery of "Barnfloor and Winepress," but Dante's *Paradiso* provides the most obvious precedent for his use of the rose as a type for it in "Rosa Mystica." Hopkins's rose is also a type of Mary who as mother of the physical Body of Christ was considered mother of the mystical Body as well. Finally, Hopkins's rose is a type of Christ himself, the head of the mystical Body by whose blood it was given life.

The Tractarians invited Hopkins to invoke all these vertical correspondences, to create images capable of sustaining many hierarchies of meanings and levels of parallelism. Their conception of a medieval type was Hopkins's primary model for the symbolism of a poem like "The Windhover," which has many levels of meanings, exploits ambiguity, and exhausts the linguistic fields of words. The type was also a perfect objective correlative for the sense of mystery Hopkins wished to convey in "Rosa Mystica," for the profusion of signification in a type endowed it with a vivid but ambiguous reality which defied simplistic reduction. In Pusey's definition, as romantic as it is medieval, the type's "very indefiniteness adds to its reality, comprehensiveness, energy. . . . No deep saying was ever uttered which was not capable of many applications and a variety of meanings, which might very possibly float before our mind together or severally."[33]

This generation of a multiplicity of denotations, however, demands an effort to integrate them: unification had actually been the primary function of typology ever since the church fathers first advanced the polysemous interpretation of biblical types to harmonize the Old and New Testaments. Consequently, the individual talent of the medievalist poet was usually expended not on the selection of objects to be compared, as in the metaphysical conceit, but on the traditional amplification and unification of conventional types deriving from the Bible, the sacraments, the fathers, or primitive Christian symbolism (as in "Rosa Mystica") or of types found in the Book of Nature (as in "The Windhover").

Both activities are carried on in Hopkins's poetry, as we have seen, by a pattern of highly structured auditory recurrences which, when read aloud, activate a conventional type like the mystical rose, make it come alive for the reader, and at the same time help harmonize its various denotations and connotations, for phonic harmony implies semantic harmony. Thus, convinced that "marked parallelism" in structure "begets more marked parallelism in the words and sense," Hopkins discovered at least one poetic arena in which he could give his individual talent free rein. He could create an unprecedented concentration of parallelisms in the sound of his poems and exploit more fully than any of his ancestors the extraordinary potential for auditory consolidation, amalgamation, and fusion of meaning in the unique linguistic context of a poem. He could generate an incredibly high "bond density" between the words in his poems which would not only heighten the emotional impact of his images and reinforce their parallels, but also create a powerful supralogical atmosphere of harmony. By subordinating the originality of his subject matter to the density of his auditory parallelisms he could make the phonic harmony of a poem its ultimate "message."[34] This was the kind of emphasis recommended by Dante, who criticized showy innovations and displays in Christian teaching, yet gloried in technical ingenuity (*Paradiso*, 29:85–126).

The dynamism of Hopkins's auditory performance is answered by the drama of his parallelism in thought, moreover; Hopkins's rose is a metaphor of growth and change—the rose's "birth, and its bloom, and its breathing its last." In this and subsequent poems Hopkins exploits the dramatic potential of such images to integrate them, a potential often neglected in his static word-painting. He learns how to sustain the illusion of consistent, unifying vertical movements analogous to his vertical parallels. Again Dante's example comes to mind: Dante's parallels or "cords" between earth and heaven and his hierarchical imagery of positions on the heavenly rose were not static. In the *Paradiso* Christ is represented as "the wisdom and the might who opened the ways between heaven and earth" (32:26) and these "ways" or roads are well traveled: Gabriel descends to Mary and Beatrice to Dante and they all ascend eventually to the heights of heaven. That upward movement of man to God which integrates much of Hopkins's poetry as well as Dante's is evident in the first half of "Rosa Mystica" while the second half reveals that even more pervasive descending movement of God to man which is the key to Hopkins's sacramental imagery as well as his literalism.

The transcendental movement is evident from the outset. The rose is elevated from its origins in "earth's mould" to heaven and eternity, and, following Hopkins's definition of poetry as an increasing emphasis of thought on a greater and greater scale which leaves behind minds unequal to further ascent, the speaker of "Rosa Mystica" exalts his rose higher and higher above the literalist vision—the unidealized imitation of things as they are—until finally it breaks free from its roots in mundane reality:

> White to begin with, immaculate white.
> But what a wild flush on the flakes of it stood
> When the rose ran in crimsonings down the cross-wood!

It no longer matters that the colors of earthly roses do not run off onto their stems. Imagery becomes a vehicle for reenacting a sacred event, here the Crucifixion, and the alliteration of subject and verb, "rose ran," epitomizes the fusion of matter and motion in one dynamic allegory.

Yet this focus on the color and shape of the blossom in the second half of "Rosa Mystica" shows how as the image surmounts the strictly sensory reality of the literalist vision and the speaker aspires to it as a purely spiritual archetype of his heavenly home, it seems to meet him halfway, as if imitating the descending movement of the Incarnation, becoming more vivid, more accessible to the senses. The drama is reminiscent of Robert Browning's "Abt Vogler": "And the emulous heaven yearned down, made effort to reach the earth, / As the earth had done her best, in my passion, to scale the sky." But the specific process by which rejection of the strictly literal picture leads to the purely spiritual vision and finally to a synthesis of the two was the central dialectic of Tractarian poetics.

The final, beatific vision was to be an indissoluble union of the Imitative and the Symbolic according to Pusey: "God has appointed, as it were, a sort of sacramental union between the type and the archetype, so that as the type were nothing, except insofar as it represents, and is the medium of conveying the archetype to the mind, so neither can the archetype be conveyed except through the types. Though the consecrated element be not the sacrament, yet neither can the soul of the sacrament be obtained without it. God has joined them together, and man may not and can not put them asunder. . . . Neither the letter without the Spirit, nor yet the Spirit without the letter."[35]

Hence in the second half of "Rosa Mystica," as in so many of the poems which follow, the operative concept of metaphor is reversed, from an allegorical parallelism in which the unknown is described in terms of the known to a sacramental symbol of convergence modeled on the Incarnation and the Eucharist in which the unknown meets and mixes with the known. In Hopkins's typologies drawn from nature this incarnational symbolism, by promoting what Keble called "a profound veneration for the letter itself and literal meaning, the garb and outward vehicle of truths so revered and precious," sometimes inspires extreme fidelity to the details of nature, a focus on the surface common in Victorian typological symbolism.[36] Hopkins's typological imagery usually unifies poems which may appear to be mere collections of details, however, by that combination of the imitative and the symbolic, the incarnational and the transcendental which he identified as the "coexistence of realism with broad conventionalism" in "Middle Age Art."

Hopkins thus seemed to combine the multivalent free figuralism of the Tractarians and the strict literalism of the Evangelicals. The seventh refrain in "Rosa Mystica," "Make me a leaf in thee," for instance, reveals that the speaker, with his image at its farthest remove from a literal, earthly rose, is on the verge of taking it "literally," as we say, treating it as if it were literally there in front of him. Even in this, however, he was still following the example of the church fathers who, according to Pusey, "fearlessly blend the sign and the thing signified, and speak of the reality under the terms under which it was set forth."[37]

Hopkins's speaker asks that his imagery assimilate him, that the rose bush which produced and multiplied the five-leaved blossom transform him also into an image bearing the sign of the mystical Body, a member of the communion of saints. He tries to step into the world of total metaphor, become himself a part of the sacred mythopoesis he has represented. There are few better examples of

Keble's version of sacramental poetry: "Poetry lends Religion her wealth of symbols and similes: Religion restores these again to Poetry, clothed with so splendid a radiance that they appear to be no longer mere symbols, but to partake (I might almost say) of the nature of sacraments."[38]

Ultimately, the "splendid radiance" of Hopkins's types defies analysis, for they are necessarily mysterious. While they were more public than we have supposed, there is a sense of mystery in them that eludes translation—the rose's "place is a secret and shut in the skies." Yet, though we cannot expect to reduce them to simplistic matter-of-fact definition, we can appreciate their significance by locating the parallels they generate in the contexts of Victorian religious medievalism and the specific Judeo-Christian traditions the medievalists revived. Pusey's advice about the Old Testament prophecies applies to Hopkins's art as well: "In the word, as in the works of God, impression depends, not so much on single objects as on their combination . . . the whole effort is made up of numerous other parts . . . take these prophecies singly, nakedly as men are now wont to do, apart from the whole system, and the impression will be diminished."[39]

This advice is as valuable for understanding "The Starlight Night" and "Hurrahing in Harvest" as it is for "Rosa Mystica," because Hopkins's sacramental poetry of nature was almost as much a product of medievalism as his patristic typology. Keble's incredibly popular *The Christian Year*, the link between Wordsworth and the Oxford Movement, freed medievalists from the constraints of the literal words of God, the Bible, and the sacraments, and encouraged them to seek types also in the works of God, the Book of Nature. One of the many books of poetry Keble inspired was *Pietas Metrica* which opens with these words: "The books of Nature and Revelation have been laid side by side and read together. For the types of the former the antitypes are sought in the latter. The suggestions and analogies in the natural world are followed out in the revealed Word of God, and clothed in the language of Poesy."[40] The authors of this proclamation were, as we know, Hopkins's father, Manley, and his uncle, Thomas Marsland Hopkins.

The nature sonnets of their protégé, Gerard, owe much to the free typology they preached and practiced. The religious themes and imagery of his sonnets, like those in *Pietas Metrica* and *The Christian Year*, are generally even more common, public, and accessible than those in "Rosa Mystica," and the use of audible, structural parallelisms to integrate and animate image and meaning is even more striking in these concentrated forms. The union of universal typology with sensory particularity continues as in "Rosa Mystica," though necessarily weighted more in favor of the latter because of the greater proximity to nature. For the same reason horizontal parallels are more frequently mixed with the vertical, but even in poems dominated by the former, like "The Starlight Night" and "Pied Beauty," a final theistical emphasis gives a vertical impetus to the imagery.

The multiplication of denotations and connotations reaches its apogee in "The Windhover," but the generation of a variety of meanings is evident in many other sonnets as well. Emphasis on multiple vertical parallels becomes explicit in later Marian poems such as "The Blessed Virgin compared to the Air we Breathe" ("Minds me in many ways") and "The May Magnificat" ("but there was more than this. . . . Much, had much to say"). More importantly, the imagery of the nature sonnets retains the dynamism of "Rosa Mystica" and its medievalist models of vertical movement, with the incarnational descent dominating poems such as "The Windhover," the transcendental aspiration governing poems like "The Starlight Night," and ascent and descent converging in poems such as "Hurrahing in Harvest."

Chapter Five
The Dragon in the Gate

Standing between "Rosa Mystica" and the nature sonnets, however, like a "dragon in the gate" barring entrance to Hopkins's other poems, as Robert Bridges put it,[1] is *The Wreck of the Deutschland.* We must come to terms with it, for critics agree that it is his "masterwork, the poem which combines latently all the later poetry, both the poetry of nature and the poetry of self."[2] Moreover, it was the manifesto of Hopkins's new style: more concentration and a higher level of generality than prose; emphasis on poetry as drama, as speech, and as music as in "For a Picture of St. Dorothea"; recurrences in sound begetting parallelism in thought as in "Rosa Mystica," along with all the attendant features of mystery, multivalence, vertical correspondences and movements, sacramentalism, and reliance on tradition and convention.

Hopkins recalled that the wreck of the *Deutschland* "made a deep impression on me, more than any other wreck or accident I ever read of" (*F*, 135). This statement is all the more impressive when we consider the number of shipwrecks he must have discussed with his father. Hopkins wrote a poem about this particular disaster at the suggestion of Fr. James Jones, Rector of St. Beuno's College, Wales, where Hopkins studied theology from 1874 to 1877. Hopkins recalled that

What I had written I burnt before I became a Jesuit and resolved to write no more, as not belonging to my profession, unless it were by the wish of my superiors; so for seven years I wrote nothing but two or three little presentation pieces which occasion called for [presumably "Rosa Mystica" and "Ad Mariam"]. But when in the winter of '75 the Deutschland was wrecked in the mouth of the Thames and five Franciscan nuns, exiles from Germany by the Falck Laws, aboard of her were drowned I was affected by the account and happening to say so to my rector he said that he wished someone would write a poem on the subject. On this hint I set to work and, though my hand was out at first, produced one. I had long had haunting my ear the echo of a new rhythm which now I realized on paper. (D, 14)

The "sprung" rhythm which first began to haunt Hopkins's ear when he revised his "For a Picture of St. Dorothea" was fully "realized" in *The Wreck of the Deutschland,* a two-part ode composed of thirty-five eight-line stanzas. The first part, consisting of ten stanzas, is autobiographical, recalling how God touched the speaker in his own life. The second begins with seven stanzas dramatizing newspaper accounts of the wreck. Then fourteen stanzas narrow the focus to a single passenger, the tallest of the nuns, who was heard to call to Christ before her death. The last four stanzas address God directly and culminate in a call for the conversion of England.

When Hopkins sent *The Wreck of the Deutschland* to his friend Robert Bridges, Bridges disliked it so much that he refused even to reread it, despite Hopkins's pleas. The poem was also rejected by the Jesuit magazine, *The Month,* and many subsequent readers have had difficulty with it. However, many of the problems readers have had with the poem, including the contradictory interpretations, especially of the nun's motives; the apparent lack of unity and logical development; the seemingly excessive emotion, apparently neither fully motivated nor objectified; and Hopkins's sudden break with his previous style, can be better understood in terms of one of the traditions Hopkins invokes in the poem, the literature of the "sublime" or infinite in nature. This particular tradition also presents a specific context for the vertical movements of his poetry and shows how even the intensely personal response in this poem is a product of tradition and convention.

A second set of reader difficulties—the apparently simplistic analysis of the causes of the wreck, the exaggeration of its violence, the apparent exclusion of Protestants from salvation, the hint of predestination, and the obsession with coincidences—can be alleviated by focusing on the role of providence, the aspect of Hopkins's theology which explained the role of destructive nature. Finally, equipped with an understanding of the paradoxical simultaneity of opposites implied in Hopkins's concept of providence, we can evaluate *The Wreck of the Deutschland* in comparison with its predecessors and see how it encouraged the sacramentalism of Hopkins's nature sonnets.

Manifesto of a New Style

First of all, because the poem was based on the newspaper accounts of the shipwreck, a comparison of them with the poem gives us a unique opportunity to test Hopkins's definition of poetry as distinguished from prose. One newspaper described people being chilled by the cold, falling onto the deck, and being washed off by the waves, for instance. Another reported people numbed by cold falling into the sea. Still another described men, women, and children swept away from their holds on the deck, one by one.[3] Hopkins concentrates all these cruel dramas in a single moment, ascending to that higher level of generality that distinguishes his poetry from prose:

17.

They fought with God's cold—
And they could not and fell to the deck
(Crushed them) or water (and drowned them) or rolled
With the sea-romp over the wreck.

This passage also makes it obvious that Hopkins has added another dimension, the dramatic imitation of action, to his definition of poetry as parallelism. Instead of merely condensing the details of factual accounts, Hopkins frequently adds his own details to heighten the drama. Despite testimony that the "wind was right astern" and they were drifting slowly when they struck, for instance, Hopkins says the ship "drove" to "leeward" (st. 14). Similarly, although the accounts describe the people in the rigging as besieged by the three elements of the cold, the wet, and the rising tide,[4] Hopkins emphasizes a fourth, the fierce wind.

These added details not only emphasize action but also supply the unifying theme of this great drama of man, God, and nature: providence. The inquest and the reporters were primarily interested in explanations of the wreck "beyond that which the snow storm may supply,"[5] but Hopkins focused on the snow storm and the wind behind it as the single cause of the wreck, rather than the captain's errors or the breaking of the propeller, in order to emphasize man's utter impotence when confronted with the terrifying forces of nature.

Many of Hopkins's most striking "sprung" rhythms in the poem are representations of these terrifying forces. For instance, the basically anapestic rhythm of stanza sixteen is "sprung" in the middle of the final line, making the line itself "buck" like the wave: "With the búrl of the fóuntains of áir, búck and the flóod of the wáve?" Likewise, the words "sea-romp over" in "With the séa-romp óver the wréck" (st. 17) imitate the sea rising up out of the horizon (unstessed syllables fore and aft) to roll over the wreck. Hopkins frequently "springs" the rhythm in this way and juxtaposes the stresses, imitating the way "Súrf, snow, ríver and eárth / Gnáshed" (st. 21).

This dramatic use of rhythm is reinforced by the auditory parallelisms. The words "wiry" and "white-fiery" (st. 13), for instance, are not only stressed but rhymed and thus the two attributes seem to merge as they do in the swirling wires of white fire in J. M. W. Turner's *Snowstorm—Steamboat off a Harbour's Mouth* (1842). Similarly, the violence of the expression "black-backed" is communicated not only by the heavy stresses, but also by the alliteration of the hard *b* sounds and the rhyme of the harsh "ack" and "acked." Moreover, the rhyme of "rock," "knock," "shock" and the related consonance of "struck" (st. 14) all dramatize the violence of the shipwreck, while *b* alliteration itself represents the battle between the ship and the shoal: "beat," "bank," "bows," "breakers," "beam."

These rhymes and rhythms obviously must be performed aloud. Hopkins's diacritical marks on the manuscript, recalling the medieval tradition of marking Bibles for oral delivery, emphasize the fact that this poem must be heard as an "utterance," as "heightened speech," as a "cry," a lexical echo of the cry of "yes" of Jesus and the tall nun,[6] an "ark / For the listener" (st. 33). The role of the speaker is thus conspicuous in the poem and the implied presence of an audience with all the collective, indeed tribal associations of oral culture, along with Hopkins's invocations of various rhetorical traditions, reminds us of his definition of poetry as speech and music as well as drama.

Conscious of the association of poetry performances with music in religious ritual and Victorian public readings, Hopkins stressed connections between speech and music. In his "Author's Preface" to his poems Hopkins connects his version of metrical "counterpoint" with music, sprung rhythm being not only the "rhythm of common speech" but also "the rhythm of all but the most monotonously regular music, so that in the words of choruses and refrains and in songs written closely to music it arises."[7] The poem which follows, *The Wreck of the Deutschland,* then exemplifies this musical analogy, becoming a "madrigal" of the various voices, a virtuoso score which could test the skills of the greatest performers of multiple character parts, the "polyphonists" or "monopolylogues" of the Victorian stage.[8]

The music of this "madrigal" (st. 18) is an excellent illustration of Hopkins's definition of poetry as parallelism. First of all, by rearranging words and substituting his own, Hopkins increases the auditory parallelism of the newspaper accounts. Take, for example, the *Times's* account of an attempted rescue: "One brave sailor, who was safe in the rigging went down to try to save a child or woman who was drowning on deck. He was secured by a rope to the rigging, but a wave dashed him against the bulwarks, and when daylight dawned his headless body, detained by the rope, was swinging to and fro with the waves."[9] Hopkins wrote:

16.
>   One stirred from the rigging to save
>   The wild woman-kind below,
>   With a rope's end round the man, handy and brave—
>   He was pitched to his death at a blow,
>   For all his dreadnought breast and braids of thew:
>   They could tell him for hours, dandled the to and fro
>   Through the cobbled foam-fleece. . . .

With the exception of the fifth line, emphasizing the unifying theme of man's impotence, and the deletion of the morbid details of the decapitation, here Hopkins has "simply" transformed the prose into song.

This increased parallelism in sound throughout the poem "begets" more parallelism in thought—comparison, metaphors, types. We become aware that the ship itself is a type rich in parallelism, for instance. Ever since the account of the ark and the flood in Genesis, to which Hopkins alludes by calling the nun's cry (and by extension his echo of it) "an ark / For the listener" (st. 33), this type has been "riding time like riding a river" (st. 6). The New Testament recurrence or antitype to the ark is the boat upon which Jesus asks his disciples in a storm, "Why are you so frightened, you men of little faith?" (Matt. 8:26). This boat, cited in stanza 26, was sometimes identified with Peter's and therefore, along with the ark, became a type of the church, whose unity in Hopkins's eyes was "wrecked" by Luther (st. 20).

Rich as these implications are, this type was made still more multivalent by its use in the almost two thousand years of literature which intervened between Hopkins and the Bible. The greatest Catholic writer, Dante, to take just one example, often represented the individual life, as Hopkins was to do in part 1 especially, as a journey liable to shipwreck (*Paradiso*, 2:1; 13:136–38), a meaning which has survived even in the modern secular age. Indeed, it has been said that "the image, the *situation,* of the person shipwrecked or castaway has compelled the Western imagination more than almost any other since the beginnings of romanticism, because it has answered to the needs of the age to figure forth the new universe in which man found himself."[10] We still use this type to describe group situations as well, especially when we refer to the "ship of state."

Parallelism pervades the representation of the passengers as well as the ship. The tall nun, like St. Dorothea, is represented in the "mold" of Mary, reincarnating Christ in the world (st. 30). Mary's traditional enemy, the dragon, embodied in the "endragoned seas" (st. 27), is a type of sin and/or paganism. The most important parallels are of course to Jesus, however.

Hopkins's invocation of this, the ultimate archetype, is illuminated by *The Teaching of the Types,* a book listed in his diary: "We must regard the type as possessing a kind of living continuity of application, like the actions and words, the sufferings and death, of our blessed Lord, Who was once the Man of Sorrows and is ever the Man of Sorrows, once the Crucified, and ever the Crucified."[11] Hence the speaker in *The Wreck*, after asserting that "His mystery must be instressed, stressed," reveals that although the stress is in some sense historical—"It dates from day / Of his going in Galilee" —insists that it transcends time itself, "rides time like riding a river" (sts. 6, 7).

A good illustration of how Jesus's example rides time like riding a river is Hopkins's rose imagery, the metaphor most in need of explication in the poem. This is the same type Hopkins meditated on in "Rosa Mystica," moreover, and thus illustrates how that transitional poem contributed to the composition of *The Wreck*. After representing the colors of the rose in "Rosa Mystica" Hopkins focused on its five-leaved shape, a shape which recurred in the wreck most explicitly when the five nuns on the *Deutschland* joined hands before they died.

The "living continuity of application" of this five-leaved type of Jesus' wounds is first illustrated in *The Wreck* in stanza 22 when the speaker incorporates the "ruddying of the rose-flake" and "cinque-foil" typology from "Rosa Mystica" with all its attendant levels of meaning. ("Cinquefoil" is the name of a genus of the five-leaved Rosaceae.) Then in stanza 23 he cites St. Francis, the founder of the nun's order who also bore the pentameral sign in this world (the stigmata). Finally he turns to the nuns themselves who had so recently embodied the signal:

> And these thy daughters
> And five-livèd and leavèd favour and pride,
> Are sisterly sealed in wild waters.

By offering their deaths to Christ, extending the ramifications of the Crucifixion in this world, multiplying the significance of the pentameral "Stigma, signal, cinquefoil token," they became members of the communion of saints forever in heaven, petals of the mystical rose Dante saw in the gardens of God. This conventional type appears in the center of part 2 because it is the central mystery, the ultimate demonstration of the significance of the deaths of the five nuns in the context of the traditions to which they dedicated their lives.

The Wreck exemplifies all the features associated with this kind of parallelism, moreover: mystery, multivalence, unifying vertical correspondences and movements, and emphasis on poetry as sacrament as well as speech, drama, and music. Hopkins acknowledged, first of all, that *The Wreck of the Deutschland* "needs study and is obscure, for indeed I was not over-desirous that the meaning of all should be quite clear, at least unmistakeable" (*B*, 50). Hopkins's attempt to preserve some mystery was not, however, the kind of insistence on a private or coterie meaning we associate with modern literature, but rather a medievalist desire to preserve the awe originally associated with the types, paradoxes, and mysteries of early Christianity. In *The Wreck* Hopkins was following Jerome and all the Tractarians, including Pusey, Newman, Isaac Williams, and Keble who agreed that no one should "expose the sacred mysteries either of Nature or Religion to public view without regard to the temper and training of his hearers. He would rather be charged with obscureness than pour forth all truths, secret and open alike, without restraint."[12] This "reserve" is usually achieved, according to Keble, through original and ingenious meters and by focusing on nature as mediator between man and God,[13] both dominant features of *The Wreck* and most of Hopkins's other poems of the seventies.

As I have suggested elsewhere, obscurity is also one of the consequences of the multidimensional, polysemantic character of Hopkins's art.[14] This obscurity is not merely intentional, however; it is to some extent inevitable. The multiplication of names in the decoding stanzas of "Rosa Mystica"—Mary the Virgin, Mary the rose, Mary the tree, Christ, Jesus, our Lord, her God, her son— and in the corresponding stanza in the subsequent poem—"The Master, / *Ipse*, the only one, Christ, King, Head" (st. 28)—demonstrates how a religious mystery ultimately exhausts and defies the power of language.

The Dynamic Sublime

The emphasis on a religious mystery ultimately beyond the power of language is reinforced by one of the most pervasive sets of conventions in the poem: those features traditionally associated with the representation of the "sublime" or the infinite in nature. These conventions not only help explain Hopkins's love of vertical correspondences and movements and emphasis on poetry as sound rather than sight, but also help us deal with many of the "problems" which have given the poem its reputation as "the dragon in the gate."

One of the problems is that, attempting to understand the development of Hopkins's art by reading his works in the order in which they were written, we feel a break sharper than the shift from prose to poetry alone would lead us to expect between the last entry of his journals (dated February 7, 1875) and *The Wreck,* conceived less than a year later. Reading Hopkins's journals we come to expect a Pre-Raphaelite preoccupation with nature's lights, colors, and sharply delineated forms, a surface more self-consciously impersonal and objective than in similar journals of scientists of the time, a quiet stasis, and the occasional mention of God here and there in the midst of descriptions of nature. Turning to the poem we are confronted with a darkness which drowns all light, color, and form, a violent collision of great forces of nature, continual authorial intrusions and outbursts of emotion, and one of the most direct and intimate relationships between God, man, and nature in literature.

The title and epigraph of the poem suggest a vision of nature different from that of the journals, but there is nothing that prepares us for the astonishingly direct and personal address to God with which the poem begins. Expecting from the title and dedication a representation of the nuns and the wreck of the *Deutschland,* the reader finds instead Hopkins's personal response to "lightning and lashed rod." Moreover, before the second stanza has ended the subject shifts from the terror of the storm to the "horror of height," another sensation apparently not related to a storm at all. At this point, with the poem barely begun, but its psychological progression already obscured, we are tempted to agree with previous readers who have felt that Hopkins's inability to successfully integrate "the objective physical literalness" of the wreck with the "subjective and spiritual matter that precedes and follows it" results in too much emotion and too little unity.[15]

The Wreck of the Deutschland has thus been called "startlingly unconventional"[16] because of the frequency with which it has defeated attempts to discover unity both within it and between it and other works of Hopkins. The poem *is* startlingly unconventional— until we find the right conventions. Recognizing that our appreciation depends to an extraordinary degree on the context in which we perceive the poem, Hopkins's critics have searched for the most useful set of conventions to bring to a reading of the poem. Romanticism, the poetry of meditation, Pindaric odes, and two versions of religious literature, the Ignatian and the Victorian, have been invoked as models which enable us to comprehend more fully Hopkins's aims and methods in the poem.[17]

One of the most pervasive and useful sets of conventions in the poem are those features traditionally associated with the representation of the "sublime" in nature. Hopkins transforms his response to the snowstorm in which the *Deutschland* perished into a general response to "the infinite air" (st. 13), the unlimited power of the forces of God and nature, what Kant called the "dynamic sublime."[18] In the second stanza Hopkins adds lightning, for instance, and later in the poem he includes thunder, even though neither are typical of a snowstorm, and he goes on to include the "Yore-flood" of Genesis (st. 32) and the whirlwind of Job (st. 13). The "horror of height" and "hurtle of hell" phrases in the second and third stanzas bring in a related complex of conventions, expanding the speaker's response to include what Kant called the "mathematical sublime," the sense of infinite space.

The second and third stanzas also express the traditional response to the sublime: a sense of "terror" and "horror" that is unusually personal (note the prominent position of the "I") because the self is "astrain" with the effort to preserve itself in the face of annihilating infinity. In the more "objective" account of the shipwreck in part 2 the passengers of the ship share this "horror of height" as they fall from the shrouds onto the deck or into the sea. Psalm 55, recalled by Hopkins's dove imagery (st. 3), expresses the ultimate source of this horror: "My heart is troubled within me: and the fear of death is fallen upon me. Fear and trembling are come upon me and darkness hath covered me. And I said: Who will give me wings like a dove, and I will fly and be at rest? . . . I waited for him that hath saved me from pusillanimity of spirit, and a storm." The speaker's personal "fear and trembling" is made public in the wailing, shaking, and quailing of the passengers that "frightful" night. In addition to this conventional response, moreover, Hopkins's direct representation of God; his proselytizing; his emphasis on darkness, mystery, and obscurity; his reliance on sound at the expense of color and form; and his recurrent pattern of vertical movements are also characteristics of the traditional representation of the "sublime" in nature.

If we consider *The Wreck* as, among other things, a response to the sublime, all these features share a special interdependency as parts of a traditionally consistent approach to nature. We thereby perceive a principle of unity and a specific logical progression in the poem—the traditional psychology of our response to the sublime. The literary history of man's response to the sublime in nature reveals that even the intensely personal response in this poem is a product of tradition and convention.

Placing the poem in the context of the literature of the sublime does not exclude perceiving it in terms of other contexts and conventions, however, for the poetry of the sublime in nature can be defined as a species of the romantic, the meditative, the religious, even the Ignatian lyric, in its special focus on infinity. Yet this somewhat more precise definition gives us at least one interpretation that enables us to move beyond vague statements about the coalescence of subject and object in the poem to a consideration of *why* and *how* Hopkins realizes the storm "so vividly that he is in it, and it is at the same time in him."[19]

Reading the poem as a response to the sublime also puts our suspicion of an "unresolved dualism" in the poem, and the related sense of sharp breaks with the works which precede and follow it, in a significantly different context. *The Wreck of the Deutschland* is seen as a movement in Hopkins's literary career parallel to the historical movement which led to the cult of the sublime: the tran-

sition from the ideal of limited, proportioned beauty to the ideal
of the irregular, the infinitely great. This ability to switch from the
beautiful to the sublime in nature is a capacity which not only James
Thomson, Thomas Gray, and Thomas Warton developed in the
eighteenth century but which Byron, Shelley, Emily Bronte, George
Eliot, George Meredith, and others in the nineteenth century cultivated. Hopkins's accession to it allowed him to achieve that depth
and range of feeling, thought, and technique which makes his mature poetry so much more successful than his earlier work.

Consequently, *The Wreck* became the occasion for his incarnation
as a poet in his own right. He broke with the Keatsian word-painting
style with which he began, replacing his initial prolixity, stasis, and
lack of construction with a concise, dramatic unity. He rejected his
original attraction to Keats's sensual aestheticism for a clearly moral,
indeed a didactic, rhetoric. He saw nature not only as a pleasant
spectacle as Keats had; he confronted its seemingly infinite destructiveness as few before or after him have ever done.

As I have suggested elsewhere, the power of the ocean, especially
as expressed in the wrecking of a ship, was viewed as the most
"sublime" of subjects about the time Hopkins recorded his response
to the wreck of the *Deutschland*.[20] Disaster at sea was in fact a subject
that fascinated the public generally and Hopkins's family in particular. Hopkins, however, was primarily interested in writing about
the wreck of the *Deutschland* because the base conduct of many
Englishmen in the rescue operation had raised important questions
about the moral and religious character of the nation.

Yet Hopkins's renunciation of poetry in 1868, with the exception
of "Rosa Mystica" and "Ad Mariam," and the presence of only four
brief references to God in more than a hundred pages of nature
description in his journal suggests that he had not yet found a way
to use his approach to the beautiful in nature to further his religious
aims. The accounts of the storm, however, no doubt reminded him
that the literature of the sublime in nature traditionally offered many
opportunities for sermons on the immediate presence of God. Thus
he perceived the possibility of a theodicy, a vindication of God's
justice, which would counter the growing sense of the disappearance
of God among the Victorians. For Hopkins, therefore, seeing more

clearly than ever before the proselytic possibilities of literature, his rector's suggestion that someone write a poem about the wreck became the catalytic theological sanction he needed to begin reconciling his religious and poetic vocations.

The most important aspect of the literature of the sublime for Hopkins was its traditional association of nature's sublimity with God's sublimity, a connection as old as the Book of Job and dating in English literature at least from Gray's response to the Alps: "Not a precipice, not a torrent, not a cliff, but is pregnant with religion and poetry. There are certain scenes that would awe an atheist into belief, without the help of other argument. . . ."[21] Hopkins's first line, "Thou mastering me," invokes this convention of the direct representation of a present God which is found in a wide variety of eighteenth-century examples of the literature of the sublime, ranging from James Thomson's *The Seasons* to Ann Radcliffe's *The Mysteries of Udolpho*.

Romantic poets continued to be prompted by sublime scenes in nature to speculate about some at least quasi-religious, infinite Presence. Byron chose the ocean as the sublime image of this Presence in "Childe Harold"—"Thou glorious mirror, where the Almighty's form / Glasses itself in tempests . . . boundless, endless, and sublime / The image of eternity, the throne of the Invisible" (4:183). The Victorians maintained this link between the dynamic sublime and God. The heroine of George Eliot's *The Mill on the Floss*, for instance, driven out upon the "immeasurable" flood, feels the full fury of the destructive forces of nature that her generation had forgotten and experiences that "awful visitation of God which her father used to talk of" (bk. 7, chap. 5). Even Charles Darwin felt that "the sense of sublimity" in nature was "intimately connected with a belief in God."[22] For Hopkins the representation of the sublime in nature, especially the ocean storm, thus offered a tried and proven means of communicating that immediate sense of the power of a present God which was diminishing in his own generation.

Another convention of the representation of the sublime in nature, the emphasis on terror and dread, also served Hopkins's proselytic purposes. For many of his contemporaries a fear of God was seen as inconsistent with a conception of Christ as a lover of men,[23] and they tended to neglect, ignore, or actually discount the destructive aspect of God. However, with instructive examples before him of the use of shipwrecks to teach dependence on providence ranging from Defoe's *Robinson Crusoe* to Frederick Marryat's *Masterman Ready*, Hopkins was inspired by the nun's fate to reemphasize the presence of the Old Testament giant God, the God of the dynamic sublime.

The god with a frowning face who lashed Hopkins's speaker with His rod and "Trod / Hard down" on him (sts. 2–3) is clearly the fiery blacksmith God of Job 41, Psalm 18, and Blake's "The Tyger" who pounds his victim on an anvil and "with fire in him" forges His will (st. 10). He is also Orion the hunter who, with his dogs, the gnashing elements, drives his "prey" to its last resort where, "dogged in den," it is "at bay" (st. 21). This anthropomorphic giant God is "fetched in the storm of his strides" (st. 33), moreover, merged with the God of the dynamic sublime. His "finger," for instance, which in the first stanza the speaker "feels" and "finds again" is associated with lightning in Hopkins's second stanza, as it is in the Old Testament.

Hopkins's emotional response to this giant God of storms is not as ably motivated as it should be, however, according to many readers. Responding to this complaint, many critics have looked beyond the immediate occasion of the poem for various experiences in Hopkins's life which would explain its emotional intensity. The "walls, altar and hour and night" of the second stanza, for instance, have been assigned to various conversion experiences, and the frequency of such renewals of conversion in Hopkins's life has thus been demonstrated. This is useful, but not absolutely necessary if we take seriously the spiritual experience suggested by the title, dedication, and second stanza: the attempt to overcome terror at the recognition of potentially infinite destruction, suffering, and death in the world of a supposedly benevolent God. That the experience of meditating more deeply than ever before on the infinity of destructive power in God should resemble, even recall, previous conversion experiences would be only natural. Yet, if the desire to justify the ways of God to man is sufficient to account for the emotions of, say, the Book of Job, surely it will do for *The Wreck of the Deutschland* as well.

A more serious objection is the complaint that Hopkins's response does not fully objectify his feelings and hence remains too personal, too private. When we consider such problems of expression, however, we must take into account what Hopkins was trying to express. Identifying the "infinite air" with God (st. 13), the destructive power was perceived as illimitable. Perceiving *why* the literature of the sublime might be appropriate to his proselytic intentions, Hopkins was still faced with the question of *how* to represent this infinity, how to express the inexpressible. Stanza 28 dramatizes this problem, recreating Hopkins's futile search for spatial models for the nun's discovery of the infinite in the finite, the presence of God in the storm: "How shall I . . . make me room there: / Reach me a. . . . Fancy, come faster." The "Fancy" for Hopkins included the ability of the mind to discover parallels, to make appropriate comparisons, to find objective correlatives,[24] but his fancy fails him and all he can do is ask the reader himself to imagine God's infinite presence: "Strike you the sight of it? look at it loom there, / Thing that she. . . ." He cannot even select one name for God's sublimity, because no single title is sufficient: "the Master, *Ipse,* the only one, Christ, King, head."

As Kant predicted, the sublimity seemed so vast that it exceeded the ability of the imagination to fashion any single, integrated image for it. Hopkins found that he, like so many Old Testament prophets, had reached the limits of language, had confronted something that is "Beyond saying . . . past telling of tongue" (st. 9), a "past all / Grasp God," whose infinity is as a "Staunching, quenching ocean" to his "motionable mind" (st. 32). This imagery recalls not only the Old Testament (especially Prov. 8:27), but also the "protestations of incapacity" common in medieval literature.[25]

The problem is particularly common in the literature of the sublime. Kant argued that the idea of infinity is to be located in the mind, and objects only excite and call this idea into the mind. Thus while natural objects may be beautiful, they are never sublime, for no object is limitless, infinite, absolutely great. Kant's example, significantly, was the ocean agitated by a storm: it could be called horrible but not sublime for the sense of sublimity was simply a specific personal response on the part of the observer. This response is particularly obvious in, say, Burke's description of a flood in Dublin: "It gives me great pleasure to see nature in these great though terrible scenes. It fills the mind with grand ideas and turns the soul in upon itself."[26] Along with such "grand ideas" as the proximity of nature's sublimity to God's, Hopkins had to accept another convention of the literature of the sublime: the soul turning in upon itself, the unusually personal response. Unable to find satisfactory correlatives for an almost inconceivable limitlessness of power, he found his best evidence of it to be simply his personal experience of it.

Generally in his previous poems and invariably in his journals Hopkins preferred to be more objective but, confronted with the sublime, many conventions of romanticism and Christianity encouraged him to reveal his inner world. The romantics' belief in genuine personal feeling, the heart, as the only true source of inspiration; their conception of the central self as modifying consciousness; and their focus on empirical experience and autobiographical authority as a form of proof; combined with the Christian beliefs in personal suffering as the way to the most profound communion with Christ, and in establishing your qualifications (being an example to your flock) before proselytizing, all facilitated the personal response necessitated by his confrontation with the sublime.

Hopkins thus had many precedents for beginning with the state of his soul rather than with the wreck itself, not the least of which was Newman's *Apologia Pro Vita Sua* which presents Newman's personal situation before focusing on the special imputation against him. Adopting a similar strategy, realizing that the only real corollary to the idea of infinity he was trying to communicate was within him, Hopkins begins *The Wreck* not with an attempt to represent the external storm but with the most persuasive evidence, his response, the storm within, and he continually shifts back to it even when attempting to recreate the wreck itself.

The first three words of *The Wreck* summarize Hopkins's technique: "Thou mastering me." The reason for this "me" and the numerous first-person singular pronouns throughout the poem is

"Thou" seen in His aspect of the infinite "I AM" that overmasters, overwhelms the finite "I" and drives it in upon itself, forcing Hopkins's speaker to address his own heart: "My heart, but you were dovewinged, I can tell" (st. 3), "Ah, touched in your bower of bone . . . heart. . . . Why, tears! is it?" (st. 18).

In place of correlatives for the idea of infinity itself, Hopkins relies on immediate dramatizations of his and the nun's responses, flashbacks, and other genetic explanations of their "heart-throe, birth of a brain." These dramatizations are based on the belief that "tho' he is under the world's splendour and wonder, / His mystery must be instressed, stressed" (st. 5). The verb "stress" meant for Hopkins "the making a thing more, or making it markedly what it already is" (*F*, 327) and "instress" in this poem on the simplest level means to stress within the self. Hence the idea is first to emphasize the mystery within the self, make it more in the soul, then to emphasize it outwardly, to make it more in the outside world, to incarnate the sacramental presence. Parts 1 and 2 correspond to this sequence, which is also repeated in smaller movements within both parts.

This "stressing" required that Hopkins transform his word-painting technique into a means of dramatization of himself and other people as well as God and nature. In *The Wreck* Hopkins uses the adjectival techniques of his journals to "instress" his own inner world, to represent his feelings in such dramatic terms as "lashed," "sifted," "mined," "roped," and "glowing." He also "stresses" or dramatizes the inner worlds of others as "anvil-forged," "heart-wrung," "trenched with tears," "carved with cares." In addition, he intensifies the sweep, hurl, and hurtle of the dynamic sublime and the wrecking of the ship, and he adapts the long participial phrases he developed in his early word-painting to dramatize God as "fire hard-hurled" (st. 34), "our passion-plungèd giant risen" (st. 33), and

> Double-naturèd name,
> The heaven-flung, heart-fleshed, maiden-furled
> Miracle-in-Mary-of-flame,
> Mid-numberèd he in three of the thunder-throne!

(st. 34)

This stressing or (if you will) exaggeration is quite obvious in stanza 13 which represents the ship as "Hurling the haven behind" and in stanza 14 which represents it as driving to leeward and beating the bank down with her bows.

However, it is not so much this "stress" as the "instressing," the dramatization of the inner world with exclamation marks, interpolated "oh's," and searching for words that has resulted in the charge of unmotivated emotional intensity in the poem. Comparing the poem to the previous literature of the sublime we feel less of a discrepancy between the emotion and its represented cause; we can more easily account for the emotional intensity within the poem itself. The "me" of the first line and the emphasis on the personal throughout the poem is to some extent necessitated by the confrontation with the infinite and justified by various conventions of romanticism and Christianity.

Yet it should be remembered that the "me" metamorphoses into a more generally proselytizing voice, that it is but one of a number of voices in the poem. *The Wreck* is a "madrigal" or "glee" (st. 18), a polyphonic song of three parts—the autobiographical, the narrative, and the sermonical—singing in canon, repeating and amplifying the theme provided by a fourth voice, the nun's.[27] Shifts from one voice to another are sometimes quite evident: the first transition from autobiographical to sermonical, for instance, is begun in stanza 5, as the speaker turns from his inner world to the outer world, and is completed in stanza 6, when the first-person singular disappears altogether, replaced by the parenthetical interjections of a preacher to "the faithful" and the "faithless."

Though there is a great deal of counterpoint and imitation, the basic sermonical movement is to higher and higher levels of generalization, a movement summarized by the echoes set up by the iteration of the word "flash." It is first used to describe Hopkins's own recognition and acceptance of Christ's mercy: his heart did "flash from the flame to the flame then" (st. 3). It is heard again in the representation of how any heart, upon acceptance of Christ, will be flushed and will be "in a flash, full" (st. 8). Finally, it echoes again at the conclusion in which Christ's appearance to all men is a "released shower, let flash to the shire" (st. 34). Each time the word recurs it represents an increasing level of generalization, another step from the personal to the universal, yet it still echoes the personal experience.

This recurrent emphasis on personal experience customary in responses to the sublime distinguishes *The Wreck* from the far more objective writing which immediately preceded it in Hopkins's journals, but not as much as another convention of the representation of the sublime, the attraction to darkness. The "poet whose verse is more filled with joy in light than any other among the Victorians,"[28] whose journals record a painterly love of color and sharply delineated forms, gives us a dark canvas. Though a full day occurred between the wreck that Hopkins represents in stanza 14 and the night he represents in stanza 15, his seascape is darkness; there is nothing but the "black-about" air and the "black-backed" sea. The only natural illumination is the "electrical horror" of lightning and the rockets and lightships, fitful flashes quickly swallowed up in night. With the exception of one painterly touch, a description of the snow as "Wiry and white-fiery and whirlwind-swivellèd" (apparently inspired by Turner's *Snow Storm*) more is heard than seen. "Night roars" in the sounds of the storm-bugling thunder, the drum of death, the "woman's wailing, the crying of child without check," and our attention is directed to the voice of the tall nun like a bell ringing the poor sheep back and to the many voices of the poet himself.

This emphasis on sound rather than sight is, as we have seen, the essence of Hopkins's new style. Yet the appeal to the ear rather than the eye in *The Wreck* is, like the personal response, hardly new in the literature of the sublime in nature, where it is necessitated by the emphasis on darkness. It is "in the night" that the whirlwind carries off its victim in the Book of Job and darkness is closely associated with God's sublimity in Psalm 18, one of the biblical undercurrents of *The Wreck:* "He bowed the heavens, and came down: and darkness was under his feet. . . . And he made darkness his covert, his pavilion round him: dark waters in the clouds of the air" (9–11). In English literature, night is invariably the setting of the poems of a group of eighteenth-century poets who flirted with the sublime, the graveyard school, and it recurs in such nineteenth-century examples as Tennyson's "On Sublimity" in which the speaker cries, "Thy joy is in obscurity, and plain / Is nought with thee; and on the steps attend / Shadows but half-distinguished" (ll. 61–63).

Obscurity and mystery, another feature of Hopkins's new style, is also common among poets of the sublime because it gives the imagination greater range, freeing it for the attempt to apprehend sublimity, especially the infinity of God, as Burke's version of Job suggests: "In thoughts from the visions of the night, when deep sleep falleth upon man, fear came upon me and trembling, which made all my bones to shake. Then a spirit passed before my face. . . . I stood still, *but I could not discover the form thereof.*"[29] Hopkins chose to set his poem in "unshapeable" night (st. 29), rejecting that attention to the forms and limits of objects which characterized his approach to the beautiful in his journals, because he too recognized that sublimity must be, as Kant put it, a sensation of formless limitlessness.

As Burke indicates, one of the fears associated with the sense of an infinitely threatening might looming up out of darkness is the fear of total annihilation of the self. Hopkins makes this traditional association explicit in stanza 14 where night is actually dramatized as the agent of destruction ("night drew her / Dead to the Kentish Knock") and in stanza 33 in which the phrase "Lower than death and the dark" alludes to a passage about the great flood in Peter's first epistle.

Yet, paradoxically, night saves as well as destroys; "thy dark descending" (st. 9) can be "the dark side of the bay of thy blessing" (st. 2). The nun sees, though the "brine / Blinds her," much as Dante discovers true sight when he is blinded in the *Paradiso* (26). Both Dante and Hopkins (st. 10) cite the parallel of the conversion of Paul (Acts 22). The use of the imagery of darkness and light in fact pervades Christianity and we, the readers, are explicitly asked to learn to "see" in the light of this tradition. "Strike you the sight of it: look at it loom there," Hopkins writes, but "loom" suggests a distorted or indistinct image and the night is "shock" (heavy) and "unshapeable" (st. 29). We must learn that if we are to see it must be with the mind's eye rather than the natural eye.

The nun sees not the colors of nature but the "scarlet" of Christ's sacrifice (st. 22) and the "fall-gold" of his mercies (st. 23). The only form to be "seen" in the usual sense is the nuns' "five-livèd and leavèd" sacrifice repeating the ultimate type, the "cinquefoil" pattern of Christ's "Lovescape crucified" (st. 23). By reiterating this type they join "the hosts of Christ's triumph" revealed at dawn in the *Paradiso* (23:19). If, like Carlyle's Teufelsdrockh, we are to find truths "sweeter than the Dayspring to the shipwrecked,"[30] we too must "let Christ easter in us, be a dayspring to the dimness of us" (st. 35). In short, we are asked to see Christ as the Light of the World, not with the natural eye as in Holman Hunt's painting of that title, but with the "single eye" of the spiritual imagination.

Thus, while Hopkins shares a great deal with predecessors in the literary tradition of the sublime—his attraction to great destructive forces, his direct representation of God in nature, his evocation of terror and dread, his unusually personal response and his choice of darkness as a setting—his spiritual imagination differs from most of theirs. In general, as Kant suggested, the response to the sublime in nature was ultimately an exaltation in the self, a discovery of a capacity for a sublimity in the self corresponding to, if not transcending, that of nature. Even in the case of the representation of God in a storm, though Kant recognizes that the religious response is usually prostration and submission, he argues that the perceptive observer will recognize a sublimity in himself corresponding to that of God's and thus will be raised above the operations of nature. Hopkins's response, however, is a complex mixture of submission and exaltation that is basically not this deification of self associated with romanticism but the denial of self associated with Victorian Christianity.

In theological terms Hopkins and the tall nun respond to three different kinds of grace: afflictive, elective, and sacramental.[31] The general archetype for their response is of course Christ, represented in the vertical movements characteristic of Hopkins's typology as "Our passion-plungèd giant risen." Afflictive and elective grace are both associated with Christ's downward movement, his plunging into passionate submission, but elective grace is ultimately associated also with his rising, a transcending movement similar in some ways to the traditional response to the sublime. When these two responses have been instressed within the self, they are stressed, "uttered . . . outright," in response to sacramental grace. This is the basic movement of *The Wreck* and, in the tradition of the Victorian prophets, Hopkins repeats it from several different perspectives and levels of generalization much as Carlyle's tripartite movement of negation, indifference, and affirmation is repeated in *Sartor Resartus*. The first three stanzas of *The Wreck* reveal Hopkins's personal response; stanzas 4 through 8 interpret it on higher levels of generalization; and the last fifth of part 1, stanzas 9 and 10, summarize it. Similarly, in part 2, stanzas 11 through 17 represent the movement in the nun; stanzas 18 through 29 interpret it from various perspectives; and the last fifth of part 2, stanzas 30 to 35, summarize it.

The first element in this pattern is the iteration of the "afflictive" fall, the descent of Christ's sacrificial Incarnation, the plunging into passion of the giant God. In part 1, first of all the poet himself is "trod / Hard down" with the horror of falling into the abyss, the Puritan fear familiar from works such as Jonathan Edwards's "Sinners in the Hands of an Angry God" (which like Hopkins's poem also stresses the flood) and Edmund Gosse's *Father and Son* (chap. 1). This fear is also obvious in High Church poetry (especially in Hopkins's "No worst, there is none") and even in secular novels of the day such as Thomas Hardy's *A Pair of Blue Eyes* (chaps. 21–22). Hopkins escapes this basic dilemma of falling into the abyss of nothingness or of infinity, the Calvinistic double predestination, by perceiving a third alternative. He flees "with a fling of the heart to the heart of the Host" (st. 3). This represents not an attempt to escape from suffering but a desire, in response to elective grace, to imitate the incarnate God, Christ, ultimately a decision to accept suffering and transform it into conscious sacrifice. Hence Hopkins focuses on the fall of Christ's "frightful sweat," his submission in a "dense and driven Passion" to the afflictions of suffering and death (st. 7). Finally, we are given the example of St. Paul's prostration, his falling to the ground before the thundrous "crash" and flash of the lightning of God (st. 10).

Parallels to this falling motion are set up in part 2 as the dense and driven snow "Spins to the widow-making unchilding unfathering deeps" (st. 13) and the passengers fall from the rigging into the sea or onto the deck (sts. 15–17). This downward movement toward submission is then repeated in the fall of the speaker's tears (st. 18) and in his ultimate surrender in which he asks God to cure the extremity where he had "cast" her by triumphantly riding down her pride (st. 28). Finally, the "heaven-flung," "passion-plungèd" Christ is called upon to descend upon England as a released shower (st. 34).

Throughout, Hopkins repeatedly emphasizes that the proper response is not the self-exaltation traditional in the literary responses to the sublime but the submissive prostration, the total surrender demanded by St. Ignatius. He explicitly denies the possibility that the nun was "asking for ease," the response of the apostles to the great sea storm of Genesareth (st. 25), one of the few instances of the dynamic sublime in the gospels. He also specifically rejects the idea that her response was essentially the transcendental upward movement of ascetic idealism that focuses on heaven as a place where the treasure won by tears on earth shall be enjoyed (st. 26; see *Paradiso,* 23:133–34). Rather, her response is seen as the love in her "of the being as her lover had been" (st. 25), a desire to be as Christ was in the garden of Gethsemane when he said, "Father . . . not my will, but thine, be done."

There have been many different readings of these controversial stanzas, but support for this interpretation is provided by a recently discovered letter of Hopkins to his sister Grace about the death of her betrothed, Henry Weber, in 1883.[32] Hopkins begins, "My dearest Grace,—I feel though at a distance some of the force of this dreadful blow by which once more death shows its power suddenly to darken our hopes and disenchant us." We recall *The Wreck of the Deutschland,* his meditation again "at a distance," on the "force" of another "dreadful blow" by which death showed "its power suddenly to darken our hopes." Hopkins's choice of the word "wreck" in his letter to characterize the danger to those who grieve—"it makes mere wrecks of them"—reminds us that the protagonist in *The Wreck* had also been a "sister." His response to Grace, moreover, "I have not written this without tears," echoes the testimonial of tears in *The Wreck* (st. 18).

Hopkins's attempt to comfort Grace then takes a fascinating turn which parallels and explicates the interpretation of the nun's motives in *The Wreck*. His initial suggestion in the letter that God "in striking so hard pities your poor heart and means for you something far better, the brighter that seeming future was the better this real one" recalls the kind of reward-oriented asceticism in which future gains are proportional to present losses which appealed to Christina Rossetti and many of Hopkins's contemporaries in the Oxford Movement. The ethos of the early poems Hopkins wrote under their influence is distilled in stanza 26 of *The Wreck* which, like the letter, invokes the image of a "brighter" future to compensate for a death which "darkens" our hopes.

In the letter, however, it is clear that Hopkins rejects the idea that "being unhappy" earns any proportional future rewards: "But you are not to think, my dear, that you are somehow to be made happy some day for being unhappy this: there is no sense in that." With this straightforward language before us, we more readily perceive that the opening words of stanza 27, "no, but it was not these," represent a similar rejection of any simplistic reward-oriented motives. With the phrase, "keener to come at the comfort for feeling the combating keen" in stanza 25, the narrator of the poem asks if the reason for the nun's cry, "Christ, come quickly," was her natural urge to get relief from her suffering. The answer is obviously "No." Hopkins does not reject the idea of a reward *per se,* but insists that it is brought about by love rather than suffering. Jesus would have preferred to do without suffering, but he embodied the kind of love which could accept it. Such a love is ascribed to the nun in the poem: "The cross to her she calls Christ to her, christens her wildworst Best" (st. 24).

This response is radically different from the one Kant described; yet, paradoxically, some elements of the traditional response to the sublime are retained. Obviously, there is a literal transcendence of nature in Christ's resurrection and ascension to heaven, a pattern the nun repeats in that after having been "passion-plungèd" and finally drowned, she, like St. Dorothea and like Mary in "Rosa Mystica," is represented as having "risen" into the "heaven-haven of the reward" (st. 35).

Moreover, besides this literal ascension, Hopkins associates the decision to imitate Christ with a sense of exaltation and upward movement in the self as well as with a falling movement. He represents his own election, for instance, as his whirling out wings "that spell" so that he could "tower" from the grace to the grace, recalling similar wing imagery in the *Purgatorio* (31:57–63). The phrase "that spell," moreover, while it means basically "that moment," as a North Wales variant of "speel" also means "to mount or ascend to a height."[33] This sensation of towering upward is explained in one of Hopkins's comments on the operation of "grace which is elevating, which lifts the receiver from one cleave of being to another and to a vital act in Christ: this is truly God's finger touching the very vein of personality . . . the aspiration in answer to his inspiration. Of this I have written above and somewhere else long ago" (*S*, 336–38). The "long ago" was no doubt in *The Wreck* in which the nun as well as the poet "towered in the tumult" and both were lifted up, elevated to a vital act in Christ.

In Hopkins's representation of his response and how the nun reared herself to divine ears so that her call "rode over the storm's brawling" (st. 19) we sense a sublimity in the self corresponding to God's sublimity which does seem to raise the self above the operations of nature. Nevertheless, the exaltation that Hopkins and the nun experience differs from that described by Kant in that their transcending upward movement, their sense of the "passion-plungèd giant" as finally "risen," is essentially a response to Christ's mercy given only after the supplicant has denied himself, submitted completely and utterly to the mastery of God and the dynamic sublime. It was clearly the ultimate archetype, Jesus, who inspired the vertical correspondences and movements which unify this poem as well as "Rosa Mystica" and the great nature sonnets which followed.

Providence

In addition to the vertical correspondences and movements associated with Hopkins's representation of types, the poem is integrated by another basic principle of the Christian belief in types: trust in God's providence. As Thomas Aquinas put it, through His providence, God so ordained the chain of secondary causes that one event could prefigure a future event; that is, the assumption that an event in the Old Testament can be a type of an event in the New is based on a belief in God's providential organization of the world throughout history. This belief pervades *The Wreck,* yet remains difficult for some modern readers to grasp. Fortunately, Hopkins's letter to Grace about the death of her betrothed helps us understand this as well. His resolution for both Grace and the nun was to recommend apprehension and acceptance of the paradoxes of God's providence.

In the poem the mystery of Christ's salvific grace is often shrouded in obscurity, "And here the faithful waver, the faithless fable and miss" (st. 6). The language of the letter is more direct and practical, however, because Hopkins intended to make the nature of that grace clear enough so that even those without his faith could grasp it; hence by explaining its role in his letter, often he clarifies its part in the poem. He sheds a great deal of light, for example, not only on the interpretation of the nun's motives, but also on Hopkins's focus on natural rather than mechanical or human causes of the wreck, his dramatization of the violence and suddenness of death, the hint of predestination in his representation of the ship's departure, the question of the fate of the drowned Protestants, the emphasis on the coincidences involving the date, the number of nuns and their order, and the use of the deaths as warnings.

Hopkins's statement that Grace's tragedy involved "things providential, always meant (more than permitted) by God to be," for instance, illuminates his focus on God's storm rather than the breaking of the propeller or the captain's error as the cause of the deaths of the passengers. Hopkins's intent is apparently to replace the popular belief that God does not "cause," merely "permits" the physical evils of suffering and death[34] with the more rigorous Old Testament concept of providence. He is clearly asking with Amos, "shall there be evil in a city and the LORD hath not done it?" (3:6), and hearing the same answer as Isaiah: "I form the light and create darkness, I make peace and create evil" (45:7).

The letter reveals that Hopkins does not focus on the secondary causes of the wreck because, like the Old Testament prophets, he wants to emphasize our direct dependence on providence. His insistence that Grace recognize sorrows as "of God's giving" along with blessings for which she would have "been bound to return him thanks" reiterates the teaching of the prophet echoed most frequently in *The Wreck,* Job: "If we have received good things at the hand of God, why should we not receive evil?" (2:10). In his 1880 sermon, "Divine Providence," Hopkins again emphasized "that there is good" in wrecks, disease, and death as well as in blessings "for if we were not forced from time to time to feel our need of God and our dependence on him, we should most of us cease to pray to him and to thank him" (*S*, 90).

In both the letter and the poem he stresses that dependence by dramatizing the violence and suddenness of death which place it beyond our control. The death of Grace's betrothed, Henry Weber, was not in fact entirely "without a warning," as Hopkins put it in his letter, for he was in frail health when Grace met him. Nor was it a violent death, but Hopkins emphasizes in the letter "the force of this dreadful blow" by which death, "striking so hard," "shows its power suddenly to darken our hopes," hopes "without a warning at one blow swept away." "Swept," "striking," "blow" all echo his earlier dramatization of the "sweep" of God (st. 2) and its effect both on the *Deutschland*—"Into the snows she swept," "She struck" (sts. 13–14)—and on the sailor, "pitched to his death at a blow" (st. 16). In Hopkins's view, this shocking unpredictability of death requires our reliance on God's omniscient and omnipotent providence which remains the only means by which deaths are controlled, their "times and circumstances appointed," as Hopkins put it in his letter.

That phrase illuminates the hint of predestination in his representation of the departure of the *Deutschland* "nor ever as guessing / The goal was a shoal?" (st. 12) and it suggests one level of meaning in the representation of Christ's sacrifice which "rides time like riding a river" (st. 6). Predestination in Catholic theology does not interfere with the power to choose freely, however, since we remain free to say *yes* or *no*, to "lash with the best or worst word last" (st. 8) and thus determine our own destiny.

Hopkins's notorious description of Luther as the "beast of the waste wood" in *The Wreck* (st. 20) presents another theological problem, however, for it has encouraged the erroneous impression that Hopkins believed Catholics to be the only Christians "chosen" to receive the protection of providence. Yet in the very first stanza he composed of that poem he was reluctant to consign all the Protestants who died in the wreck to eternal damnation: "Yet did the dark side of the bay of thy blessing / Not vault them, the million of rounds of thy mercy not reeve even them in?" (st. 12). The idea that providence governs not only the chosen but all the peoples of the world gradually emerges in Hopkins's poem as it did in the Old Testament, until finally Hopkins answers his own question: he extends the protection of "lovely-felicitous Providence" to even "the unconfessed" (st. 31).

The key is the mediation of the nun who was able to "Startle the poor sheep back!" (st. 31). Hopkins's own family and many of his friends, of course, also fell into this category of "poor sheep" led astray by the "beast of the waste wood." Though he had little hope of leading them back to the fold, this letter confirms that, like the nun, he believed he might be able to intercede with providence for them at the moment of their death. He based this belief on the following observation: "It is seen again and again, I have seen it myself and speak of what I know, that people get the last sacraments just in time, that some happy chance or other falls out in their favour. And when we do not see the providence it may still be there and working in some secret way" (S, 292). In his letter to Grace, Hopkins referred to "motions from God" which might have endowed him with some access, however small, to these secret ways and workings of providence.

He writes that he has "often before now received" these motions. The first we know of occurred in 1873, when he received "as I think a great mercy about Dolben" (J, 236), Hopkins's friend who drowned in 1867 just before he was to be received by Newman into the church. Stanza 31 of *The Wreck of the Deutschland* is apparently the record of another such motion. In 1877 he wrote to his mother about still another motion from God, this time concerning the death of her father, and he cites six previous motions (F, 147–48).

Thus, Hopkins's emphasis in his letter to his mother on the coincidence of his grandfather's death with one of Mary's feast days is particularly interesting in view of his fascination with the coincidence that the five Franciscan nuns celebrated in *The Wreck of the Deutschland* died on the seventh of December, the night before the Feast of the Immaculate Conception (st. 30). This letter makes it clear that readers should not regard his interpretation of that coincidence and of the correspondences between the number of the nuns and the "mark" of Christ's wounds and the stigmata of Francis (sts. 22–23) as merely a self-regarding display of wit inspired by the metaphysical poets, as some critics have suggested.[35] These correspondences are analogous to the parallel between Hopkins's grandfather's death and Mary's feast day and to all those other "happy chances" Hopkins so frequently associated with what he called the special providence over death (*S*, 248, 250).

All three coincidences in *The Wreck* were clearly "things providential" for Hopkins, illustrations of the basic assumption of his sermon on "Divine Providence": "search the whole world and you will find it a million-million fold contrivance of providence planned for our use and patterned for our admiration" (*S*, 90). Hopkins's advice to his mother applies equally well to his readers: "Do not make light of this."

The Wreck was clearly intended to be the instrument of providence: "One of God's providences is by warnings—the deaths of others . . . a sudden thought: beware, beware of neglecting a warning. . . . A warning leaves a man better or worse, does him good or harm, never leaves him as it finds him" (*S*, 252). This consciousness of the significance of warnings was but one side of that extraordinary sensitivity to providence, the key to many aspects of Hopkins's art and life, evident in Hopkins's letters, in his poem, and in one of his Dublin meditation points: "Pray to be on the watch for God's providence, not determining where or when but only sure that it will come. And apply this to all your troubles and hopes" (*S*, 258).

Theodicy

Once Hopkins's speaker in part 1 says "yes," accepts his dependence on God's providence, he achieves the eternal poise of a pool fed by streams from a mountain (st. 4), streams of God's grace. This everlasting source of mercy and love is connected to man by

the "veins" or "ropes" of vertical correspondences and movements
between heaven and earth, imagery recalling the vision of Paradise
granted to Dante after he too said "yes" on the mount of Purgatory
(31:13). *The Wreck* then proceeds to strike a balance between the
initial Old Testament emphasis on God's terrible destructive power
in the storm and the final New Testament focus on his "mercy that
outrides the all of water" (st. 33). God's "dooms-day dazzle," his
"lightning of fire hard-hurled," eventually yields to images of God
as a "released shower" renewing the landscape (st. 34) and "a dayspring," a "crimson-cresseted east" (st. 35).

Yet the Being who destroys in the beginning is the same as He
who saves in the end: "God" is a "Double-naturèd name" (st. 34).
He is the "Lord of living and dead," He who fastened and yet almost
unmade the poet, both the strand which destroyed the ship and the
sea which sustained it (st. 1), both the "arch and original Breath"
and the "body of lovely Death" (st. 25). The last two stanzas of
part 1 in fact emphasize the beauty and terror of nature as paradoxical
aspects of the same God, a God who is both "lightning and love,"
"a winter and warm," who can strike with a "crash," an "anvil-
ding," or steal "as Spring."

The Wreck is thus one of the best examples in Western tradition
of the contrapuntal imagination, the "stereoscopic" vision becoming
increasingly prized in the sciences as well as the humanities. Scientists have celebrated Hindu paradoxes, especially those associated
with Shiva and Kali, for this effect, and some have begun to recognize
that Western drama also offers "a training ground for stereoscopic
vision needed to cope with the successes and limitations of today's
science,"[36] but *The Wreck* reveals that Western poetry and religious
traditions offer such a training ground as well.

One of Hopkins's own training grounds was Christian theology,
of course; he was able to reconcile the terror and beauty of nature
primarily through his deep commitment to the mystery of the three
persons of the Trinity as different aspects or modes of being of the
same God. Terrified by God as the paternal giant, for instance,
Hopkins could flee to Him as Jesus, the heart of the Host. He was
but flashing "from the flame to the flame," towering "from the
grace to the grace" (st. 4), responding to the one God, the "Christ

of the Father compassionate, fetched in the storm of his strides"
(st. 33).

Just as the nun "that weather sees one thing, one; / Has one fetch
in her" (st. 19), Hopkins in *The Wreck* sees that "God" is the word
for that ultimate unity embracing all of nature that he sought in
his journals and in his study of Parmenides and Greek philosophy;
God is the "Stanching, quenching ocean of a motionable mind" (st.
32) that absorbs all, the unmoving and all-encompassing One, the
"Ground of being, and granite of it" (st. 32).

This perception of beauty and love in the midst of terror and
destruction was not a new but an ancient revelation; yet it eluded
most of Hopkins's predecessors as well as his contemporaries. Hopkins's ability to perceive the unity of God as Scotus and Dante had
perceived it distinguishes *The Wreck of the Deutschland* from most
romantic attempts to confront the pain, death, and destruction
inflicted by nature. Wordsworth, for instance, faced with the death
of his brother in a shipwreck, found in "Elegaic Stanzas" that his
vision of benevolent nature was a "fond illusion" (l. 29), that "a
power is gone, which nothing can restore" (l. 34). Unable to reconcile nature's beauty and its terror, he despaired and commended
Beaumont's painting of the sea in anger as the true picture of nature.
Shelley, at first glance, seems to have moved closer to Hopkins's
vision in "Ode to the West Wind" when he calls the wind both
"Destroyer and preserver" (l. 14), hoping that destruction will prepare the way for a rebirth. However, he soon loses his sense of
balance, and affirmation becomes negation, a request to the wind
to destroy him as well as the foliage, echoing Job's cry to the wind
to put an end to his suffering.

Hopkins's bold identification of God with the dynamic sublime,
on the other hand, distinguishes *The Wreck* from most Christian
theodicies. Unlike traditional Christian apologists, Hopkins refuses
to explain disaster as either the absence of God or the presence of
some negative power which resists God. Nor does he allow an act
of the victims of the disaster to be labeled as its cause. A line such
as "what could he do, / With the burl of the fountains of air, buck,
and the flood of the wave?" (st. 16) reinforces the reader's sense of
the storm as the sole cause of the wreck. Hopkins then identifies

this storm with God in such phrases as "Thy terror" (st. 2), "Thou art lightning" (st. 9) and "God's cold" (st. 17), leading up to the climactic recognition of the identity in the twenty-eighth stanza.

Yet this God is not simply the God of the Old Testament. The Oxford Movement had transmitted to Hopkins the church fathers' mission of unifying the Old and the New Testaments, the ultimate aim of their language of types. As a theodicy, therefore, *The Wreck* is an attempt to show that the Old Testament God and the New Testament God are one and the same God, present in both destructive and beautiful nature. Hopkins's emphasis on this paradoxical simultaneity of opposites makes *The Wreck* one of the best reconciliations of the two Hebraic traditions, as well as a vision of the ultimate unity of the benevolent and destructive aspects of nature and God.

Previous literary theodicies were less satisfying in this respect. In *Paradise Lost,* for example, Milton's basically dualistic Christianity makes a genuine unity between a merciful God and a nature that inflicts pain and death virtually impossible. The traditional assumption underlying his defense of the ways of God to man is that cruel, destructive nature is more directly related to man's behavior than to God's and is to be associated with the other afflictions man allowed into this world, primarily sin, that other pole of this inevitably dualistic conception. In the Book of Job, on the other hand, God is indeed identified closely with cruel, destructive nature, but His benevolent aspect is not considered and the basis of the vindication is simply man's inability to understand. Man's ignorance of God's ways is also the basic argument of Pope's "Essay on Man," Mark Akenside's *The Pleasures of the Imagination,* and many others. Hopkins recognizes that in some respects God is "past all / Grasp" (st. 32), but in general he rejects the Thomistic stress on man's inadequate grasp of God's being, preferring Scotus's emphasis on man's natural knowledge of God through His univocity of being with nature.

These features also distinguish *The Wreck* from the most famous Victorian theodicy, Tennyson's *In Memoriam.* Unlike previous theodicies, both poets locate their responses more in the heart than in the mind, writing elegies rather than didactic essays or religious epics such as Pope's "Essay on Man" or Milton's *Paradise Lost.* Breaking with the indirect invocations of Pope and Milton, both Tennyson and Hopkins address themselves directly to God's power; both recognize the destructiveness of nature and reject it as a model of benevolence; both also affirm personal immortality and find Christ the ultimate answer. Tennyson's Hallam and Hopkins's tall nun are represented as semidivine prophets in heaven—Hallam as an ideal Victorian sage, the tall nun as a "prophetess" (st. 17) who transmits the message of Providence (st. 31)—and both are "noble types" of Christ (*In Memoriam,* epilogue).

Nevertheless, though Tennyson's invocation bears some resemblance to stanzas 2 and 11 of Hopkins's poem, he usually addresses only the merciful Christ, He who resurrected Lazarus. Hence in *In Memoriam,* as in most other traditional theodicies, God and nature are "at strife" (no. 55). Hopkins, however, because he can affirm both the resurrection of Lazarus and the great flood, finds that God and nature are one. The tall nun reads the storm right, recognizing its participation in the being of God. She finds what Tennyson could not—the immanent as well as the transcendent God truly present everywhere, even in cruel nature. Hopkins is thus able to accept what Tennyson could not: the terrible, frightening aspects of the paternal Old Testament God.

Yet Hopkins remains less overtly mystical than Tennyson: although Hopkins also locates his response in the heart, Hopkins does not rely, as Tennyson does, on dreams or trances for the surrender of the self. Nor does Hopkins compromise with science by adopting spiritual or sentimental evolutionism. Though Tennyson knows that "Well roars the storm to those that hear / A deeper voice across the storm" (no. 127), more overpowered by grief, he is less sure of that voice, of personal immortality, of the meaning of life. Hence where Tennyson's faith, in the central lyrics of *In Memoriam,* is doubting, questioning, and apologetic, Hopkins's faith is certain, firm, and unequivocal. As a result his theodicy is more compact and unified.

Sacrament

Hopkins is more sure of himself because *The Wreck of the Deutschland* was a great breakthrough to the vision of God immanent in nature that he had been seeking, and thus to the sacramentalism that was to be the basis of the great nature poems of the following years. As we have seen, he had written earlier in "Half-Way House," "I must o'ertake Thee at once and under heaven / If I shall overtake Thee at last above." His first step toward overtaking God under heaven had been his discovery of the immanence of God in the Host in the Mass. Then he expanded his sense of God's immanence until he could find Him in nature as well. "Sway" in "sway of the sea," in the opening stanza of *The Wreck,* for instance, suggests God as the surge of the sea as well as holding sway or command over it, striking the keynote of the simultaneity of God's immanence in and transcendence of nature to be played throughout the poem. In the fifth stanza, Hopkins represents God not only "above" nature in the "lovely-asunder starlight," but also "under the world's splendour and wonder," echoing Shelley's brief glimpse in "Adonais" of the simultaneous immanence and transcendence of "that Power" which "wields the world with never wearied love, / Sustains it from beneath, and kindles it above," itself an echo of the conclusion of Dante's *Paradiso.* Following Scotus, Hopkins then asserts Christ's Real Presence in nature since the beginning of time, "Though felt before, though in high flood yet" (st. 7).

Finally, in the climactic twenty-ninth stanza we learn that the nun has read this Book of Nature right,

> Read the unshapeable shock night
>   And knew the who and the why:
> Wording it how but by him that present and past,
> Heaven and earth are word of, worded by?—

She discovered how even destructive nature was the Word of God, His utterance, His expression. In the coda, stanza 32 ("I admire thee, master of the tides, / Of the Yore-flood, of the year's fall") reminds the reader that the present Master of the tides is the one who controlled the first flood, that the vast forces of nature are still expressing the same God—the Incarnation is riding time like riding a river. Finally, the phrase "Ground of being, and granite of it" suggests the idea underlying Hopkins's sense of "immanence," Scotus's idea of nature participating in the being of God.

The Wreck not only evokes this belief in the immanence of God in nature, this key to approaching nature as something holy, a sacred opportunity for worship, but also suggests the appropriate sacramental response. Perceiving Christ in the storm, the nun responds by "calling 'O Christ, Christ, come quickly' / The cross to her she calls Christ to her, christens her wild-worst Best" (st. 24). Hopkins adds the words "here was heart-throe, birth of a brain, / Word, that heard and kept thee and uttered thee outright" (st. 30) to make it clear that it is the uttering outright, the explicit gesture that consitutes the sacramental response. The result is a kind of renewal of the Incarnation in the nun, making God "new born to the World" once again, imagery recalling Dante's sense of the world swollen with the birth of True Belief sown by the messengers of the Everlasting Kingdom (*Purgatorio,* 22:76–78).

Stanza 5 presents the generalization for which the nun's response is one example:

> I kiss my hand
> To the stars, lovely-asunder
> Starlight, wafting him out of it; and
> Glow, glory in thunder;
> Kiss my hand to the dappled-with-damson west:
> Since, tho' he is under the world's splendour and wonder,
> His mystery must be instressed, stressed;
> For I greet him the days I meet him, and bless when I understand.

The kissing of the hand to the stars and the sunset is apparently the symbolic gesture of uttering outright denounced in the Book of Job: "If I beheld the sun when it shined and the moon going in brightness: and my heart in secret hath rejoiced, and I have kissed my hand with my mouth: which is a very great iniquity, and a denial against the most high God" (31:26–28). But Hopkins, in the light of the Incarnation, Transubstantiation, romanticism, and Keble's poem for Septuagesima Sunday in *The Christian Year,* reverses this Old Testament injunction. Finding God under the splendor of nature as well as above, Hopkins asserts that kissing his hand to the stars or to the sunset is not an iniquity or betrayal of God but a sacramental sign of worship based on nature's participation in the being of God.

Such a gesture of explicit recognition, an uttering outright, is required because, though God is indeed under the splendor and wonder of nature, his unity, his simultaneous transcendence and immanence, and his sacramental presence are mysteries not to be taken for granted. They must be "instressed, stressed." As we have seen, "stress" for Hopkins meant "making a thing more, or making it markedly what it already is; it is the bringing out of its nature." Thus "His mystery" requires the observer to make more, to mark or emphasize to himself, bring out to his senses and his mind, make actual in himself, the mystery of God's immanence as it is revealed in the unifying and individualizing force of being in the object.

As he suggests in the last line of the stanza, when he meets this force of being in nature and recognizes nature's participation in the being of God he "greets" God with an actualizing sacramental gesture which can "waft" God out of nature, bring Him closer to the observer, renewing Christ's presence in him so that God can be "reborn to the world." Hopkins's uttering outright, his kissing of his hand, his greeting of God when he meets him in nature, his sacramental gestures, are his nature poems.

Chapter Six
Poet of Nature

The sacramental concept of poetry implied in *The Wreck of the Deutschland* is related, as we have seen, to the Oxford Movement's concept of a "type" which could become an "instrument" as well as a sign of "real things unseen." If "Rosa Mystica," the source of the rose imagery in *The Wreck*, is a good example of how Hopkins applied biblical typological principles to traditional images in his poetry, "The Windhover" is the paradigm of how he adapted the hermeneutics of the Book of Nature developed by Keble and by his own father and uncle in their *Pietas Metrica*.

The question of how to assimilate the multidimensional, polysemantic character of Hopkins's art, first posed by *The Wreck*, is raised again by "The Windhover" because, as Marshall McLuhan put it, "there is no other poem of comparable length in English, or perhaps in any language, which surpasses its richness and intensity, or realized artistic organization."[1] Indeed, there are so many different interpretations of this poem that readers are tempted to quit trying to sort them out and simply retreat into pure subjectivism and relativism. Thus it could be argued that "The Windhover" is not only the best illustration of Hopkins's poetics—for the concentration of parallelism and multivalence is higher than in any of his other poems—but is the ultimate test of one's ability to explicate a poem.

One way of assimilating all the diverse, contradictory readings of this, the most explicated poem of its length in the language, is to apply the techniques of biblical hermeneutics we discussed in our reading of "Rosa Mystica" and the related sections of *The Wreck*. A return to some of the principles of this, the first literary criticism (if we may call it that), the interpretation of the Book of western civilization, can help us organize our responses to "The Windhover." The four levels of medieval biblical interpretation which Dante applied to the *Divine Comedy* are particularly valuable for discussing multivalent works such as "The Windhover" because they assimilate complexity and ambiguity of meaning yet resist tendencies to solipsism and relativism both by insisting on the primary reality of things over words and by affirming the existence of the primal unity from which Hopkins's apparently endless permutations emanate.

The Literal Level

The best antidote to pure subjectivity in interpretation may in fact be a reemphasis on the first of the four levels of medieval hermeneutics: the literal. The literal level has always been essential in the Christian interpretation of the Incarnation, for it was a bulwark against the assertion of Manicheism that Jesus had no physical reality, only a phantasy body, an assertion which reduced the Incarnation to a fiction. For a poem to be interpreted typologically in the biblical sense, therefore, rather than merely allegorically, we must be conscious of a level of literal truth. Hence the famous typological problem in the Divine Comedy: defining what is literally true, that is, Dante's own conversion experience.

Hopkins was far more explicit about this literal level than Dante, however. He wrote to Bridges about *The Wreck*, for instance: "I may add for your greater interest and edification that what refers to myself in the poem is all strictly and literally true, and did all occur; nothing is added for poetical padding" (*B*, 47). The literal level is especially important for Hopkins's poetry because most of his poems are lyrics, a genre even more dependent than the ode or the epic on conceiving of poetry as autobiographical.

In the tradition of lyric poetry, moreover, romantic lyrics place unusual stress on a literal interpretation of the poet's self in the poem. Heavily influenced by medieval hermeneutics,[2] romantic imagery is almost by definition typological in that it implies not merely a comparison but one in which there is a discernible relation between the image and reality, at least the reality or personal experience of the speaker. In romantic nature lyrics in the tradition of Wordsworth especially, such as those Hopkins composed in 1877, the emphasis on literal reality extends to nature as well as to the speaker. Wordsworth was "well pleased to recognize / In nature and the language of sense / The anchor of my purest thoughts" ("Tintern Abbey," ll. 108–9). The anchor was William Tyndale's metaphor for the role of the literal sense in biblical criticism. This sense of "thingness," the physical presence of nature, is important not only for readers familiar with biblical typology but for all modern readers influenced by science and its basic assumption that nature does have an existence independent of ourselves and our symbols.

The neglect of this literal level in our reading of Hopkins's own poetry is epitomized by the absence of notes in texts of the poem to explain adequately the physical reality upon which "The Windhover" is based: the unique flight patterns of this particular bird. The word "riding" in "The Windhover" refers specifically to the famous flight pattern for which the bird is named: by rapidly beating its wings it seems to hang stationary in one spot like a helicopter rather than circling or gliding like other birds of prey.[3]

This is what Hopkins "caught" sight of that morning. This falcon, itself dappled like the dawn, was drawn forth by the dappled dawn to hunt. Hopkins saw it hovering over one spot as if drawn or painted against the background of the rising sun, much as the "flake-leaves light" in Hopkins's "Epithalamion," "painted on the air, / Hang as still as hawk or hawkmoth." Hopkins was fascinated by his hovering, his "riding of the rolling level underneath him steady air," his "striding high there," that is, astride of, straddling the wind, "reining" or controlling it with his undulating, "wimpling" wings. The windhover "rung" upon his wings much as a bell ringer pulls up and down on the bell ropes or the rider of a horse "undulates" his belled reins.

On certain occasions windhovers have also been known to fly in rings or semicircles: the male has been known to fly in circles above the female in courtship and sometimes the bird takes a circular path to a new hunting location. Thus the secondary senses of "ring" here, as a term in falconry meaning to rise upward in spirals, and as an equestrian term denoting the training of a horse to run in circles with a long rein, are not entirely inappropriate.

In any case, after catching sight of the hovering, Hopkins then sees the windhover move off to a new location, either by hurling itself down and then suddenly "gliding" up to a new spot, or else by hurling itself horizontally into the wind and then gliding in a "bow-bend" pattern until it reaches a new spot. In either instance, it manages to "beat back" the wind once again, the root meaning of "rebuff." The "achieve" and "mastery" of the bird in the maneuver are like that of a skater approaching along one side of a bow-shaped bend at high speed and then gliding swiftly around it, as ice hockey players often do behind the goal.

As we move from the octet to the sestet, there is an abrupt change in the rhythm. The striking initial double stress on "Brute beauty" imitates the new movement of the bird climaxed by the word "Buckle." The bird buckles its wings together and falls from the sky, as if it were wounded or buckling under, collapsing, crumpling under pressure, but in fact it is buckling to, buckling down, preparing for action, getting ready to come to grips with its prey. In this dive all its features, all its "brute beauty," "valour," "act," "air, pride, plume," come together, are buckled together. The fiery flash of light that breaks from it as it dives with the rising sun behind it is far "lovelier," for the sight of a diving windhover is even more rare than that of a hovering one, and it is obviously far more "dangerous" when it dives down upon its prey.

With the pause between tercets, the attention shifts from the heavens to the earth to which the falcon has descended. The V-shape made by the windhover in its dive (its wings are more pointed than those of the American kestrel) is that of the ploughshare, that of the furrow a plough makes when it buckles up the earth, and the shape of embers collapsing or buckling through a grate.[4] The blue-gray color of the upper part of the bird, moreover, corresponds to the blue-bleak color of both the embers and the ploughshare, while the russet color on the lower part of the bird recalls both the shining on the ploughshare after ploughing and the fire breaking through the bottom of the buckling ember. Thus the colors as well as the shape of the diving windhover resemble both a ploughshare ploughing through the air and a falling ember.

The sense of "fire" breaking from the bird is caused by the fiery flashes of the colors of the diving bird as well as the effect of the rising sun, directly behind the bird as it dives. The result is a "shining" like that of the bursting ember, the gleaming surface of the ploughshare being polished by use, the shine of the moist, new sillion (the strip between the furrows), the sparks produced when the ploughshare strikes the blue-bleak rocks, and the colors revealed by shearing them open. The implication is that if even the "sheer plod" of ploughing can produce such a "shining," there should be "no wonder" that a handsome bird of prey can.

The Metaphorical Level

Of course the bird does not literally catch on "fire," nor is it really a "dauphin" or horse-rider. The second level of interpretation is a more systematic exploration of the metaphors which deny merely literal explanation. We soon discover that many of the metaphors in this poem are connected, moreover, especially the chivalric and fire images, suggesting the possibility of a consistent "underthought" in the poem, to use Hopkins's term (*F*, 253).

The key "underthought" is suggested by the subtitle, "To Christ our Lord," added six years later as a dedication and/or a way of addressing the entire poem to Christ. The subtitle thus reminds us that Hopkins dedicated all of his life and art to Christ and emphasizes that in this poem as in biblical typology the most consistent "underthought" is Christological, that is, most of the metaphors point to Christ.

The first obvious metaphors are "minion," meaning loved one and servant of the monarch, among other things, and "dauphin," a royal son and heir apparent, terms that also fit Jesus as the Son of God. This particular "dauphin" is the heir apparent to the "kingdom of daylight," moreover, echoing the recurrent stress in the New Testament on the "kingdom of heaven," Hopkins's emphasis on the "daylight divine" in "Rosa Mystica," and the close association of dawn imagery with God throughout his poetry, especially in "Barnfloor and Winepress," "Easter," "God's Grandeur," and the chivalric imagery concluding *The Wreck of the Deutschland.*

Accompanying this symbolism of Jesus as the Son of God is the related undercurrent of imagery of Christ the King, especially important to Hopkins because of the pervasive emphasis on the Kingdom of Christ and on chivalric imagery in the Society of Jesus. It has been suggested that Hopkins's splitting of "king" and "dom," for instance, reminds us that "dom" is a shortened form of "dominus" or "Lord," and thus an echo of the dedication to Christ, "our Lord." The rest of the chivalric imagery of minion, kingdom, and dauphin is then developed in the riding, striding, and rein imagery in the octet. Most of this imagery echoes the speech in Shakespeare's *Henry V* in which the dauphin praises his flying horse: "When I bestride him, I soar, I am a hawk. He trots the air, the earth sings when he touches it. [He is a] beast for Perseus. He is pure air and fire. . . . His neigh is like the bidding of a monarch, and his countenance enforces homage . . . for a sovereigns' sovereign to ride on, and for the world, familiar to us and unknown, to lay apart their particular functions and wonder at him. I once writ a sonnet on his pride and began thus: 'Wonder of nature—' " (III, vii, 11–42).

Hopkins reverses the negative connotations Shakespeare gives this speech by replacing the French dauphin with a more obviously Christian rider for his Pegasus, the flying steed traditionally symbolizing poetry. In his "St. Thecla" Hopkins had already suggested St. Paul as the proper rider for Pegasus and in "Andromeda" it is Christ himself who, like the windhover, "Pillowy air he treads a time and hangs." The metaphor of "riding" itself recalls Jesus who "on wings dost ride" in Hopkins's "Half-Way House" and the striding, hurling, gliding, mastery, and pride imagery all echo *The Wreck of the Deutschland,* especially the representation of "The Master, / *Ipse,* the only one, Christ, King" who can "ride, her pride, in his triumph" (st. 28), yet also "with a love glides / Lower than death and the dark" (st. 33).

Moreover, when the undercurrent of the chivalric imagery culminates in the "valour," "plume," and "pride" of the sestet of "The Windhover," it is clearly the chivalric imagery of Christ the King of the conclusion of *The Wreck.* This constellation of images is epitomized in "Buckle!" which evokes not only the "buckler" of medieval armor but also "buckling," a word for the combat of knights in Shakespeare's *Henry VI* plays. The fire breaking from their lances hitting the armor is clearly more "dangerous" an activity than merely riding, because it results in "gashing" and "galling," in this context meaning "abrasion."

This is the imagery of the "hero all the world wants" described in Hopkins's sermons: Christ as a "warrior and a conqueror," a "king" who "was feared when he chose," who "took a whip and singlehanded cleared the temple." "I should have feared him," Hopkins makes clear. Yet "in his Passion all this strength was spent," all "this beauty wrecked, this majesty beaten down" (*S*, 34–38). For Hopkins, Christ's triumph was inherently paradoxical: "doomed to succeed by failure; his plans were baffled, his hopes dashed, and his work was done by being broken off undone" (*D*, 138). "Poor was his station, laborious his life, bitter his ending; through poverty, through labour, through crucifixion his majesty of nature more shines" (*S*, 37).

The essence of Christianity for Hopkins, as we saw in *The Wreck*, was the concept of the sacrificial Incarnation, here postfigured in the dive of the windhover from the heavens to the earth. In this view, Christ could have remained above the earth, but he chose to swoop down, not to destroy but to save his prey, the hearts of men, to restore them to the kingdom of heaven. To this end he, rather than his prey, suffered the insult of the "gall" offered him to drink and the "gash" of the spear. When His "valour" and "act" were buckled together in the "brute beauty" of the Crucifixion, it was an apparent collapse or buckling under which was actually the preparation, the "buckling to" of the warrior for the victory of the Resurrection and the triumph of Christianity throughout the Western world. The V-shape of the diving windhover prefigured the collapse of Christ's pinioned arms "when his body buckled under its own weight," yet the result was the release of grace for "billions" of souls.[5]

The "fire that breaks from" Christ then, the fire lit on the cross ("I have come to bring fire to the earth," Luke 12:49), is the fire of love, the fire of God Himself: "For love is strong as Death. . . . The flash of it is a flash of fire, / A flame of Yahweh himself" (Song of Sol. 8:6). This flash of fire from the cross is "a billion / Times told lovelier" and more "dangerous" to the prey, men's hearts, because it demands complete commitment. This is the purging Pentecostal fire of the Holy Spirit (Luke 3:17) and the fire of the God of Psalm 18 who soared on the wings of the wind and came down from the heavens and kindled live embers with his consuming fire.

The "danger" is that of Christ the Master who preys on men's hearts, claims them totally, tears them away from their families, becoming their "sword / strife," as Hopkins put it in "To seem the stranger." This "dangerous" call to die unto the old self is reinforced by the plough imagery: "Once the hand is laid on the plough, no one looks back who is fit for the kingdom of God" (Luke 9:62), a phrase which haunted Hopkins throughout his life. The "sheer plod" that must follow putting one's hand to the plough may be a bleak life but, like the buckling ember, it can burst into the "lovelier" fire if the ploughman deliberately imitates the type of Christ's sacrifice, evoked by the final gold and vermilion imagery, the traditional colors of the Crucifixion in art.

The conclusion thus seems far removed from the initial chivalric imagery of the falcon—a contrast developed in Hopkins's "St. Alphonsus Rodriguez" (1888)—but the windhover is actually an appropriate type of one who was valiant though his "station was poor" for, according to the medieval hierarchy of falconry, it was "at the bottom of the social ladder, reserved for knaves, servants, children."[6] Thus the basic paradox of Christianity is present from the beginning in the poem, the paradox so well expressed in the conclusion of "That Nature is a Heraclitean Fire":

I am all at once what Christ is, since he was what I am, and
This Jack, joke, poor potsherd, patch, matchwood, immortal diamond,
           Is immortal diamond.

The Moral Level

In quadrivalent biblical typology the third level is as closely related to the second and first as they were to each other. The assumption is that if a reader makes a genuinely Christological interpretation he will be changed as a result; he will "turn," the root meaning of "trope," hence the label *tropologia* for this level. Hopkins's hero, Origen, emphasized this level, the most popular one in the Middle Ages, though Jerome was the first to restrict the term to this meaning.

For Hopkins the Book of Nature as well as the Bible demanded a tropological reading, a moral application to the self: "This world then is word, expression, news of God," he wrote; "it is a book he has written . . . a poem of beauty: what is it about? His praise, the reverence due to him, the way to serve him. . . . Do men then do it? Never mind others now nor the race of man: DO I DO IT?" (*S*, 129, 239).

Hopkins's attempt to answer that question, it could be argued, is the most literal meaning of "The Windhover," just as Dante's own conversion is the literal meaning of The Divine Comedy, and Christ's fulfillment of the Law is the literal meaning of Old Testament types in Luther's theology. The sense of a dialectic between Hopkins's own history and that of Christ, whether perceived in the Bible or the Book of Nature, is in fact evident in the very shape of Hopkins's poems. His sonnets, like *The Wreck,* are divided into two parts, with the second answering the first, like the New Testament answering the Old, with the pause before the sestet signaling a shift from one level of interpretation to another.

The initial "I" of "The Windhover" foreshadows this shift because it stresses the experience of the self as the literal meaning of the poem. The obvious tropological application of the lesson of the Book of Nature to the self begins with "My heart in hiding / Stirred for a bird" at the conclusion of the octet. The most literal meaning is that his heart was not visible, that he was trying to avoid being seen by the falcon, but one does not need to hide to observe windhovers, and in any case the bird could not see "his heart." To discover what his heart is hiding from the reader is again forced to another level of interpretation.

One biographical answer is that he was hiding from fulfilling his ambitions to be a great painter and poet. Instead of ostentatiously pursuing fame in that way, wearing his heart on his sleeve, he had chosen to be the "hidden man of the heart" (1 Pet. 3:4) quietly pursuing the *imitatio Christi.* As Hopkins put it, Christ's "hidden life at Nazareth is the great help to faith for us who must live more or less an obscure, constrained, and unsuccessful life" (*S*, 176).

Hopkins did live such a life, but the windhover reminded him of Jesus' great achievements after Nazareth. The windhover "stirred" his desire to become a great knight of faith, one of those who imitate not only the constraint but also the "achieve of, the mastery of" this great chevalier. The fluttering wings of the falcon are an image of zeal in the *Paradiso* (19:34–36) and its "ecstasy" recalls Hopkins's initial desire in "Il Mystico" to be lifted up on "Spirit's wings" so "that I may drink that ecstacy / Which to pure souls alone may be" (ll. 141–42). Ultimately, Hopkins became aware that he had been hiding from the emotional risks of total commitment to becoming a "pure" soul. The phrase "in hiding" thus means not only hiding from the world, or from worldly ambition, but also hiding from God, the meaning it has in Hopkins's "Thee God, I come from": "Once I turned from thee and hid, / Bound on what thou hadst forbid; / Sow the wind I would; I sinned."

This is the basic predicament of stanza 2 of *The Wreck*. The "hurl and gliding" of the windhover recall how once before his heart swooned before the "sweep and hurl" of God. The solution in "The Windhover" is the same as that of stanza three of *The Wreck*, a renewed conversion to Christ, again conveyed by heart and flight imagery. The "mastery" that "stirred" his heart in "The Windhover," therefore, was ultimately that of the "mastering me / God" of *The Wreck* (st. 1), the "Master" who could "ride" down our "pride," convert "at a crash Paul," and "master" Augustine.

The words "here / Buckle!" thus mean "here in my heart," as well as here in the bird and here in Jesus. Hopkins's heart in hiding, Christ's prey, now senses him diving down to seize it for his own. Just as the bird buckled its wings together and thereby buckled its brute beauty and valour and capacity to act; so the speaker responds by buckling together all his considerable talents. He renews his commitment to the *imitatio Christi,* deciding anew that "his truth shall be thy shield and buckler" (Ps. 91). Like Spenser's Redcrosse knight, he buckles on all the chivalric imagery of Eph. 6 in order to buckle down, buckle to, in serious preparation for the combat, the grappling, the buckling with the enemy. As Paul said, "Put on the whole armour of God, that ye may be able to stand against the wiles of the Devil."

Hopkins wrote this poem only a few months before his ordination as a Jesuit priest, the ultimate commitment to sacrifice his worldly ambitions. Just as Jesus' paradoxical triumph was his buckling under, his apparent collapse; so the knight of faith must be prepared for the same buckling under or collapse of his pride, for a life of "sheer plod" and "blue-bleak" self-sacrifice, if need be. Nevertheless, the knight of faith has the promise that a fire will break from his heart then—galled, gashed, and crucified in imitation of Christ. The fire will be "a billion times told lovelier" than that of his "heart in hiding," and far more "dangerous, both to his old self (for the fire is all-consuming) and his enemy, Evil.

In Hopkins's case the fire also became far more "dangerous" to his worldly poetic ambitions. "The Windhover" also represents Hopkins's Pegasus, the classical flying steed of poetry. The collapse of his own poetic self is implied in this imagery, for Pegasus threw off Bellerophon because of Bellerophon's pride. Fearing his pride in his own poetry, Hopkins burned his poems upon entering the Society of Jesus, believing that poetry always had to give way, buckle under, to the "greater cause" of his religion. As a result, there was a very real danger that his poems would never reach the public they deserved, that he would have to sacrifice all the worldly fame promised him as "the star of Balliol" for a life of "sheer plod." "Plod," echoing "on you plod" in his "Soliloquy of One of the Spies Left in the Wilderness," evokes the dreary lot of the Israelites crossing the wilderness from Egypt to the Promised Land, the standard *typos* of conversion among the Victorians.

Yet the Israelites did reach the Promised Land and the "plod" makes the plough "shine" in "The Windhover." The plough scratching the field was in fact also a common medieval metaphor for the writer's pen scratching across the paper, the furrows corresponding to the rows of letters. Hopkins's paradoxical triumph as a poet is that, although his poems were created out of that life of sheer plod and remained as obscure as blue-bleak embers to most of his contemporaries, now that they have found an audience to appreciate them they have burst into fire, shining like multifaceted diamonds.

Hopkins's new self, in short, was able to mount Pegasus again, transforming the classical flying steed into a Christian symbol of poetry as Dante had (*Paradiso*, 18:81). In this very poem in fact the steed carries him, its chevalier, to fame.

In other words, "The Windhover" is, among other things, as Michael Sprinker has shown, an allegory of Hopkins's rediscovery and renewal of his poetic vocation.[7] "I caught" thus not only means "I caught sight of," I grasped with my senses and my mind, I attained full possession or knowledge of an object, coming upon it unexpectedly or by surprise, "catching it in the act," as we say. "I caught" also means here "I was caught by" the windhover, that is, the "dapple-dawn-drawn Falcon" caught my eye and drew me forth, drew me out of myself that dawn, drew a poem out of me, summoned my lyrical voice to an act of creation. The result is quite properly dedicated to "Christ our Lord," for like the nun in *The Wreck of the Deutschland* this speaker, looking at nature, is "wording it how but by him that present and past, / Heaven and earth are word of, worded by" (st. 29). The result is a "catch," in still another sense: a canonical, rhythmically intricate composition for several voices.

One of those voices, though only one, is the voice of a poet attempting to find himself again as a poet. The bird's "mastery" of its environment inspires him to attempt a poetic "mastery" of the symbols of the Judeo-Christian tradition to which he had dedicated his life. Consequently, Hopkins constructed, or "achieved," not only an extraordinarily successful mimesis of the bird's "achieve," and a brilliant conversion of the bird's hovering and dive into a symbol of Christ's Incarnation, but also simultaneously a symbol of his own plunging into poetry, his own incarnation as a Christian poet.

The "buckling" of the bird and the crucifixion imagery of the sestet represent the poet's askesis as well as the terrible askesis of Christ's Passion. One could argue that the secret of Hopkins's eventual success was indeed his sacrifice of his early poems and his willingness to spend seven years in a hidden life, like Jesus' at Nazareth, waiting for the right occasion to write again; in other words, that it was Hopkins's ascetic restraint that made his poems so compressed, so rare, so much like diamonds.

Hopkins's application of the moral sense of the Book of Nature to himself is only the beginning of the tropological interpretation of "The Windhover," however. The primary moral application is to you, the reader. Hopkins's aim is clearly to call upon you to effect a similar change in your life. By virtue of his approaching ordination as a priest, Hopkins felt a special urgency about communicating this need for change to others. His poetry thus resembles the biblical tradition of typology in that "by its very nature," it "fastens on an event of conversion with the aim of effecting another . . . with a call to a radical re-alignment, with a challenge to change your mind, your way of life, your allegiances."[8]

The Anagogical Level

The fourth level is related to the third level in biblical criticism in that it too focuses on the life of grace in the soul—Dante's example is the soul leaving sin for a life of sanctity and freedom—but the fourth level is ultimately the "mystical" level that teaches "ineffable mysteries" according to Origen. In *Contra Celsum* he used the word now translated as anagogical, meaning "leading up," to distinguish this from the literal or historical senses. The most common "ineffable mystery" associated with this level is that of "eternal things" or the "future life," especially heaven and the Second Coming. In the Middle Ages, however, an equally, if not more important "ineffable mystery" was the discovery that the Creation and the Incarnation were being constantly reenacted in a "kind of continuous present."[9] The anagogical level was thus basically a breakthrough to alternative conceptions of human time.

Following Rom. 1:20 ("For the invisible things of Him . . . are clearly seen, being understood by the things that are made") some medieval theologians believed that the anagogical level could be attained by reading the Book of Nature as well as the Bible. For them nature became the universal symbolism of the Incarnate Word, eventually conceived of as equal to the Bible and to the liturgy in which the two converged. As Hugh of St. Victor put it, types could be discovered *per creaturam,* in creatures, as well as *per doctrinam,* in doctrine. Thus there was a double book for a double universe.[10] Because of the Fall, the Book of Nature had become obscure, hiding God, but it could still reveal Him to readers who reached the anagogical level. According to the theory of universal symbolism in Aquinas's *Summa,* this belief is based on the inclusion of material things, as well as Old Testament prefigurations of Jesus, in the category of "symbols of sacred things which are sacred in themselves."[11]

The romantics revived this tradition of discovering types of eternity in nature. Wordsworth, for instance, discovered that the features of nature

> Were all alike workings of one mind, the features
> Of the same face, blossoms upon one tree;
> Characters of the great Apocalypse,
> The types and symbols of Eternity,
> Of first, and last, and midst, without end.
>
> (*The Prelude*, 6:636–40)

The influence of Wordsworth, therefore, as well as the medieval poets and critics, is evident in Hopkins's response to the Aurora Borealis: "This busy working of nature wholly independent of the earth and seeming to go on in a strain of time not reckoned by our reckoning of days and years but simpler and as if correcting the preoccupation of the world by being preoccupied with and appealing to and dated to the day of judgment was like a new witness to God and filled me with delightful fear" (*J*, 200). *The Wreck of the Deutschland* and a number of his other poems express not only his sense of the providential ordering of human time but also the delightful fear inspired by this discovery of Apocalyptic time in nature.[12]

Most of his nature poems suggest not so much that sense of the end of the world common in Protestant anagogical typology, however, as his experience of the beginning of the world. Nature could lead him back as well as forward in time. When he contemplated the sacramental quality of St. Winefred's Well in Wales, for instance, he wrote: "The strong unfailing flow of the water and the chain of cures from year to year all these centuries took hold of my mind with wonder at the bounty of God in one of His saints, the sensible thing so naturally and gracefully uttering the spiritual reason of its being (which is all in true keeping with the story of St. Winefred's death and recovery) and the spring in time to its spring in eternity: even now the stress and buoyancy and abundance of the water is before my eyes" (*J*, 262).

Nature was thus a corridor through time, giving the viewer access to the very beginnings of the world, to Eden itself. The "ecstasy" of the windhover is that of the creatures in Hopkins's "Spring" (1877)—"What is all this juice and all this joy? / A strain of the earth's sweet being in the beginning / In Eden garden"—and of Tennyson's "Wild bird, whose warble, liquid sweet, / Rings Eden through the budding quicks" (*In Memoriam*, no. 88). The windhover's "ecstasy" was also a taste of that second Eden, the Incarnation, that "ecstasy all through mothering earth" which "Tells Mary her mirth till Christ's birth" ("The May Magnificat").

Such a breakthrough to Edenic time was not as rare as we might think. Even as late as the nineteenth century, thousands of miles from Wales, for instance, during the same years Hopkins was describing nature's "ecstasy" in "The Windhover" and "The May Magnificat," Dostoevski was focusing the climax of part 2 of *The Brothers Karamazov* on Father Zosima. Zosima's doctrine of the worship of sinless nature was based on a sense that "Christ has been with [the creatures] before us," a feeling that "every leaf is striving to the Word," that "paradise" is at hand. Hopkins's "ecstasy" in "The Windhover" almost seems to be a response to Father Zosima's injunction: "pray to the birds too, consumed by an all-embracing love, in a sort of transport, and pray that they too forgive you your sin. Treasure this ecstasy, however senseless it may seem to others."

The "fire" that breaks from the windhover when it dives, then, is the fire of the Word becoming incarnate, the revelation of the spark of divinity in each and every creature, the fire of "God's Grandeur" and "As kingfishers catch fire." As McLuhan says, "familiarity with Hopkins soon reveals that each of his poems includes all the rest."[13] "As kingfishers" opens with virtually the same image as "The Windhover." Like windhovers, kingfishers usually hang stationary (in their case on a branch) overlooking their prey before descending. The invitation to compare them with Christ is even more obvious because Christ the King was known as a fisher of men. The meaning of the octet of "As kingfishers catch fire" is simpler and more direct, however: "Each mortal thing does one thing and the same: / Deals out that being indoors each one dwells."

The "being" that dwells "indoors," the "fire" within all mortal things which can be "dealt out," is the fire of "God's Grandeur," to turn to still another sonnet, one composed just before "The Windhover." "God's Grandeur" is also dominated by an image of a bright winged bird suspended over the world at dawn. It too states simply, "The world is charged with the grandeur of God. / It will flame out. . . ." The dearest freshness "deep down" in things which will "flame out," in the windhover, then, as well as any other creature, is nothing less than the grandeur of God.

Thus, as Hopkins put it in "As kingfishers catch fire," "Christ plays in ten thousand places," not only in "just men," the immediate subject of the sestet of that poem, but in all things; "All things therefore are charged with love," he wrote in his commentary on Ignatius, "are charged with God and if we knew how to touch them give off sparks and take fire . . . ring and tell of him" (S, 195). Hopkins found support for this idea, as we have seen, in Scotus's concept of the Incarnation continuing in nature, that is, in the idea of nature as the mystical body of Christ. This world is charged with God's grandeur because it too is part of His mystical body. When the speaker in "Hurrahing in Harvest," another sonnet of 1877, discovers that "hills are his world-wielding shoulder," his heart is snatched up, as if by a bird of prey, and it "rears wings bold and bolder / And hurls for him, O half hurls earth for him off under his feet." There should be "No wonder of it," "The Windhover" reminds us, for the symbolism of the Incarnate Word is a universal symbolism, including ploughs and coals as well as hawks and hills.

Inner meanings of the text such as these are revealed only to those who seek them, however, according to Clement of Alexandria, the founder of the multivalent school of biblical hermeneutics. This is particularly true of the Book of Nature, for the creatures of nature, from the medieval perspective, were not descriptive symbols like words, that is, mere signs, but rather interpretive symbols which have an obvious meaning but "at the same time they contain, in their capacity as signs, a hidden meaning which will be revealed only to the one who knows how to interpret it . . . the one who allows himself time for meditating upon created things."[14] Origen felt that only those who were endowed with a special "grace" could achieve the highest spiritual level, the anagogical: "the more beautiful the soul, the more divine beauty it can perceive in things."[15] This idea recurs in Hopkins's theory of perception of inscape, as we shall see, and especially in stanza 5 of *The Wreck of the Deutschland* which emphasizes how rare and mysterious is the discovery of divine beauty in nature: "For I greet him the days I meet him, and bless when I understand."

Welsh Eden

In *The Wreck*, "The Windhover," and his other sonnets of 1877, Hopkins clearly did attain the highest "spirituality," the mystical sense, the "anagogical" interpretation of the Book of Nature. In other words, if we look back to some of the melancholy poems of the 1860s, he moved from *acedia* to "ecstasy." Because the inner way sometimes resulted only in a discovery of that inner emptiness and ennui that Pascal defined, many religious before Hopkins had turned to the outer way to find a unity in the external world that would lead them to God. Thus, these poems represent another movement in the ongoing dialectic Hopkins experienced between the two ways.

Indeed, his great outburst of nature poetry in the late 1870s may be represented as a natural reaction against the *acedia* which often accompanied his overemphasis on the inward way. Dante defined *acedia* as a joylessness most conspicuous in the victim's inability to appreciate God's creation, a sense of *acedia* also relevant to the romantic melancholy of Goethe's Werther, Senancour's Obermann, and Coleridge's "Dejection" Ode. A traditional way to escape *acedia*, therefore, from St. John Chrysostom on, was to love God's creation. Even the primarily inner-directed *Spiritual Exercises of Saint Ignatius* include "The Contemplation for Obtaining Love" in which "The second point is to consider how God dwells in His creatures. . . . The third point is to consider how God works and labors for me in all created things on the face of the earth, that is, He conducts Himself as one who labours; in the heavens, the elements, plants, fruits, flocks, etc. He gives them being, preserves them."[16] Hopkins uses the same verb, "dwells in," in "As kingfishers catch fire."

As we have seen, as early as "Half-Way House" Hopkins felt a need to approach God in this way: "I must o'ertake Thee at once and under heaven / If I shall overtake Thee at last above." As "The Windhover" and Hopkins's other sonnets of 1877 reveal, Hopkins found such a halfway house not only in the communion bread and wine but also in the Vale of Clwyd and the rest of the countryside around St. Beuno's College, Wales, where he studied theology from 1874 to 1877. His swing from *acedia* to enthusiasm is evident in his earliest letters from there (*F*, 124–27). Wales provided the occasion for his greatest experience of nature, as it had for Wordsworth (at Mt. Snowdon and Tintern Abbey), John Dyer (at Grongar Hill), and Henry Vaughan.

Hopkins's awakening to an unfallen world of nature in Wales is recounted in "Moonrise" (1876) and in his Welsh poem, "Cywydd" (1876), in which he asserted that the appearance of the earth shows an eternal share of virtue; only the human element is defective, man alone is backward. For Hopkins nature seemed not only unfallen, but in a sense eternal due to God's presence and protection: because the Holy Ghost broods over it, "nature is never spent" ("God's Grandeur").

Some of the most luminous symbols of that presence in Hopkins's Welsh poetry are the sunrises and the "sea-sunsets which give such splendour to the vale of Clwyd," as Wordsworth put it in his preface to "Descriptive Sketches." Such sights were distilled in Hopkins's nature poetry in his imagery of sunlight which "sidled like dewdrops, like dandled diamonds" ("The furl of fresh-leaved dogrose down," 1879). Everything from ploughed furrows to clouds to their reflections in pools is shining and gleaming. Even night reveals a world of strangely translucent moonshine or of stars that gleam like "bright boroughs" or "diamond delves" or "quickgold" in grey lawns; all of nature was perceived as a "piece-bright paling" that was Christ's "home," as Hopkins put it in "The Starlight Night":

> Look at the stars! look, look up at the skies!
> O look at all the fire-folk sitting in the air!
> The bright boroughs, the circle-citadels there!
> Down in dim woods the diamond delves! the elves'-eyes!
> The grey lawns cold where gold, where quickgold lies!

> Wind-beat whitebeam! airy abeles set on a flare!
> Flake-doves sent floating forth at a farmyard scare!—
> Ah well! it is all a purchase, all is a prize.
> Buy then! bid then!—What?—Prayer, patience, alms, vows.
> Look, look: a May-mess, like on orchard boughs!
>   Look! March-bloom, like on mealed-with-yellow sallows!
> These are indeed the barn; withindoors house
> The shocks. This piece-bright paling shuts the spouse
>   Christ home, Christ and his mother and all his hallows.

Hopkins clearly found in the Vale of Clwyd what the Pre-Raphaelite painters were seeking: "They chased, as it were, all the year round over the bright valleys of the earth, their ideals of luminosity; from the backcloth of bright earth and sky they cut out, as if with sharp knives, square panels of eternal paint; they gave to material phases of nature a relative permanency, a comparative immortal life."[17]

Pre-Raphaelite color and brightness convey immortal life in a poem such as "The May Magnificat": Hopkins's "strawberry-breasted" thrush, "bugle-blue" eggs, "drop-of-blood-and-foam-dapple" bloom, and "azuring-over" greybell, all shades of crimson and blue, relate the Incarnation to nature; "crimson and pure blues seemed to me," Hopkins recalled, "spiritual and heavenly sights fit to draw tears once" (*B*, 283). The painter's eye is also evident in the lush colorful landscape of wheat and flowers in "The Woodlark." Its painterly terminology—"The sky is two and two / With white strokes of blue"—recalls not only the bright colors of many Pre-Raphaelite paintings, but the heavy emphasis on actual strokes of paint in such impressionist paintings of the next decade as Van Gogh's *Wheat Field with Lark*.

Hopkins anticipates Van Gogh specifically in "Miror surgentem" (undated) which focuses on Orion, the constellation used to represent the transcendent God in *The Wreck of the Deutschland*. In the Latin poem Hopkins wonders how Orion rises in the sky and flashes its fire which a force not its own makes brilliant in the heavens. Its soft luster comes and goes, he says, giving the impression that the wind could whirl its seven star-points round and round. The most appropriate analogue for this particular vision is not so much the Ruskinese search for the evidence of an underlying force in recurrent forms, or the Pre-Raphaelite ideal of luminosity, as it is the dramatized vision of nature in such impressionist paintings as Van Gogh's *Starry Night*. In Hopkins's "The Starlight Night" the stars are indeed animated in Van Gogh's fashion. They seem to be firefolk and elves-eyes revealing sudden flashes of movement, like leaves of whitebeam or abeles when they are dramatically flipped over by sudden gusts of wind and flash the whiteness of their undersides, or like doves suddenly flying into the sky "at a farmyard scare."

As the primary symbol of nature's energy and God's grandeur, fire dominates Hopkins's imagery. The poppy buds in "The Woodlark" are "flame-rash rudred," "aflash" with the colors of fire. "Fire" breaks from the falcon and embers reveal the fire within in "The Windhover." Chestnuts are fresh "firecoals" and finches' wings flash the colors of fire in "Pied Beauty." Kingfishers "catch fire" and dragonflies "draw flame" in "As kingfishers catch fire." God's grandeur "will flame out" ("God's Grandeur"). Once again Hopkins seems to prepare the way for Van Gogh, especially Van Gogh's flamelike plants such as the cypresses in *Road with Cypresses and Stars*.

Both artists use fire imagery to convey their sense of the great forces molding and shaping nature. Hopkins's use of the word "vital" in his description of an internal fire, a "vital" candle in the heart in "The Candle Indoors" (1879), moreover, suggests affinities between his conception of nature and the "vitalism" of Carlyle, Browning, and Van Gogh, among others. When Hopkins translated Parmenides' Being as an "ethery flame of fire, comforting the heart" he added, "he is thinking of it perhaps as a vital principle" (*J*, 130).

Hopkins's vital principle, his sense of a divine spark within all creatures, was an explicitly Christian one, however, based on the idea of the Incarnation. In *The Wreck* we perceive God not only as a transcendent Orion of light in heaven but also in the thundering storm itself, but one instance of that presence of God in the world invoked in the fifth stanza of that poem. The first signs of the extension of the sacramentalism suggested in that stanza are found in Hopkins's poems about St. Winefred's Well, a spring in the town of Holywell not far from St. Beuno's reputed to have the power of curing the sick and the lame. As we have seen, Hopkins discovered in this well an accepted example of sacramental nature, a holy "sensible thing" (*J*, 261) which offered in itself a sacred opportunity for worship. His poem "On St. Winefred" (undated) closely identifies the activity of the spring with St. Winefred herself: "she lends, in aid of work and will, / Her hand from heaven to turn a mill." In "In S. Winefridam" (undated) Hopkins suggests that if he followed "the traces of the ancient deed" properly, they would still be "full of holy power." In his Welsh "Cywydd" Hopkins extended this sense of the sacramental quality of St. Winefred's Well to other springs and streams near St. Beuno's, which he also described as "a holy remnant kept for us by Beuno and Winefred." Having moved from a sense of the sacramental quality of one fountain to a sense of the sacramental quality of many fountains and streams, it was but one step further to the conception of all of nature as a sacrament, offering sacred opportunities for worship everywhere.

That Hopkins took that step is nowhere more obvious than in the line, "and the azurous hung hills are his world-wielding shoulder," in "Hurrahing in Harvest," words which fulfill Ruskin's injunction to give up mere realism and treat "the pure and holy hills" as "a link between heaven and earth" (3:449). Following that advice, Hopkins obviously went beyond purely transcendental religious views which allow admiration for nature solely as a source of analogies, a pale reflection of God's beauty. He even surpasses some of the mystics and prophets who conceived of nature as the garment, the time-vesture of God. As we have seen, for Hopkins nature was more than a veil for a transcendent God: it actually shared in the presence, the Being of God.

God is immanent in nature, moreover, not only in the general sense that the earth is part of the mystical Body of Christ but, more particularly, He dwells inside of creatures in nature such as the windhover and is expressed in the action of each one in its own way, as Hopkins suggests in "As kingfishers catch fire":

> As kingfishers catch fire, dragonflies draw flame;
>   As tumbled over rim in roundy wells
>   Stones ring; like each tucked string tells, each hung bell's
> Bow swung finds tongue to fling out broad its name;

Each mortal thing does one thing and the same:
    Deals out that being indoors each one dwells. . . .

                                                          (ll. 1–6)

This is not to say that God dwells in other creatures in the same
way He dwells in the "just" man discussed in the sestet. The being
of each creature participates in the Being of God according to its
capacities; the capacity of men to imitate Christ being greater, their
potential for sharing in the Being of God is greater. Nevertheless,
as Hopkins makes clear in his Welsh "Cywydd," nature has one
very significant advantage: it is not subject to sin, it is not fallen.
The being of any one of its creatures participates fully from its
conception in God's Being according to its capacity, whereas man
must strain to achieve this potential level of participation and rarely
succeeds. Thus the evidence of God's Being is much greater in nature
than in mankind because, as Hopkins says in "Ribblesdale," nature
"canst but only be, but dost that long— / Thou canst but be, but
that thou well dost. . . ."

This sense of God's presence within creatures and their acts can
be seen even in those poems of 1877 to 1879 which seem devoted
to a transcendental conception of God. The Holy Spirit is brooding
over the world at the conclusion of "God's Grandeur," but the entire
world, everything in nature is also "charged," filled to the brim
with God's splendor, not as a vague aura about the earth, but as
an eternal freshness "deep down" in each thing in nature, something
that "will flame out" from within each one:

The world is charged with the grandeur of God,
    It will flame out, like shining from shook foil;
    It gathers to a greatness, like the ooze of oil
Crushed. Why do men then now not reck his rod?
. . . .

And for all this, nature is never spent;
    There lives the dearest freshness deep down things;
And though the last lights off the black West went
    Oh morning, at the brown brink eastward, springs—

> Because the Holy Ghost over the bent
> World broods with warm breast and with ah! bright wings.
>
> (ll. 1–4, 9–14)

Even in an apparently conventional, transcendental poem such as "The Starlight Night" there is the suggestion of the presence of Christ "withindoors," "shut home" in the stars of the night and in more earthly stars: flowers on bushes and trees, "flake" doves scattered into flight, leaves of trees turned and flashed by the wind.

The Poetry of Reconciliation

In such poems Hopkins was trying to convey both the transcendent and the immanent aspects of God. In general, his attempt to resolve any one of the tensions in his nature poetry of this period necessarily involved the reconciliation of other intimately related oppositions, a continuation of that revolt against dualism which we traced in his poetry and prose of the sixties. Just as the attempt to integrate the destructive and benevolent aspects of God and nature made *The Wreck of the Deutschland* a great poem, attempts to reconcile such opposing ideas as the transcendent and the immanent aspects of God, the beautiful and the sublime, unity and variety, formal order and formless change lend greatness to many of the poems after *The Wreck*.

For instance, as we have seen, Hopkins could embody the orthodox view of God above nature, transcending it, as well as dwelling within it, in such lines as "thou art above, thou Orion of light" in *The Wreck* (st. 21). This traditional conception of God is also evident in poems written after *The Wreck* such as "Miror surgentem," which includes an image of God's provident hand stretched out everywhere to nature. Although He extends a special protection and aid, God is clearly conceived anthropomorphically and apart from nature. Similarly, although protecting and cherishing the earth, the Holy Spirit in "God's Grandeur" is separate from and above nature, like a mother dove over her egg or Milton's Holy Spirit which "with mighty wings outspread / Dove-like satst brooding on the vast Abyss / And mad'st it pregnant" (*Paradise Lost*, 1:20–22). Likewise in "The Starlight Night" heaven seems to be represented in the conventional sense as a place just above or behind the stars. The basically transcendental approach of this poem and the representation of the moon as a "paring of paradisaical fruit" in "Moonrise" a year before recalls such poems as "For a Picture of St. Dorothea" and the many poems of Christina Rossetti in which ecstatic contemplation of ascension into a starry heaven is the reward for ascetic withdrawal from the things of this world.

Besides balancing these transcendent aspects of God with the evidence of His immanence in his 1877 sonnets, Hopkins assimilated both the beautiful and the sublime moods of nature. "God's Grandeur," for instance, uses the Italian sonnet structure and the inclusiveness of the word "grandeur" to suggest God's presence in both the sublime and beautiful aspects of nature. As we have seen, Hopkins explained that he chose to illustrate the idea "it will flame out" by the metaphor of "shining from shook foil" because it evokes images of both sheet and forked lightning (B, 169), images recalling the "lightning and lashed rod" and the chastising "lightning of fire hard-hurled" in The Wreck (sts. 2, 34). The sense of a fire that "will flame out" also recalls other instruments of the blacksmith God's forging fire in The Wreck such as Death's "flame" and the "white-fiery" snow. The violence of "shook" and "crushed" in "God's Grandeur" supports this sense of a great power, a threatening "rod" that must be reckoned with by man. Thus the "grandeur" of God expressed in the octet can be seen as the awesome majesty of infinite power associated with the dynamic sublime and the Old Testament God.

Yet the word "grandeur" can also mean the splendor of a great display of beauty. Even "lightning" can have this connotation, as in "Spring" where it is the vehicle for the union of the beautiful and the sublime in a single image: a thrush "Through the echoing timber does so rinse and wring / The ear it strikes like lightnings to hear him sing." If the octet represents the awesome "grandeur" of God, the sestet of "God's Grandeur," especially the concluding image of a sunrise revealing the bright-winged Holy Spirit brooding over the world, conveys this other meaning of the word.

The fusion of the sublime and the beautiful in a single creature in "The Windhover" represents another stage in Hopkins's revolt against dualism. The striking opening of the sestet, "Brute beauty," emphasizes through consonance, assonance, and a double stress the unity of these opposites. What is admired is both the beauty of the bird's flight patterns and its "dangerous" brute force. Likewise, in "Hurrahing in Harvest" God's grandeur in both the hills and the stallion is seen as beauty as well as strength: "And the azurous hung hills are his world-wielding shoulder / Majestic—as a stallion stalwart, very-violet-sweet!—" (ll. 9–10). The hills are "azurous-hung" like a painting as well as "world-wielding," and the stallion is "very-violet-sweet" as well as an image of God's "stalwart" power.

Hopkins went on to reconcile nature's unity and variety as well as its sublimity and beauty, moreover, a continuation of the effort begun in his definition of "inscape" in his prose. The fairly single-minded quest for unity in his search for inscapes in nature is reconciled with a delight in nature's variety, motion, and changefulness in "Pied Beauty," for instance:[18]

> Glory be to God for dappled things—
>   For skies of couple-colour as a brinded cow;
>   For rose-moles all in stipple upon trout that swim;
> Fresh-firecoal chestnut-falls; finches' wings;
>   Landscape plotted and pieced—fold, fallow, and plough;
>   And áll trádes, their gear and tackle and trim.
>
> All things counter, original, spare, strange;
>   Whatever is fickle, freckled (who knows how?)
>   With swift, slow; sweet, sour; adazzle, dim;
> He fathers-forth whose beauty is past change:
>   Praise him.

Hopkins's representation of the landscape as "plotted and pieced" implies the kind of recurrence and regularity he discovered when "the lines of the fields, level over level, are striking like threads in a loom" (*J*, 23). In "Pied Beauty," however, he also focuses on individual piedness, variegation, and change, as well as on those manifestations of a fixed pattern of unity so painstakingly collected in his journals.

The individuality of each thing that constitutes the variety of "All things" is stressed in lines 7 and 8. Each thing is "original," "counter" to all other things, "spare" in the sense of being not abundant, not repeated, and hence "strange," not known before, new. In other words, the speaker does not automatically categorize things as most adults do. Seeing some fallen chestnuts he does not simply classify them under the noun "chestnuts" and pass on, but pauses to recognize that these chestnuts are not exactly like all previous chestnuts, that to some extent they have an individuality that evades our linguistic categories, an original strangeness which ordinary language levels.

Wishing to resurrect the wonder that the counterness and spareness of all things created in us as children ("who knows how?"), Hopkins often created new words such as "unleaving," "wanwood," and "leafmeal," which he used in a poem such as "Spring and Fall" to recreate a child's wonder at the fall of leaves. In "Pied Beauty" we see his simpler method of making one linguistic unit, "fresh-firecoal chestnut-falls," out of adjective, noun, and verb, in order to suggest that what he saw could not be simply classified, that some of its individuality resided in the intersections of our categories. The cumulative effect of this recurrent perception of the individuality, the original counterness of "All things," is a sense of the infinitely rich variety of nature.

Yet, simultaneously there is a sense of unity. In one place a trout is marked by a rose-mole and in another it is not; at one moment it is swimming swiftly and is "adazzle" and at another it is resting and appears "dim." Nevertheless, throughout all these spatial and temporal changes it is the same trout. Each dappled thing unifies its own variety. The use of plurals and collectives in the poem also emphasizes the larger unity of the class: all trout are "fickle, freckled," but they are unified by certain common characteristics which place them in the species, trout. The great variety of the different species is in turn unified by the poet's most powerful tool, metaphor—the demonstration of unexpected unity between things thought to be unrelated such as trout and roses, skies and cows, chestnuts and coals. Finally, imitating the cyclical structure of nature, the poem ends where it began, with the focus on the word for the ultimate unity, "God."

In this short poem, encompassing both earth and sky and the traditional four elements of earth, water, air, and fire, the oneness of the biosphere can be heard as well as seen. The sound structure of the poem reinforces the reader's sense of a complex unity in the midst of all the counterness and spareness. Alliteration in line 4, for instance, unites the "fresh firecoals," the "falls" of chestnuts, and the "finches"; in line 9 it suggests the presence of an underlying unity between the apparent opposites. Throughout the poem, assonance, consonance, rhyme, and rhythm all work to create an intricate model of how unity and variety depend upon and sustain each other.

Yet instead of the quiet beauty of a stable, unifying order, nature in "Pied Beauty" is in constant flux. Hopkins's emphasis on action and change in the poems of the late 1870s resulted in representations of nature in which a wild willfulness of forms displaced regular patterns, and loveliness consisted not only in the forms but also in the behavior of objects such as the clouds in "Hurrahing in Harvest": "up above, what wind walks! what lovely behavior / Of silk-sack clouds! has wilder, wilful-wavier / Meal-drift moulded ever and melted across skies?" Nature is being represented here not as it was in the journals but as it was in *The Wreck of the Deutschland*: as a world of great activity. Hopkins proceeded in his subsequent poems to include both the formless dynamic energy and change of nature that he had embodied in that poem and the opposite sense of nature's unchanging stable order and formal unity that he had so laboriously cultivated in his journals.

"Pied Beauty" also reveals Hopkins's conception of the relationship between God and this world of variety and change: God "fathered-forth" this world but, paradoxically, was Himself "past change." This dual conception of God as removed from the world of mutability and yet at the same time the Progenitor of that world was an ancient paradox, of course, but Hopkins felt the necessity of a new reconciliation of the idea of nature as a world of regularly recurrent patterns of unity, reflecting a transcendent Oneness, with a concept of nature as full of variety and change being continually created by a God who was very closely identified with, actually immanent in that process.

One of his reconciliations is the representation of the recurring act, the inscape of change. The "rash-fresh" yet "re-winded" sounds of the skylark in "The Sea and the Skylark," for instance, represent ageless patterns. What Hopkins admires is the "resumption by the lark of his song, which by turns he gives over and takes up again all day long, and this goes on, the sonnet says, through all time without ever losing its first freshness, being a thing both old and new" (B, 164). The skylark's song is both a pattern of sound which recurs throughout the day and throughout all time, typifying and thereby uniting the species, and yet a song that seems to be new, an original utterance of one individual, unique creature. Thus the song is an instance of both unity of recurrence and diversity of original expression, immutability and mutability, stability and change.

Hopkins's most successful reconciliations in his next set of nature sonnets, in 1879, were often achieved by limiting his search in this way to individual objects, acts, or scenes which had a formal unity, thereby revealing the force within them to be both a diversifying and a unifying power. The landscape of "Binsey Poplars," for instance, the first of his pair of elegies for the countryside around Oxford in 1879, combines specialness with recurrent regularity. Part of the attraction of the Binsey poplars for Hopkins was the regularity of their form, their "following folded rank." This regularity contrasted with the willful variation of the "river and wind-wandering / Weed-winding bank," phrases which echo the "wind-walks" and "wilful-wavier" clouds of "Hurrahing in Harvest." This balance of regularity and variety constituted the "sweet especial scene," an expression or "selving" of the tender "being" of the country. When the "following folded rank" of the poplars was cut down, the entire scene was "unselved."

"Duns Scotus's Oxford" enlarges the focus to all of the landscape surrounding the university town, and considers the special balance between town and country. The city had its man-made towers, for instance, but it was also "branchy between towers"; it was swarming with bells, but also with cuckoos, larks, rooks, and shepherds. The result was "rural keeping." "Keeping," according to Webster's, means among other things "the harmony or correspondence between the different parts of a work of art," as in "the foreground of this painting is not in keeping." In Hopkins's notes on painting in 1874 he uses the term "inscape of composition" in a similar way to define the qualities of correspondence, regularity, and often internal recurrence necessary in an individual painting to give it "keeping" in this sense, that genuine unity which he so admired (*J*, 248).

Hopkins's interest in the "special" scenes of "Duns Scotus's Oxford" and "Binsey Poplars" reveals the same painterly interest in an unusual harmony and balance, a special unity destroyed by the addition of any foreign element or the removal of any part. The harmony between the "coped and poised" powers of Oxford and its rural surroundings, for instance, was destroyed by the new "graceless growth" of brick suburbs. Similarly, the balance between the regularity of the "following folded rank" of the Binsey poplars and the variety of the "wind-wandering weed-winding" river upon which their shadows swam was destroyed when the poplars were chopped down. (Incidentally, poplar shadows upon a stream is the same image of harmony as that of several Monet landscapes.) The result in both cases was an "unselving," the destruction of a special unity. A striking manifestation of the tender "being" of the "country" disappeared from both scenes. Evidence of the immanent unifying and diversifying force was lost to all "after-comers."

Hopkins's attraction to that force is also embodied in the celebration of the "forged feature," the rehearsal "Of own, of abrupt self" in "Henry Purcell" in 1879. Hopkins clearly intended to praise individuality and the special case in this poem. Yet, "beyond that," he admired Purcell because, as he said in his preface to the poem, Purcell "uttered in notes the very make and species of man as created both in him and in all men generally." The analogy to the great stormfowl in the poem works in the same way: "the seabird opening his wings with a whiff of wind in your face means the whirr of motion, but also unaware gives you a whiff of knowledge about his plumage, the marking of which stamps his species" (*B*, 83). Hopkins is fascinated by both the unique individual and that pattern in the plumage which, recurring throughout the plumage of all birds of that species, unifies the species and thus reveals the evidence of an integrating force in nature.

The Tragic Vision

Hopkins believed that if other people could see this unifying force in nature as he did, they could be brought closer to God. The chief difficulty with this idea of nature as a mediator between man and God, however, has always been that even a poet cannot effectively communicate a sensitivity to his environment if his community is not ready for it. The Psalms suggest how old this problem is: "The heavens are telling the glory of God; and the firmanent proclaims his handiwork. Day to day pours forth speech, and night to night declares knowledge. There is no speech, nor are there words; their voice is not heard; yet their voice goes out through all the earth and their words to the end of the world" (19:1–4). This is the Psalm echoed in "Where are the Nine?" in *Pietas Metrica*. This lament for man's inability to appreciate and respect nature increasingly dominated nineteenth-century literature as industrialization and urbanization spread. Wordsworth and Coleridge had already registered their complaints when Thoreau wrote of how "The morning wind forever blows, the poem of creation is uninterrupted; but few are the ears that hear it."[19] Eventually Hopkins came to a similar conclusion, realizing how sadly "beauty of inscape was unknown and buried away from simple people and yet how near at hand it was if they had eyes to see it and it could be called out everywhere again" (*J*, 221). Yet it was not only simple people who lacked the requisite vision: the eyes of the vast majority of people, then as now, had not been trained to see the beauty of inscape, the beauty of the intricate unity intrinsic in nature's richest variety. As Origen observed centuries before, a "special grace" was needed to reach the "anagogical" level.

Hopkins was more isolated than most poets, moreover, because, though nature still testified to him of God's presence and offered mediation, for many of his contemporaries who also responded to nature God was a transcendent deity who did not live in the world or had disappeared altogether. In either case, for most of his contemporaries, nature existed only to be exploited. As Hopkins put it in "God's Grandeur," the shod feet of modern men "have trod, have trod, have trod; / And all is seared with trade; bleared, smeared with toil; / And wears man's smudge and shares man's smell. . . ."

The anguish that Hopkins and other nineteenth-century writers felt because industrial man not only failed to respond to the forms of nature, but in fact seemed dedicated to their annihilation should not be underestimated. One of Hopkins's journal entries reads, "The ashtree growing in the corner of the garden was felled. It was lopped first: I heard the sound and looking out and seeing it maimed there came at that moment a great pang and I wished to die and not see the inscapes of the world destroyed any more" (*J*, 230).

The pervasiveness of this unusual sensitivity to the environment and the tragic vision it produced in the nineteenth century may be suggested by Hardy's ascription of the "weakness of character," ultimately even the death wish, of his nineteenth-century man, Jude, to a similar sensitivity: "He could scarcely bear to see trees cut down or lopped, from a fancy that it hurt them; and late pruning, when the sap was up and the tree bled profusely, had been a positive grief to him in his infancy" (*Jude the Obscure,* pt. 1, chap. 2). Earlier, Thoreau had written, "Sympathy with the fluttering alder and poplar leaves almost takes away my breath . . . if any part of the forest was burned . . . I grieved with a grief that lasted longer and was more inconsolable than that of the proprietors. . . . I would that our farmers when they cut down a forest felt some of that awe which the old Romans did when they came to thin, or let in the light to, a consecrated grove *(locum conlucare)* that is, would believe that it is sacred to some god."[20] It was both the immediate loss, and the fact that the "After-comers cannot guess the beauty been" ("Binsey Poplars") that led Hopkins to plead in "Inversnaid" (1881), "What would the world be, once bereft / Of wet and of wildness? Let them be left, / O let them be left, wildness and wet; / Long live the weeds and the wilderness yet."

Industrialization continued to consume the wilderness as it still does, however; whole landscapes like those around Oxford were destroyed by what Hopkins called "base and brickish" suburbs. Finally in 1882 he wrote of the Ribble river valley:

> . . . strong
> Thy plea with him who dealt, nay does now deal,
> Thy lovely dale down thus and thus bids reel

> Thy river, and o'er gives all to rack or wrong.
>
> "Ribblesdale"

Though in 1882 Hopkins felt that nature's plea was still strong with God, that nature was still somehow "never spent," in this poem he at first puts God's rule over the river in the past tense—"dealt"—and concludes the octet replacing the image of God brooding protectively over nature ("God's Grandeur") with a new image of God giving all of nature over to "rack or wrong."

The source of this wrong being done to nature was, as the sestet reveals, the egoism of the stewards of the earth:

> And what is Earth's eye, tongue, or heart else, where
> Else, but in dear and dogged man?—Ah, the heir
> To his selfbent so bound, so tied to his turn,
> To thriftless reave our rich round world bare
> And none reck of world after. . . .

Hopkins discovered anew the aptness of the motto that Ruskin chose for the title page of *Modern Painters*: a citation from Wordsworth on how Nature and Truth revolt "offended at the ways of man" who

>   prizes
> This soul, and the transcendent universe
> No more than as a mirror that reflects
> To proud Self-love her own intelligence.

A chief cause of this proud self-love according to Wordsworth was increasing urbanization. In *The Prelude* Wordsworth focused on the dangerously narcissistic introversion of city life, where the self is "Debarr'd from Nature's living images. / Compelled to be a life unto itself" (6:313–14). Hence it is not surprising that it was in Hopkins's first extended comparison of the city and the country, "The Sea and the Skylark" (1877), that his tragic vision of environmental degradation received its first full expression. Hopkins tried to suggest that an Edenic purity was there, just outside the cities and towns, that other men also could feel how the cleansing song of the thrush could "rinse and wring" the ear ("Spring"). He admired the sea and the skylark because they had "the cheer and charm of earth's past prime," they were as "rash-fresh" and "pure" as if they were still in Eden.

But when he turned from this "freshness deep down" in nature to urban civilization symbolized by the nearby town of Rhyl, he felt the vulnerability of man and nature to each other. The town seemed "frail" both because its temporal existence seemed so negligible beside the apparent immortality of nature itself, and because the seemingly infinite power of the sea that roared around its edges could crush it. Yet man also posed a serious threat to nature's frailty: Hopkins's "Our make and making break, are breaking, down" suggests not only that man's basic structure, his make, is disintegrating, but even his attempts at construction, his making, is itself a breaking. This paradox is defined more fully in "Binsey Poplars":

> Since country is so tender
> To touch, her being só slender,
> That, like this sleek and seeing ball
> But a prick will make no eye at all,
> Where we, even where we mean
> To mend her we end her,

For Ruskin in "The Two Paths" it was the names "of great painters" that were "like passing bells" of decaying civilizations (16:342). For Hopkins it was the sounds of the sea and the skylark that ushered out like bells at the end of the year his own "sordid turbid time." Hopkins's representation of this "sordid turbid" time breaking down to man's last "dust," draining fast toward man's first "slime," recalls similar accounts of dust, slime, and pollution in the works of Tennyson, Dickens, Ruskin, and others.[21]

Not long after he completed "The Sea and the Skylark" Hopkins was assigned to Chesterfield. From this time until his death the pollution of the industrial cities to which he was assigned took a mounting toll of his energies and his spirit. Of his life in Chesterfield in 1878 he wrote, "Life here is as dank as ditch-water. . . . My muse turned utterly sullen in the Sheffield smoke-ridden air" (*B*, 47–48). After a brief sojourn at Oxford he was sent in 1879 to Bedford Leigh, near Manchester, which he described as "very gloomy . . . there are a dozen mills or so, and coalpits also; the air charged with smoke as well as damp" (*D, 29, B, 90*). In 1880 Liverpool was his assignment: there "the river was coated with dirty yellow ice from shore to shore" (*B*, 116). Sent to Glasgow in 1881, Hopkins wrote, "My Liverpool and Glasgow experience laid upon my mind a conviction, a truly crushing conviction, of the misery of town life . . . of the degradation even of our race, of the hollowness of this century's civilisation: it made even life a burden to me to have daily thrust upon me the things I saw" (*D*, 97). Finally, in 1884, after teaching at Stonyhurst for two years, Hopkins was sent to Dublin, "a joyless place and I think in my heart as smoky as London is" (*B*, 190).

Throughout the whole of his career in the Victorian cities a remarkably modern concern for pollution weighed heavily upon him: "our whole civilisation is dirty, yea filthy, and especially in the north; for is it not dirty, yea filthy, to pollute the air as Blackburn and Widnes and St. Helen's are polluted and the water as the Clyde and the Irwell are polluted? The ancients with their immense public baths would have thought even our cleanest towns dirty" (*B*, 299). From this sense of physical pollution Hopkins moved to a sense of the general pollution of the human race: "the filthy, as the scripture says, are filthy still: human nature is so inveterate. Would that I had seen the last of it" (*B*, 110). Such connections between physical and moral pollution were not uncommon in Victorian writers. Dickens's *Dombey and Son* (1848), Ruskin's "The Stormcloud of the Nineteenth Century" (1884), and other Victorian works anticipated many recent findings in the human sciences about the relations between environmental and human deterioration.

Eventually, Hopkins "saw the last of it." He died in Dublin at the age of forty-four of typhoid fever, apparently caused by the polluted urban water supply. The continuing attraction of nature for him even toward the end, however, his desire to snatch brief moments of light and joy in nature before the night overwhelmed all, is evident in his last nature poem, the fragment "Epithalamion" (1888). It was intended as an ode on the occasion of his brother's marriage but the result is a tale of one man's encounter with nature which anticipates some of the nature poetry to follow Hopkins.

The direct personal voice and the primary action, a man swimming alone in nature, anticipates Lawrence's "Wild Common," for instance, and the diction and syntax sound often like that of another lover of Wales, Dylan Thomas:

Hark, hearer, hear what I do; lend a thought now, make believe
We are leafwhelmed somewhere with the hood
Of some branchy bunchy bushybowered wood,
Southern dean or Lancashire clough or Devon cleave,
That leans along the loins of hills, where a candycoloured, where a gluegold-
   brown
Marbled river, boisterously beautiful, between
Roots and rocks is danced and dandled, all in froth and water-blowballs,
   down.

                                                                                      (ll. 1–8)

"Epithalamion" also summarizes Hopkins's own experience of nature:

Till walk the world he can with bare his feet
And come where lies a coffer, burly all of blocks
Built of chancequarrièd, selfquainèd, hoar-huskèd rocks
And the water warbles over into, filleted|with glassy grassy quicksilvery
   shivès and shoots
And with heavenfallen freshness down from moorland still brims,
Dark or daylight on and on. Here he will then, here he will the fleet
Flinty kindcold element let break across his limbs
Long. Where we leave him, froliclavish, while he looks about him, laughs,
   swims.

                                                                                      (ll. 35–42)

Hopkins obviously had discovered the applicability of Wordsworth's preface to *The Excursion:*

           Paradise and groves
        Elysian, Fortunate Fields, like those of old
        Sought in the Atlantic Main—why should they be
        A history only of departed things,

Or a mere fiction that never was?
For the discerning intellect of Man
When wedded to this goodly universe
In love and holy passion, shall find these
A simple produce of the common day.

Hopkins's poetry, wedded to the universe in love and holy passion, is a modern record of Eden found—and lost. To retrace the final result of that marriage, the increasing sense of man's destruction of nature and the desire to enjoy some fleeting moments with her before it is too late, is to define what is essentially our own relationship with nature.

Evaluation

Our evaluation of Hopkins as a poet of nature often depends to a great extent on how well we think he relates to the "scientific" response to nature, however. Aldous Huxley, for instance, felt that he had to reject a poem such as "The Starlight Night" because it was so out of touch with the scientific forefront of thought that it was "not at all legitimate," "simply inadmissable."[22] Admittedly, this and many of Hopkins's other nature poems challenge our basic assumption that art must mirror "our sense of the age," as Robert Langbaum put it. Langbaum argues that our age is mirrored in "the new nature poetry" of Marianne Moore, D. H. Lawrence, Wallace Stevens, Ted Hughes, and others who extend Ruskin's attack on personification as "pathetic fallacy," rejecting even the vestigial anthropomorphism of Swinburne and Hardy in order to focus on the true "mindlessness of nature, its nonhuman otherness."[23]

It is true that a poem such as Wallace Stevens's "The Course of a Particular," with its fierce rejection of any trace of personification of nature, is more of a midwife to our new scientific world. Hopkins's "The Starlight Night" and his other nature poems seem to breathe life into the old world, the age of faith in the "pathetic fallacy," in the personification of God and nature, and the verbal imagination generally. Yet this apparent opposition between science and the ancient traditions of personification in religion and the humanities is simplistic, for metaphor is the scientist's as well as the poet's most powerful tool.[24]

A creative scientist recognizes the value and validity of any and all metaphors which provide access to important dimensions of reality, whether or not they happen to operate in his own field of specialization. Hence he should have little difficulty perceiving that one of the most powerful and meaningful of all the dominant metaphors of Western civilization is the personification of nature—the assertion of some sense of identity between man and nature. This is one of the languages that puts man in the landscape and the landscape in man. It has been abused more than most theoretical models in science, of course, but it can still be made responsible to feedback and remains congruent with significant aspects of reality.

Yet Huxley rejects Hopkins's metaphors of stars as "fire-folk sitting in the air" as anachronistic in an age of science, and presumably on the same grounds, Hopkins's imagery of "elves' eyes," the "piece-bright paling" which "shuts Christ home, Christ and his mother and all his hallows." Admittedly these are not the metaphors of science. Why should they be? Hopkins no more thought of his discipline as a mirror of popular science than a scientist thinks of his as a mirror of popular poetry. A creative scientist and a poet can each respect the other's work because they are both interested not in mirroring but in modeling and changing our conception of reality, and to this end the more powerful the metaphor the better.

Thus, refusing to limit himself to the models fashionable in Victorian science, Hopkins resurrected a sense of a universe animated by powerful cosmic forces, employing metaphors at once more precise and suggestive than those of his contemporaries, metaphors which enabled him to fill and satsisfy our imagination as a great nature poet must. Compare Hopkins's nature poetry with Matthew Arnold's in this respect, for instance. Afraid of committing the "pathetic fallacy," Arnold's representation of a thrush is tentative, an admission of ignorance: "Sometimes a thrush flit overhead / Deep in her unknown day's employ" ("Lines Written in Kensington Gardens"). Sure of the presence of God in this world, Hopkins's representation of a thrush is an enthusiastic celebration of communion: "Thrush's eggs look little low heavens, and thrush / Through the echoing timber does so rinse and wring / The ear, it strikes like lightnings to hear him sing" ("Spring").

Hopkins achieves what other nature poets of his day could not partly because he recognized the importance of personification; in his case the significance of the ultimate personification: the cosmic Christ. Unlike most of his contemporaries, imagining God in the flowers and waters Hopkins approached them with a belief that they were alive, and thus kept his poetry free of the debilitating shame, hesitation, and alienation which plague the "modern" view of nature according to Ruskin (5:231). Because Hopkins rediscovered part of what Arnold called the great medieval "Sea of Faith," especially the belief in the verbal imagination and the vitality of tradition, as we have seen, Hopkins could resurrect Hebraic pastoral even in the age of science: "What is all this juice and all this joy? / A strain of earth's sweet being in the beginning / In Eden's garden" ("Spring").

Unlike the speaker in Wallace Stevens's "The Course of a Particular," Hopkins does not merely hear the cry of a bird, therefore; he makes a real attempt to see it as "part of everything," as a "cry of divine attention" concerning everyone rather than "no one at all," as Stevens puts it.[25] Compared with Stevens's poem and a surprising number of Arnold's and Wordsworth's poems, moreover, Hopkins's poems seem fiercely reactionary in their insistence on richness of image and sound as perceptible emblems of order and splendor in the world, flashes of the grandeur with which the world is "charged." Ironically, this supposedly archaic, anthropomorphic attitude toward the universe produced poems such as "Binsey Poplars" and "Ribblesdale" which place Hopkins in the forefront of the current struggle in the environmental sciences to overcome the anthropocentrism threatening our environment. Hopkins thus shares a common cause as well as a common language (metaphor) with innovative scientists and, as Robert Lowell has suggested, should still be considered "probably the finest of English poets of nature."[26]

Chapter Seven
Poet of Modernity and Medievalism

Although Hopkins composed nature poems from his departure from Wales in 1877 to his death, his assignments in Victorian cities forced him to change the focus of his life and art from nature to man, and finally to one man—himself. Hopkins's difficulty in maintaining his positive, hopeful response to nature in the eighties is epitomized in "Spelt from Sibyl's Leaves." In addition to its traditional Hebraic and Hellenic theme of a personal descent into hell, which we shall discuss shortly, it also conveys a modern sense of irreversible environmental deterioration.

Like James Thomson's "The City of Dreadful Night" and many other poems, Hopkins's "Spelt from Sibyl's Leaves" employs nightfall as the central symbol of the nineteenth century's destructiveness. Modern civilization is represented as an earthless, hollow waste which makes all things equal by leveling the individuality of each: "self ín self steepèd and páshed." The selfness of one thing is forced into the selfness of another until they both become steeped in the sameness of night.

The preceding line, "For earth her being was unbound," invokes the accompanying sense of enervation, so typical of the late nineteenth century, suggesting that even the energy which has been bound up in the variety of forms is dissipating. "Pied Beauty" is no longer visible: "her dapple is at an end." As in Ruskins's "Deucalion," the earth in the modern age is represented as being "unsculptured or deformed," "suffering a deliquescent and corroding change. All character . . . being gradually effaced" (16:123).

Hopkins goes beyond Ruskin and his other contemporaries, however, by describing the earth as God's Body now actually "dísmémbering," and even "Disremembering"—losing even its memories of its own variety and all possibility of again becoming part of the mystical body of Christ. Hopkins's sense of the all-powerfulness of evil in the world eventually grew to the point where it included nature as well as urban civilization. The "worldwielder" who had been perceived as God in "Hurrahing in Harvest" is identified quite differently in Hopkins's more orthodox notes on Ignatius's *Spiritual Exercises*: "Satan, who is . . . the worldwielder . . . wreathing nature and as it were constricting it to his purposes" (*S*, 98–99).

The effect of this more orthodox view of decaying nature on Hopkins's earlier vision of unfallen nature is evident in "On the Portrait of Two Beautiful Young People," a counterpoise to the sestet of "Spring." In the later poem the "worm" invades the imagery of formerly Edenic nature: "Worst will the best. What worm was here, we cry, / To have havoc-pocked so, see, the hung-heavenward boughs?"

In "The Sea and the Skylark" we hear the lark's "rash-fresh re-winded new-skeinèd score / In crisps of curl off wild winch whirl," but in "Spelt from Sibyl's Leaves" this imagery belongs to quite a different song. Nature's complex unity in variety is still expressed by piedness of sound ("skéined stained véined variety") and by metaphor—the comparison to an intricate network of veins and skeins tying everything together in one unity. Yet all this wondrous unity in variety is reduced by the analytical, categorizing verbs ("párt, pen, páck") into a simple dualism. With nature often assigned to the "black," the "wrong" half, the speaker must withdraw into his own divided self. With nature no longer his household (the root-meaning of "ecology"), orphaned from his own body as well as the surrounding world, he is "sheathe- and shelterless." Shifting from the outward way back to the inward, he decides to strip down to the essential self to concentrate on the generation of a "new self and nobler me," as he put it in "The Blessed Virgin compared to the Air we Breathe" (1. 69).

This shift of attention from nature to man following Hopkins's more orthodox sense of nature as unredeemed, subject to the Fall, is perhaps most obvious in one of his simplest and most popular poems, "Spring and Fall." The speaker suggests to a young child named Margaret that a shift of concern from nature to mankind and finally to the self is a normal progression for all of us. Fallen nature can inspire "grief" and "sorrow" but "as the heart grows older / It will come to such sights colder" for it will discover that "It is the blight man was born for, / It is Margaret you mourn for." This change to a more human focus is obvious also in "Harry Ploughman" which is about rural man rather than nature, but the shift is most explicit in "To what serves Mortal Beauty" which commands us to love "love's worthiest, were all known; / World's loveliest—men's selves."

Shifting his energies from "indifferent" admiration of nature (*S*, 166) to attempts to bring love and grace to urban man, Hopkins often succeeded, as "Felix Randal" (1880) so eloquently testifies. But he also frequently experienced frustration and the increased sense of social degeneration lamented in "Tom's Garland" (1887) and in "The Times are nightfall" (undated):

> . . . Nor word now of success:
> All is from wreck, here, there, to rescue one—
> Work which to see scarce so much as begun
> Makes welcome death, does dear forgetfulness.

In this poem, a prototype of "Spelt from Sibyl's Leaves," Hopkins can find only one alternative:

> Or what is else? There is your world within.
> There rid the dragons, root out there the sin.
> Your will is law in that small commonweal.

"Rooting out sin" in the "world within" was the subject of previous poems such as "The Candle Indoors" but it soon became the preoccupation of most of the poems of Hopkins's final years, his sonnets of desolation: the six original "terrible sonnets" of 1885— "Carrion Comfort," "No worst, there is none," "To seem the stranger," "I wake and feel," "Patience," and "My own heart"— and three sonnets of 1889, "Thou art indeed just," "The Shepherd's Brow," and "To R. B."

Modern Poet of Ennui

The last line of "No worst, there is none," implying that the only comfort is that "each day dies with sleep" and that "all / Life death does end," is generally regarded as the nadir of Hopkins's desolation, the most despairing lines in all of his poetry. As we have seen, according to his own testimony Hopkins was subject to melancholy all his life (*F*, 11; *B*, 183; *S*, 262) but his "terrible pathos," as Dixon called it (*D*, 80), is most obvious in his late sonnets of desolation. Melancholy dominated the poems of his conversion in the sixties as well, however, and thus may be said to be as pervasive and consistent a theme in his poetry as nature or religion. Our final evaluation of Hopkins's life and art, therefore, is determined to a great extent by our response to this "melancholy" epitomized in the last line of "No worst."

The poem as a whole is often considered his greatest poem and/ or the poem which best expresses his modernity. Thus it offers an obvious opportunity not only to discuss his last sonnets but also to evaluate Hopkins as a modern poet, for "these astringent later sonnets crystallize that sense of frustration, of separation from God, which is the peculiar psychic disease of the twentieth century."[1]

As one of the seminal expressions of romantic "world-sorrow" or *Weltschmerz*, "No worst" reveals Hopkins's deep affinities not only with twentieth-century writers but also the nineteenth-century continental romantics who were more dominated by ennui than the English romantics:

> No worst, there is none. Pitched past pitch of grief,
> More pangs will, schooled at forepangs, wilder wring.
> Comforter, where, where is your comforting?
> Mary, mother of us, where is your relief?
> My cries heave, herds-long; huddle in a main, a chief-
> woe, world-sorrow; on an age-old anvil wince and sing—
> Then lull, then leave off. Fury had shrieked 'No ling—
> ering! Let me be fell: force I must be brief'.
> Oh the mind, mind has mountains; cliffs of fall
> Frightful, sheer, no-man-fathomed. Hold them cheap
> May who ne'er hung there. Nor does long our small
> Durance deal with that steep or deep. Here! creep,

> Wretch, under a comfort serves in a whirlwind: all
> Life death does end and each day dies with sleep.

Hopkins's "cliffs of fall" are like those facing Lord Byron's Manfred and Arnold's Empedocles, but even more like those confronting the Vicomte de Chateaubriand's René and J. W. Goethe's Tasso. Indeed, like Hopkins's persona, Goethe's confronts the whirlwind as well as the "cliffs of fall":

> Where, O where do I direct my steps
> To flee from the vortex of the whirlwind of loathing,
> To escape from the abyss that lies before me?
> > *(Torquato Tasso,* ll. 2238–40)

It may be argued that "No worst" is in fact a paradigm of all of modern humanism in that it expresses the syndrome of ennui much as Francesco Petrarca (Petrarch) did at the start of the Renaissance: a sorrow, caused not by a single blow of fortune but by a plenitude of causes, leading to despair and finally to a longing for death. One of the causes, for Petrarch as for Hopkins, incidentally, was living in a crowded, polluted city. Hopkins's affinities with Petrarch are important because Petrarch's unusually personal account of his sorrow in his *Secretum* has been "justly hailed as the first, intensely vivid portrayal of the new *Lebens-und Weltgefühl* of modern man . . . 'the foundation charter of Humanism and the Renaissance, and the Renunciation of the Middle Ages' . . . the first articulation of that bitter-sweet disgust with the world and with life which the Elizabethans were to call melancholy, and the Romantics, *ennui* or *Weltschmerz*. To be even more specific, it is the *voluptas dolendi* in Petrarch's analysis, his feeding with great delight on his own sorrows, which has been read as foreshadowing figures such as Goethe's Werther or Chateaubriand's René."[2]

Hopkins's seminal expression of this "age-old" literary emotion is important also because, like "The Starlight Night," "No worst" has aroused the opposition of the rationalist temper of modern science and technology. The rationalist perspective which has increasingly dominated the last two centuries is a source of objections to Hopkins as a modern poet of ennui as well as a modern poet of nature. "No

worst" has been criticized by one of Hopkins's most famous oppo-
nents, Yvor Winters, for instance, essentially for being too much
like Petrarch's *Secretum*, for being so "particular and personal" that
"we can feel no certainty regarding the nature of the experience";
so "emotional" and "romantic" that it is "a violation of our integrity;
it is somewhat beneath the dignity of man."[3] Winter's critique is
important because, as one critic has observed, "whether or not one
be in accord with Winters' 'moralistic' theory of poetry, his basic
accusation is repeated by implication, one must admit, in the failure
of most Hopkins critics to deal adequately with the terrible sonnets
in general, with [this sonnet] in particular."[4]

Though "No worst" does seem quite "particular and personal,"
it is actually an excellent illustration of Eliot's assertion that "not
only the best, but the most individual parts of [a poet's] work may
be those in which the dead poets, his ancestors, assert their immortality most vigorously."[5] No doubt some readers remain uncertain about the nature of the experience on the first or second reading
of the poem, but it could be argued that this initial uncertainty is
a sign of Hopkins's maturity as a poet and part of the modernity
of the poem. One word alone, "world-sorrow," can invoke a be-
wildering combination of allusive contexts but, as Eliot put it, "the
mind of the mature poet differs from that of the immature one
. . . by being a more finely perfected medium in which special,
or very varied, feelings are at liberty to enter into new combinations
. . . a number of floating feelings . . . having combined. . . .
It is a concentration, and a new thing resulting from the combination, of a very great number of experiences."[6] Such ambiguity or
"multivalence" has become a virtue in modern literary criticism.
The Heisenberg uncertainty principle and Goedel's theorem have
even forced some of the more advanced physicists, astronomers, and
mathematicians of the twentieth century to be almost as receptive
as romantic poets to the necessity of what Keats called "negative
capability," the ability to live with uncertainty.

Yet "the crucial question" remains: "what is the 'chief-woe' which
extends to 'world-sorrow' and 'age-old anvil'? Surely 'world-sorrow'
means more than mere *Weltschmerz*. . . . If we could convincingly
explain 'chief-woe' we could know the source of Hopkins' anguish

and thus negate the charge that he only presents 'an illusion of motivation.' "[7] "World-sorrow" is indeed "more than mere *Weltschmerz*," more than an allusion to romanticism and humanism. It is essential to recognize that this allusion also imports the richer contexts of the Bible and all the texts it has generated, including all the medieval treatises on sin and their culmination in Dante's Divine Comedy.

If we miss the biblical context, we may indeed agree with Winters that Donne's "Thou hast made me" is superior to Hopkins's "No worst, there is none" because "Donne's despair, death, and sin, . . . have a body of theology behind them."[8] Once we recognize the biblical allusion, however, we have a key to a body of medieval theology which defines the parameters of Hopkins's predicament and why he feels as he does in this and the other sonnets of desolation. We also become aware of a set of medieval contexts which provide an ironic contrast to the romantic and humanistic contexts the allusion usually invokes on first reading.

Medievalist Poet of Acedia

Admittedly, "No worst," is "emotional" and "romantic." The modern romantic combination of *voluptas dolendi* (enjoyment of sorrow) and artistic pride, especially the use of language for self-deification rather than for sacramental reconciliation with God, was perhaps Hopkins's greatest temptation. Hopkins was painfully aware of this tendency in himself and in romanticism generally, however, and he struggled against it. He discovered by by extrapolating some of the more genuinely religious impulses of romantic medievalism he could find a way to resist this modern disease. Seeking not the "renunciation" but the resurrection of the Middle Ages, he was able to attain more multivalence than most modern writers achieve, that is, a medieval as well as a modern, a religious as well as a secular sense of this phenomenon.

We need to recognize, first of all, that Hopkins's representation of his cries being herded and huddled together in the one category of "world sorrow" is but one more instance of the process of moral categorization announced in "Spelt from Sibyl's Leaves," where the related imagery of "folds" and "flocks" first appears: "Part, pen, pack / Now her all in two flocks, two folds — black, white; right, wrong." For all its attractiveness, Hopkins knew that the *voluptas dolendi* of world sorrow belonged in the "black," the "wrong" side of the ledger. This romantic emotion was obviously a "sin" to be rooted out of "the world within." Indeed, in Ireland and Scotland one meaning of the word "sorrow" is "the Devil." While Petrarch de-emphasized these moral connotations of the term, no reader who really wanted to understand the "age-old" meaning of "world sorrow" unmistakably invoked by Hopkins could ignore its original spiritual meanings.

Among the various medieval definitions of the term, one of the most prominent in English is that of Chaucer's Parson who decried "the synne of worldly sorwe, swich as is cleped *tristicia,* that sleeth man . . . as seith Saint Paul. For certes, swich sorwe werketh to the deeth of the soule and of the body also; for thereof comth that a man is anoyed of his owne life. Wherefore swich sorwe shorteth ful ofte the life of man, er that his tyme be come by wey of kynde" (ll. 725–27). The relevance of this to Hopkins's life as well as his art, especially to his death wish toward the end, is quite striking. The allusion is to 2 Cor. 7:10—"For the sorrow that is according to God worketh penance, steadfast unto salvation; but the sorrow of the world worketh death"—and Chaucer concludes that "For certes, ther bihoveth greet corage again Accidie, lest that it ne swolwe the Soule by the Synne of sorwe."

What Chaucer called "accidie" (in Latin *acedia*) was the name of a set of sins that included *tristicia* or world sorrow. As we have seen, *acedia,* the fourth deadly sin, is sometimes translated as "sloth," but there is really no English equivalent because *acedia* includes spiritual as well as physical desolation. Following Ignatius, Hopkins defined "spiritual sloth" or "desolation" as "darkness and confusion of soul . . . diffidence without hope and without love, so that it finds itself altogether slothful, tepid, sad, and as it were separated from its Creator and Lord" (*S,* 204). It is differentiated from physical sloth by the fact that the victim realizes his predicament, worries about it, and tries to overcome it.

As we have seen in Hopkins's poetry of the sixties, coldness, impotence, and wastefulness are important features of *acedia,* but by far the most important is "world sorrow." Indeed, world sorrow is so prominent a component of *acedia* that Thomas Aquinas, John of Damascus, John of Wales, and Thomas of Chabham equated *acedia* with *tristicia* ("world sorrow"). The connection is quite striking in Dante's *Inferno* where certain sinners must spend eternity under the surface of a foul slime gurgling the hymn, "We were sorrowful *(Tristi)* in the sweet sunny air, bearing within a slothful *(accidioso)* breath; now we are sorrowful *(attristiam)* in the black mire" (7:121–24). The Italian *attristirsi* means both to become sorrowful and to lose one's strength, become impotent, suggesting the range of emotions "herded and huddled" together in this main, chief woe of modern as well as medieval civilization. Besides world sorrow and loss of strength or impotence, the syndrome also includes feelings of exile and estrangement, darkness, the disappearance of God, despair, the death wish, and attraction to suicide—all emotions which recur throughout Hopkins's life and art.

Ironically, Hopkins succumbed to these emotions not through laziness but probably through an overanxious response to the adjurations against sloth. As we have seen, he was preoccupied with the parallel between himself and the spy left in the wilderness. Another medieval type or *exemplum* for the *accidiosi*, according to Alanus of Lille, was the Christian who draws his hand back from the plough, again a type which haunted Hopkins throughout his life *(D, 88)*. Hopkins's response to these warnings was exaggerated religious zeal which, as the medieval treatises on *acedia* make clear, can itself lead to a kind of spiritual collapse which may deprive the victim of any real ability to do good. This was the basic predicament of Hopkins's "Spelt from Sibyl's Leaves" and the sonnets of desolation, as one of his retreat notes reveals:

I do not feel then that outwardly I can do much good. . . . In thought I can of course divide the good from the evil and live for the one, not the other: this justifies me but it does not alter the facts. . . . I was continuing this train of thought this evening when I began to enter on that course of loathing and helplessness which I have so often felt before, which made me fear madness . . . being tired I nodded and woke with a start. . . . I am ashamed of the little I have done, of my waste of time, although my

helplessness and weakness is such that I could scarcely do otherwise. . . .
All my undertakings miscarry: I am like a straining eunuch. I wish then
for death. (*S*, 262)

This confession, like the sonnets of desolation themselves, is virtually a recapitulation of the medieval treatises on *acedia*, and it is
important to see Hopkins's writings in this context. According to
one of the treatises, Guillaume Dequileville's *Pelerinage de vie hu-
maine*, for instance, sloth is also known as *tristesse*, for she is a mill
which always turns and never grinds anything except the waste of
one's own thought and thus carries "Despair" written on a card
around her neck. These and other images of the treatises, such as
Hugh of St. Victor's metaphor of a mind dashed in upon itself
through *tristitia*, provide the imagery of the conclusion of "Spelt
from Sibyl's Leaves," the opening of "Carrion Comfort," and much
of the rest of the sonnets of desolation.

The sense of exile, estrangement, and impotence so well expressed
in Hopkins's "To seem the stranger" also comes under the heading
of this chief-woe, world sorrow, and again the medieval origins are
significant. Evagrius of Pontus, apparently the source of the first
list of deadly sins, devoted more space to *acedia* than to any of the
others, pointing out that the demon of *acedia* adds the memory of
the victim's family to the other aggravations. Estrangement from
one's family is an important feature of *acedia* also in John Chrysostom's *Exhortations to Stagirius*. John, whose homily on Eutropius
Hopkins translated, begins with a summary of the *tristitia* syndrome
in Stagirius which bears a remarkable resemblance to Hopkins's
situation. A man converts, gives up his family and his position in
society, and then struggles manfully against, yet often succumbs
to *tristitia*, which in turn causes extreme physical and mental
ailments.

Just as in Hopkins's "To seem the stranger," Stagirius's problem
is exacerbated by the fact that he is exiled from his family. As in
Hopkins's "Carrion Comfort" Stagirius feels that he is both a passive
victim of various tortures and one who battles with God Himself
in nightmares. Like Hopkins's "No worst," moreover, John's final
exhortation implies that *tristitia* is a universal phenomenon, that the
whole "terrestrial kingdom" is full of causes for *acedia*, and he too

uses the imagery of mountains and cliffs to represent the lure of insanity and suicide.

Thus, although pride is usually regarded as the deadliest of the seven deadly sins, John argued that excessive sorrow was the most ruinous diabolic obsession. This excessive sorrow contributed to a similar sense of exile not only in Hopkins's "To seem the stranger" but also in the works of Dante, Charles d'Orleans, Joachim du Bellay, the countess of Winchelsea's "Pindaric Ode on the Spleen," Chateaubriand's René, and Charles Baudelaire's "Andromaque," as well as the account of Despair and the death wish in Edmund Spenser's *Faerie Queene* which is echoed in "No worst."

Just as conspicuous as this sense of exile and estrangement in Hopkins's poetry of the sixties and the eighties is the feeling of impotence or loss of strength so well expressed in the conclusion of Hopkins's "To seem the stranger," in the lament for the "ruins of wrecked past purpose" in his "Patience," in the image of "My winter world" in his "To R. B." and in the representation of God as one who defeats and thwarts "Time's eunuch" in his "Thou art indeed just, Lord."

A similar preoccupation with impotence is evident in the medieval treatises. Nor is eunuch imagery unusual in their list of features of *acedia,* which was also known as *sterilitas animae.* After the Middle Ages, Petrarch's complete collapse of will in his secularization of *acedia* is imitated by Hamlet, Goethe's Werther, Etienne de Senancour's Obermann, and Stephane Mallarmé's Igitur. Mallarmé's "The virgin, vivacious and beautiful today" also invokes the related "ennui of sterile winter" much as Hopkins's "To R. B." does.

One of the results of this sense of sterile winter is a feeling of the disappearance or withdrawal of God. It is most obvious in Hopkins's "Nondum" and his phrase, "dearest him that lives alas! away" in "I wake and feel," but is also implied in "Comforter, where, where is your comforting?" in "No worst." We think of this as a modern phenomenon but it is the normal experience of the absence of spiritual consolation, and darkness is its traditional imagery, especially in Bernard of Clairvaux, Dante, Milton, and John of the Cross, as it is in Hopkins's "Nondum," "Spelt from Sibyl's Leaves," "Carrion Comfort," and "My own heart." The "darkness and confusion of soul" (*S*, 204) represented in the first quatrain of Hopkins's "I wake and feel" recall specifically the opening of the *Divine Comedy*: "In the middle of the journey of my life I awoke to myself in a dark wood where the straight way was lost." We also recall the episode of waking "with a start" in Hopkins's retreat notes (*S*, 262).

The ultimate result of God's withdrawal from the soul and the consequent darkness is often the temptation to despair, that loss of all hope which is the state of the damned in the *Inferno*. This, the temptation resisted in the opening of Hopkins's "Carrion Comfort," was the natural culmination of *acedia* according to John Cassian, John Chrysostom, and William Langland's *Piers Plowman* (20:163), and it recurs in such secular versions as Petrarch's *Secretum* and Robert Burton's *Anatomy of Melancholy*. Despair in turn often leads to the death wish, as implied in the conclusion of Hopkins's "No worst," in his "The Times are nightfall," and in his lament in "To seem the stranger": "Not but in all removes I can / Kind love both give and get." Finally, according to John Chrysostom, the medieval *Book of Vices and Virtues,* the play *Mankind,* and the lyrics of Charles d'Orleans, the victim often must wrestle with thoughts of suicide. Even Ignatius had to fight off this temptation,[9] and it recurs in the Renaissance in Petrarch, Burton, *Lear, Hamlet,* and *Richard II*.

The death wish does not really begin to dominate the imagination until the modern era, however, and thus its presence in "No worst" makes it seem a modern poem. As A. Alvarez put it, "It was a Romantic dogma that the intense, true life of feeling does not and cannot survive into middle age."[10] The first four desperate negatives and the imagery of twisting in Hopkins's "Carrion Comfort," for instance, echo Keats's struggle with suicide in "Ode to Melancholy"—"No, no, go not to Lethe, neither twist / Wolf's bane." Thomas Chatterton and Goethe's Werther succumbed to the temptation, followed by Gustave Flaubert's Madame Bovary, Byron's Manfred, Arnold's Empedocles, and many others. This worship of Thanatos also dominated A. C. Swinburne's poetry and led to the representation of the death of all of civilization in such poems as Hopkins's "Spelt from Sibyl's Leaves," James Thomson's "The City of Dreadful Night," Baudelaire's "Spleen and Ideal," and Jules Laforgue's "The Funeral March for the Death of the Earth." In the twentieth century, of course, this suicidal impulse became still more pervasive in the lives as well as the art of many literary figures.

Chateaubriand traced the cause of this syndrome of suicidal impulses, impotence, exile, estrangement, and despair, which is epitomized in Hopkins's "No worst, there is none" and in his "terrible sonnets" generally, to the gap between the idealistic vision of Christianity and the tawdry reality the Christian must face. Pater, however, Hopkins's anti-Christian antagonist at Oxford, discovered that Christianity was the anodyne rather than the poison. The hero of his novel, *Marius the Epicurean,* published the year "No worst" was written, experiences feelings remarkably similar to Hopkins's speaker.

In this novel modern ennui is represented under the guise of Roman melancholy: "a deep sense of the vacuity in life. The fairest products of the earth seemed to be dropping to pieces, as if in men's very hands, around him. How real was their sorrow, and his! His observation of life had come to be like the constant telling of a sorrowful rosary, day after day; till, as if taking infection from the cloudy sorrow of the mind, the eye also, the very senses, were grown faint and sick" (chap. 23).

"Contrasting itself for Marius in particular, very forcibly with" this "so heavy burden of unrelieved melancholy" (chap. 22) was Christianity: "Here, it might be, was, if not the cure, yet the solace or anodyne of his great sorrows—of that constitutional sorrowfulness, not peculiar to himself perhaps, but which had made his life certainly like one long 'disease of the spirit' " (chap. 21). Just as Hopkins discovered that Ignatius (unlike Thomas à Kempis) preferred consolation to desolation, Marius discovers that the monastic codes were exercises against world sorrow, were in fact adjurations to joy: "Take from thyself grief, for (as Hamlet will one day discover) 'tis the spirit of doubt and ill-temper. Grief is more evil than any other spirit of evil, and is most dreadful to the servants of God, and beyond all spirits destroyeth man" (chap. 22).

The Context of Allusion

Raising the question of the relationship between ennui and Christianity reminds us that to recognize that the term "world sorrow" in "No worst, there is none" assimilates this "age-old" range of meanings and traditions is only the first step toward an adequate reading of this poem. "World sorrow" is not the only allusion; nor are the medieval treatises on *acedia* and romantic glorifications of ennui the only prior texts invoked. Hopkins's poetics demands a more systematic reconstruction of this context of allusion.

His use of sound and metaphor to allude to previous writers is, like Dante's, essentially a biblical technique, and the importance of this kind of allusion throughout his poetry cannot be underestimated. It makes a difference in our interpretation of the New Testament, for instance, once we recognize that Jesus' apparently despairing cry on the cross, "My God, My God, why have you forsaken me?" is an allusion to the first line of a Psalm which ends with the coming of the kingdom of God throughout the world.

This kind of allusion is particularly common in Victorian literature, moreover,[11] which was heavily 1 .fluenced by the Bible. Nor were Victorian contexts of allusion limited to the Bible and related typological imagery; Tennyson's allusions to Homer, Dante, and Milton in "Ulysses," for example, must be understood as an essential counterpoint of meaning warning against the very temptation which the speech itself represents. This use of metaphor and echo to suggest allusive counterpointed meanings was an important technique for many writers, but especially for Hopkins.

Hopkins's advice about the significance of the choice of metaphor in Greek tragedy and the New Testament applies equally well to many other lyrics, including his own:

My thought is that in any lyric passage of the tragic poets . . . there are— usually; I will not say always, it is not likely—two strains of thought running together and like counterpointed; the overthought that which everybody, editors, see . . . and which might for instance be abridged or paraphrased in square marginal blocks as in some books carefully written; the other, the underthought, conveyed chiefly in the choice of metaphors etc [sic] used and often only half realised by the poet himself, not necessarily having any connection with the subject in hand but usually having a connection and suggested by some circumstance of the scene or of the story. (*F*, 252).

Hopkins then analyzes the opening chorus of Aeschylus's *Suppliants*, pointing out what "this alludes to," what "this suggests," and extends the principle to Hebrew literature as well: "Perhaps what I ought to say is that the underthought is commonly an echo or shadow of the overthought, something like canons and repetitions in music, treated in a different manner, but that sometimes it may be independent of it. I find this principle of composition in St. James's and St. Peter's and St. Jude's Epistles, an undercurrent of thought governing the choice of images used" (*F*, 253).

The undercurrent of thought governing the selection of words in Hopkins's poems which literally "echo" words and phrases in other works creates "canons and repetitions" of Hopkins's keynotes of meaning throughout his poetry. This echoing can be simply a way of amplifying meaning, much as the song of the thrush is more striking when heard through the "echoing" timber in "Spring." Echoes are often most important, however, when the underthought they convey is "independent of" the overthought, creating a thematic counterpoint that significantly enriches the poem.

A simple example of this technique, one which need not require digressions into particular allusions here, is "The Leaden Echo and the Golden Echo." Like Jesus' cry on the cross, discovery of a more positive echo in this poem changes the response of the listener. It is particularly important for our purposes, moreover, because the initial phrases of "No worst, there is none" echo a line from the earlier "The Leaden Echo" which is preceded and followed in that poem by the keynote of "No worst"—"despair":

> Ruck and wrinkle, drooping, dying, death's worst, winding
>   sheets, tombs and worms and tumbling to decay;
> So be beginning, be beginning to despair.
> O there's none, no no no there's none:
> Be beginning to despair, to despair,
> Despair, despair, despair, despair.

> THE GOLDEN ECHO
>   Spare!

The first five lines are excellent illustrations of echoing used to amplify the overthought, but the word "Spare!" while it too echoes "despair," initiates a counterpoint of meaning, a hopeful golden echo questioning feelings of despair: "O then, weary then why should we tread? O why are we so haggard at the heart, so care-coiled, care-killed, so fagged, so cogged, so cumbered, / When the thing we freely forfeit is kept with fonder a care" by God.

As a poem of modern ennui, "No worst, there is none" is a variation on the theme of "The Leaden Echo." Yet it is more than that, for there are also some golden echoes, hints of hope, that distinguish it from many modern poems. These golden echoes are subtle and indirect, and no modern reader is obliged to hear them, but they are there.

Indeed, there are so many of these golden echoes that we cannot pursue them all here. We must concentrate on the richest set of them, the chief underthought, the most illuminating context of allusion for understanding Hopkins's sonnets of desolation. One of the most significant contexts is generated by Hopkins's recurrent allusions to *King Lear,* which have been cited many times. [12]

These allusions also support the diagnosis of *acedia,* for the figure of the dispossessed monarch, so susceptible to those feelings of abandonment and impotence which generate deep feelings of sorrow, is an archetype of ennui according to Pascal. Turning inward, the exiled monarch discovers what all men discover, according to Pascal, an infinite abyss which can be filled only by an infinite God. Both Lear and his counterpart, Gloucester, follow this pattern of conversion.

When Lear finally gives up all his worldly possessions and his pride, he learns love for the "Poor naked wretches" and, in the speech echoed by Hopkins in "No worst," makes a declaration of his *imitatio Christi,* his willingness to sacrifice himself to bear the burden of others. Gloucester gives up his sight and apparently even his life. Edgar leads him to believe he has committed suicide by jumping off a precipice, in the cliff scene echoed in "No worst," and convinces him that he has experienced a miraculous resurrection. Gloucester is then "born again," feels pity for the suffering Lear, and accepts the will of the gods. By echoing both incidents many times throughout "No worst" Hopkins invokes a sense of redemptive meaning for his own suffering as well.

Inferno

At least as important as *Lear* in this respect as a context of allusion in the sonnets of desolation, however, is the Divine Comedy. The "Fury" in "No worst" and the phrase "I can no more" in "Carrion Comfort" can be considered direct allusions to the Divine Comedy, and there are many other connections as well. Even without all the specific metaphorical and auditory echoes, moreover, one would expect that the greatest poem of the Middle Ages, indeed of Christianity, would be an important context for Hopkins's sonnets of desolation. Dante was as important a precursor, an embodiment of "Tradition," for Hopkins as he was for Ruskin, T. S. Eliot, and many others.

Of course, as Maria Rossetti put it, "some there are who, gazing upon Dante's Hell mainly with their own eyes, are startled by the grotesque element traceable throughout the Cantica as a whole, and shocked at the even ludicrous tone of not a few of its parts."[13] Hopkins, like other "earnest" Victorians, had "this feeling about *Faust* and even about the Divine Comedy," but in all other respects his response to Dante was very favorable. He began referring to Dante in his diary as early as 1863; cited a line from the *Inferno* in Italian in his "Rhythm and other Structural Parts of Rhetoric"; included the Divine Comedy in his list of "great works of poetry"; put Dante in the same class as Shakespeare; and called him "the master."[14]

Hence we should not be surprised to discover that the initial sensations of "No worst," of being "pitched past pitch of grief," each level of pain "schooled" by the one before it, surpassing it finally and producing a "wilder" wringing, are those the reader experiences when he descends from the first to the second circle of Dante's hell and discovers that it bounds a smaller space yet contains much more grief. Hopkins's internal rhyme of "pang" and "fore-pangs" in his second line even echoes the structure of Dante's "Novi tormenti e novi tormentati" ("New torments and new souls in torment," 6:4–5), a line echoed again in Hopkins's "not live this tormented mind / With this tormented mind tormenting yet" ("My own heart").

Hopkins's most distinctive allusion to Dante in "No worst," however, is "Fury had shrieked." The Furies are of course Greek spirits of revenge, but their invocation in a clearly Christian context—preceded by references to the Comforter, to Mary, to the sin of *tristitia,* and followed by the Dantesque imagery of the mountains of the mind and the whirlwind—all point directly to cantos 8 and 9 of the *Inferno,* one of the most important contexts of allusion in "No worst."

In these cantos the passage of Dante and Virgil through Hell is stopped by over a thousand devils. Virgil leaves to confront them, assuring Dante, "comfort thy weary spirit and feed it on good hope, for I will not forsake thee in the lower world" (8:105–08). But Virgil, his comforter, is rebuffed, and Dante's situation could well prompt Hopkins's cry, "Comforter, where, where is your comforting?" Virgil tries to comfort Dante again, reminding him, first of all, that the demons also tried to oppose Christ when He descended for the Harrowing of Hell and, secondly, that he and Dante have already managed to descend far into the "steep"—another image which recurs in "No worst." Virgil is confident that they will defeat the demons because "such help was offered" by Beatrice, the primary Marian figure in the poem. Nevertheless, even Virgil cries out, "How long it seems till someone comes!"—a cry akin to Hopkins's "Mary, mother of us where is your relief?" Suffering from a cowardly faintheartedness clearly related to *acedia,* Dante then asks if anyone had before descended this far into the "sorrowful" *(trista)* cavity (9:16–17).

Virgil begins to answer, but Dante's eyes are drawn to the terrifying arrival of the Furies, the handmaidens of Proserpine, queen of everlasting grief. The Furies "shriek" for Medusa to turn Dante to stone and prevent his escape from Hell. Just as this is a turning point in the *Inferno,* the "shriek" of the Fury is echoed at the traditional turning point between the octet and the sestet in Hopkins's sonnet as well. Then in both works comes the noise of a whirlwind, followed in the *Inferno* by an Angel sent from Heaven who opens the gate for Dante and Virgil.

These echoes and parallels are reinforced by the fact that the commentaries on this passage in Dante fit "No worst" and Hopkins's other sonnets on *acedia* almost as well as they fit the *Inferno*. Dante's theme is identified as "despair" and his story is also perceived as a "narrative of disablement":

a period of his life when it seemed as if the foundations were removed and when there came to him a new assurance . . . Dante underlines . . . the significance of the Furies and the Gorgon, their traditional characters as the spirits of remorse and despair. Against the forces of denial and refusal with these dreadful allies the conscience is all but paralysed and reason itself for the time baffled and disabled, and the soul's only safety is to wait on God . . . then, while he shelters Dante from the threatenings of the screaming Furies to bring Medusa, comes the sound as of a rushing mighty wind—surely suggesting the story of Pentecost and the gift of the Spirit.[15]

At this point Hopkins's "No worst" ends, but just as the conclusion of the twenty-second Psalm could not be ignored once Jesus invoked the first line, the end of this incident in the *Inferno* presents a counterpoint of meaning for "No worst" that should not be simply ignored: "and then, august, serene, untroubled [comes] 'one sent from Heaven,' at whose presence devils and Furies are silent for fear and Virgil and Dante for reverence and at the touch of whose wand the way is open." Indeed, implied in all the parallels with the *Inferno* is the fact that relief did come, that Dante did emerge from Hell to go on to Purgatory and finally Paradise.

Though "No worst" ends before the recognition that the whirlwind announces the imminent arrival of the Comforter, Hopkins's apparently despairing final line, "Life death does end and each day dies with sleep," at least differentiates the speaker from the damned who flee the whirlwind in the *Inferno* because they have no hope, even of death. The conclusion of Hopkins's "I wake and feel"— "The lost are like this, and their scourge to be / As I am mine, their sweating selves; but worse"—again alludes to Dante and clearly distinguishes the speaker of Hopkins's terrible sonnets from the damned who are continually referred to in the *Inferno* as "the lost" and the "sorrowful," those who have lost all hope, even hope of death.

This distinction is easier to understand if we recall that Hopkins regularly meditated on *The Spiritual Exercises of Saint Ignatius*. If we see "No worst, there is none" in this context, simplistic identifications of Hopkins with the speaker, even of the speaker with the torments described, are more difficult. Indeed, the speaker of "No worst" often seems to be merely an anonymous exercitant following the instructions for the Ignatian "Meditation on Hell." The second prelude of this exercise is, in Hopkins's words, "to ask for what we want, which here is such an inward feeling of the pain the damned suffer that if we ever come to forget the love of the eternal Lord, through our faults (our venial sins, lukewarmness, worldliness, negligence), the fear of hell-pains at least may help us then and keep us from falling into mortal sin" (*S*, 214). In other words, Hopkins was directed by Ignatius to identify as completely as possible with the lost in this exercise in order to avoid becoming completely identified with them later. Ignatius specifies, moreover, that the exercitant is to "hear with the ears the wailings, the groans, the cries" of the lost, and "taste" their "sadness."

Once we become aware of these comments by Hopkins on the Ignatian text, can we assume that "No worst" is as "particular" and "personal" as Winters and others have charged? Reflecting the wider contexts invoked by Hopkins's allusions, the first four lines are in fact all generalizations—the speaker does not identify himself with the cries at all. The personal "My" is not heard until the fifth line, and then only to emphasize a move to a still higher level of generality, a categorization of the pangs and griefs under a "main" or "chief" woe, "world-sorrow," an "age-old" experience of mankind. The suggestions of a multitude of cries and causes generalize the situation still further. We cannot even identify the subsequent cliff and fall metaphors in the poem with some idiosyncratic mental instability in the speaker, for this is the traditional imagery of falling into hell so frequently invoked in the Ignatian meditation on hell (*S*, 137, 243) and many other treatises on sin.

Even the personal "My" cannot be simply identified with the speaker, for Ignatius asks the exercitant to make the cries of the lost his own. We should not be surprised if he succeeds, for the contemplation of the five senses in the Ignatian exercises is one of the most effective exercises of the sympathetic imagination ever devised (see *S*, 175). Hopkins's ability to identify with the pain of the lost was no doubt particularly acute because of his poetic and religious genius; as he put it, "the keener the consciousness the greater the pain; the greater the stress of being the greater the pain . . . the higher the nature the greater the penalty" (*S*, 138).

Even if the sin being contemplated is one to which the exercitant himself is particularly susceptible, we should not ignore the therapeutic function of the exercise. "The instressing of the scope of the sin" is not only a "torment," Hopkins points out; it is also "a mitigation of pain": "the concentration of the mind on the scapes of its own sin is some relief, as we act over to ourselves again and again the very scene which costs us shame as a relief to the shame, and that the pain of sense lessens while it conditions the pain of loss" (*S*, 139, 138). Moreover, while the exercitant recognizes that his sins are like those of the lost, that recognition itself enables him to prevent complete identification with the lost: "we have the fate of others before our eyes for our warning; our sins are like theirs but not our fate—not hitherto: let us while we can make ourselves safe, *make our election sure*. How? By hope, by prayer" (*S*, 244). The mere fact that the exercitant is still alive, that he can expect the relief of sleep and death, as the final line of "No worst" reveals, is a significant difference: "we may thank God that we are not among their number" (*S*, 140).

Again the commentary on Dante is appropriate to "No worst" and Hopkins's other sonnets of desolation: "here as elsewhere in Hell Dante is distinguished as a 'living soul' from the dead souls there,— not merely as one still in the earthly life, but as one living by hope in grace."[16] Dante is in Hell because he "fell so low," as Beatrice put it in the *Purgatorio*, "that all means for his salvation now came short except to show him the lost people; for this I visited the threshold of the dead" (30:136–39). Like Dante, Hopkins also faced "the lost," and that which was most like them in his own soul, but he too remains separated from the lost in that he is a living soul still addressing God in his prayers, still trying to purge himself of his sins, and still living "by hope in grace."

Purgatorio

When Hopkins put Ignatius's definition of "spiritual sloth" into his own words he placed the emphasis on this process of purgation: "there seems to be no question of tepidity. The only class of people St. Ignatius contemplates as making the Exercises or as reading these rules are the second, *illi qui intense procedunt in purgandis suis peccatis*: they are in the Purgative way and penitents at any rate now."[17] "World sorrow" seems simply a by-product of this process of purification: "In those who go on earnestly purifying themselves from their sins, and advancing from good to better in the service of God our Lord . . . it is peculiar to the evil spirit to cause anxiety and sadness" (*S,* 203). This sorrow can be overcome, however; it is a test "that God may try how much we are worth, and how much we progress in His service and praise, without . . . bountiful pay of consolation and special graces [and] teach us not to build our nest in another's house, by allowing our intellect to be lifted up to any kind of pride or vainglory" (*S,* 204–5).

One of the goals of the struggle against "world-sorrow" is thus that the victim may conquer his pride, realize his dependence on God, and acknowledge God's mastery. This is of course the theme of *The Wreck of the Deutschland* as well, which is echoed in "No worst" in diction such as "anvil," "wring," "lingering," "fall," "whirlwind," "deep" and "frightful."

"Frightful," for instance, recalls "The dense and driven Passion, and frightful sweat: / Thence the discharge of it, there its swelling to be" (st. 7). *The Wreck* then goes on to demonstrate the continuing sacrificial Incarnation of Jesus in the nun and in Hopkins: "here was heart-throe, birth of a brain" (st. 30). In the same way the pangs and sorrows of purgation in "No worst" may be seen as the labor pains for the birth of a new self:[18] "Men here may draw like breath, / More Christ and baffle death; / Who, born so, comes to be / New self and nobler me" ("The Blessed Virgin compared to the Air we Breathe," ll. 66–69). This purgation and rebirth imagery—the traditional symbolism of the pattern of conversion in Victorian literature—is the most positive context of allusion for "No worst" and in a sense the point of the whole poem.

It is appropriate, therefore, that Hopkins proceeds in "No worst" to invoke the "mountains" of the mind, more properly the imagery of the *Purgatorio* than of the *Inferno*. Hopkins's imagery of "cliffs of fall," that "steep or deep" which is "no-man-fathomed," also refers to the mountain of Purgatory as well as the abyss of hell, for both are ringed with cliffs.

Admittedly, in the first circle of hell Dante found himself on the brink of the abyss of sorrow, the *abisso dolorosa*, resounding with the infinite cries of woe, so deep and dark that the bottom could not be fathomed (4:7–12). This "steep of grief" is said to pack and crowd—huddle and herd together, Hopkins would say—all the evil of the universe (7:17–18) and is thus an "alpine steep" to be shunned by everyone because of what it contains (12:1–3). Hopkins's sense of "cliffs of fall" into this "steep" is particularly reminiscent of Dante, because after being assigned to their positions in Hell, souls are flung downward into this abyss and many of the cantos of the *Inferno* conclude with similar falling motions.

Yet this imagery of a possible fall back into Hell is also that of the ascent of the mountain in the *Purgatorio* (13:80). When Dante and Virgil come to the foot of the mountain, for instance, they find a "cliff so steep that the nimblest legs would have been useless on it" (3:46–51). The canto of the *Purgatorio* that concludes "I can no more," the phrase cited in "Carrion Comfort," also begins with the image of a cliff more solitary than a desert where the weary, uncertain Dante and Virgil find themselves between a sheer "steep" and the edge of an empty void (10:19–23). Hopkins's reference to Mary in "No worst" also invokes the context of the *Purgatorio* more than that of the *Inferno*, for on all the terraces of Purgatory she is cited as the first example of the virtue to be achieved. In addition, Hopkins's phrases, "No lingering" and "be brief," recall the adjurations against weariness and *acedia* throughout the *Purgatorio* as well as the *Inferno*.

The most obvious allusion to the *Purgatorio* in the sonnets of desolation, however, is the phrase "I can no more" in "Carrion Comfort," the sonnet found on the same manuscript page as "No worst, there is none." The phrase is in quotes in the poem, moreover, a clear invitation to consider who may have said it before. It is an echo of Newman's "The Dream of Gerontius," for instance, with

Newman's attendant imagery of bending over "the dizzy brink / Of some sheer infinite descent" (ll. 107–12) also invoked. "I can no more" is also the last phrase of Katherine in Shakespeare's *Henry VIII* and no doubt the phrase has echoed throughout the centuries. The themes of "Carrion Comfort," however, along with its Dantesque imagery of feasting on carrion, untwisting strands of self, a devouring lion, and a winnowing tempest, all suggest a more important allusion.

The phrase "I can no more" appears in a very prominent place in the *Purgatorio:* these are the final words of the first canto devoted to the first sin, pride, one of Hopkins's most serious temptations. The next canto in fact represents situations uncomfortably close to Hopkins's own: the pride of a poet and of a "Pre-Raphaelite" painter, with the focus narrowing to the speaker's own pride in his own poetry.

Such pride was closely connected to the *acedia* lamented in "No worst," moreover. Gregory the Great traced the roots of *tristitia* or world sorrow to pride, and Bernard explained that impotence and God's apparent withdrawal from the soul were caused by pride, for which the soul was being punished. The connection between pride and *acedia* became particularly obvious in the romantics. Pride was evident not only in their attempt at self-deification, but even in their pose of ennui, for it was a claim to greater sensitivity, especially in the works of Jean Jacques Rousseau, Chateaubriand, Alphonse de Lamartine, Byron, Senancour, Giacomo Leopardi, Arthur Schopenhauer, and Paul Valéry.

It is to conquer this kind of pride that the lion, presumably the "lion of Judah," rocks the speaker of "Carrion Comfort" with his "wring-world right foot" and scans his "bruised bones" with "darksome devouring eyes." As in *The Wreck of the Deutschland* and "No worst, there is none," God merges with the storm in "Carrion Comfort." In this poem the purpose of the trial is clear: God fans "in urns of tempest, me heaped there, me frantic to avoid thee and flee? / Why? That my chaff might fly; my grain lie, sheer and clear."

The text is Luke 3:17, upon which Hopkins meditated on other occasions as well (*S,* 267–68). In this and in his other sonnets of desolation, including "No worst," Hopkins frequently alludes to the New Testament. It is the ultimate context of Hopkins's purgation, as it was of Dante's, and of course Hopkins knew it even more intimately than he knew the *Divine Comedy*. One of the biblical incidents echoed in the imagery and phraseology of "No worst," for instance, is that of the exorcism of the demons of Gadara. Like the victim in Hopkins's poem they have "seized on him a great many times" (Luke 8:29). To get rid of them Hopkins invokes the "Comforter," another name for the Holy Spirit, the power by which devils are exorcised (Acts 10:38).

But the most striking echo is Hopkins's metaphor of many cries being herded together, followed by his imagery of the mountain and the cliffs of fall. First of all, the multitude of demons—"My name is legion for there are many of us"—corresponds to the traditional sense of a multitude of causes of *acedia*, also known as the "demon" of noontide. Jesus then heaves the demons out of the victim and huddles them together in a "herd" of pigs on the "mountain." The devils plead with Jesus "not to order them to depart into the Abyss" (Luke 8:31), but He orders them off the cliff, they fall, and return to the dark underworld until the Day of Judgment (2 Pet. 4).

Like the imagery of the *Purgatorio,* this exorcism imagery obviously provides a significant counterpoint of meaning in "No worst, there is none." The suggestion is that the speaker is attempting to herd and huddle all the demons of ennui together in one category and heave them out of himself. This is essentially the same function performed by Dante's descent into Hell: facing the demons of self in order to exorcise them, for the "state of souls after death" in the *Inferno* is "the *forma perfectior,* the fulfilment of their state in this life."[19] Thus we may argue that Hopkins wrote a seminal romantic poem of ennui in order that, following Dante, he could face the *forma perfectior* of this spiritual disease in himself and exorcise it.

Hopkins's poems are especially suited to this cathartic, purging function because they are prayers as well as poems. Like Jesus' cry on the cross, Hopkins's sonnets of desolation are addressed to God and are themselves consolations. As Augustine put it, "unless we mourned in Thine ears, we should have no hope left. Whence then is sweet fruit gathered from the bitterness of life, from groaning, tears, sighs, and complaint?"[20] John Donne discovered in "La Corona" that *acedia* could create this "holy discontent" which leads to devotion: "Deign at my hands this crown of prayer and praise, / Weav'd in my low devout melancholy." Similarly, like the Psalms, even when they lament God's distance from the speaker, as renewals of spiritual commitment, Hopkins's prayers themselves help decrease that distance. Perhaps Hopkins's favorite metaphysical poet, George Herbert, expressed this paradox best in "The Pulley" which concludes, "wearinesse / May tosse him to my breast."

The most important connection between Herbert, Donne, and Augustine, of course, is that they were all dedicated to the imitation of Christ. If Jesus' cry on the cross is the prime example of world sorrow, Jesus was their ultimate paradigm for purging it. If it is true that "Chief" in Hopkins's phrase, "chief-woe," by its etymology suggests Christ as the "head" of the church, the implication is that the "chief-woe" is one that Christ Himself had experienced. As we have seen, *The Teaching of The Types* reminded Hopkins that Jesus "was once the Man of Sorrows and is ever the Man of Sorrows."

In his poem, "The Mount of Olives," Alfred de Vigny also focused on Jesus on the way to Gethsemane, "Sad unto death, his gaze somber and melancholy." Similarly, Bishop Bossuet, one of the most popular preachers of the seventeenth century, in a sermon for Good Friday remarked that "Ennui casts the soul down into a very particular kind of sorrow, which makes life unbearable and in which every moment becomes a burden. . . . There you have the condition of the Savior of souls on His way to the Mount of Olives."[21] Bossuet and Hopkins would have argued that this was but a stage on the way to the triumph of the Resurrection, however.

The echoes of Dante suggest other parallels with Jesus, the ultimate allusion in Hopkins's devotional poetry obviously. What has been said of the *Divine Comedy* may be said equally of Hopkins's descent into hell in his sonnets of desolation: "What Dante does, in his journey, Christ has done. Dante's descent into Hell, and his release from it, is a typological repetition, a 'subfulfillment' of Christ's." Like Dante's, Hopkins's experience of Jesus' sadness unto death may also be read as a typological repetition, a "subfulfillment" of the *imitatio Christi,* and the final line of "No worst" thus may be seen in the same context as Dante's *Inferno*: "Dante's fore-having of death is now shown to be more than a purgation-process. It is a 'dying with Christ,' taken to an almost literalistic extreme, which revitalizes a phrase grown perhaps overfamiliar." The result is a "paradoxical tension" for such "dying with Christ implies that *resurgi e vinci*," the triumph of the Resurrection.[22] The expectation is that the descent into the inferno will be transformed, by the process of purgatory, into an ascent into paradise.

In other words, the past, by typological allusion, is to be redeemed by the present. The anagogical collapse of time past and time future into a kind of continuous present is indicated by the tenses of the verbs and participles in "No worst." The first verb, the copula "is," is in the present tense, but is followed by the past participle "pitched" (l. 1), then by the future "will," the past "schooled," and finally by "wring" which, though grammatically connected to "will," is so far removed from it in the line that it foreshadows the assimilation of past and future in the present in the next four lines. The climax is the activation of the key allusion to the past by a series of present-tense verbs: "My cries heave . . . huddle in a main, a chief- / woe, world-sorrow; . . . wince and sing— / Then lull, then leave off." The verbs insist on the living presence of the past, its recapitulation in the attempt of the speaker to give birth to a new self modeled on previous selves. Set thus in the resonant context of tradition, the protagonist's dilemma is clearly no longer merely "personal." Deriving its significance from the past and providing an example for the future, it illustrates Eliot's concept of tradition in which "the past should be altered by the present as much as the present is directed by the past."[23]

In this poem Hopkins is obviously no longer merely the Pre-Raphaelite student of Dante, the lecturer citing Dante on meter, or the admirer of Dante's "great work of poetry." At this stage in his life, Hopkins had become a mature poet, not only in Eliot's sense of being able to combine various emotions, but also in his reading of Dante. Dante's imitation of Christ is no longer merely a vicarious experience for him; he now relives Dante's experience of hell and purgatory, earning his right to rediscover paradise. Hopkins the preacher is now practicing what he preached, trying to confront the hell within. The allusions to Jesus, Dante, and other followers of the *imitatio Christi* are no longer merely acquired, merely "literary"; they become the deepest, most personal identification with texts and authors possible. If this is the best example of how to read, it is also the best example of how to write, for Hopkins's revising, his rewriting of these texts, is clearly an attempt to completely and utterly revise and remake himself.

This is the combination of "the timeless and the temporal together" that "makes a writer traditional," as Eliot observed, yet "it is at the same time what makes a writer most acutely conscious of his place in time, of his own contemporaneity."[24] Hopkins's complex use of allusion aligns him with Eliot, W. B. Yeats, Ezra Pound, James Joyce, Virginia Woolf, and that whole "network of allusion that stands as the dominant mode of modern British literature."[25]

Yet there is a significant difference. The allusions in Joyce's *Ulysses* and Eliot's *Wasteland* are ironic, suggesting not so much the connection between past and present as the immeasurable gulf between them. Hopkins's allusions in "No worst" also suggest the ironic contrast between the romantic glorification of *Weltschmerz*, as a proof of sensitivity and a motivation for writing, and the medieval sense of it as one of the deadliest sins, to be resisted with all one's might. But Hopkins is not satisfied with mere irony. Resisting a modernist embrace of the disinheriting future, he also tries to sustain the medievalist's attempt to salvage something from the past. His aim is not merely to diagnose the disease of modern life, but to find a cure, or at least an anodyne.

His allusions are the basis not only of a parody of modern life but also an "antiparody"—the attempt not only to criticize but to elevate the subject.[26] When Hopkins was finding his own style he developed the technique of antiparody to respond to defiantly "modernist" romantic works such as Swinburne's parody of a Marian hymn, "Dolores."[27] When he became a mature poet, Hopkins concentrated many such experiences in "No worst," not merely to create a seminal expression of contemporary ennui, but also an antiparody of the whole *Weltschmerz* syndrome of romanticism and modern humanism. For Hopkins, antiparody and other forms of allusion demonstrate that the gulf between past and present is not immeasurable, that it can be bridged by the genuine identification with one's precursors possible in serious reading and writing.

Of course it could be argued that the last line suggests that Hopkins did not bridge that gulf in "No worst," but "No worst" was not Hopkins's only poem of the 1880s. Most of his other sonnets of desolation are clearly more affirmative, and one of his last poems does indeed suggest that Hopkins's "dying with Christ" gave him a glimpse of that *resurgi e vinci*, the triumph of the Resurrection.

Paradiso

That triumph is celebrated in Hopkins's sonnet of 1888, "That Nature is a Heraclitean Fire and of the comfort of the Resurrection." Apparently a direct reply to "No worst, there is none," the question, "Comforter, where, where is your comforting" is answered in the title of the later poem. *Acedia* has been conquered: "Enough! the Resurrection, / A heart's clarion! Away grief's gasping, joyless days, dejection." In this poem the light is no longer delayed; a new stage has been reached in Hopkins's "Divine Comedy." "A change comes at last like a flood upon the will," Maria Rossetti wrote in her book on Dante, "the craving for agony is satiated; the soul leaps up free for its beatitude." As Dante himself put it, "The inborn and perpetual thirst for the godlike kingdom bore us away. . . . It seemed to me that a cloud covered us, shining, dense, solid and smooth; like a diamond that is smitten by the sun."[28] As we have seen, Hopkins concludes this poem with similar imagery:

I am all at once what Christ is, since he was what I am, and
This Jack, joke, poor potsherd, patch, matchwood, immortal diamond,
      Is immortal diamond.

"The diamond," Pater remarked, "if it be a fine one, may gain in value by what is cut away."[29] One could argue that it was the cutting away, the ascetic commitment to the *imitatio Christi*, that made Hopkins compress so much meaning into the seemingly endless echoes and extraordinarily allusive metaphors of his poems, with the result that they do indeed seem to shine like multifaceted diamonds.

Thus we are left with the final irony that the cries of impotence in Hopkins's sonnets of desolation are themselves the best evidence of the author's potency. Our very familiarity with such lines as "not I build; no, but strain / Time's eunuch, and not breed one work that wakes" ("Thou art indeed just, Lord") gives the lie to the lines, showing that Hopkins did build, that he was not Time's eunuch, that he bred not one, but many works that wake. The "winter world" for which he apologized in "To R. B.," has been revealed, by the help of R. B. (Robert Bridges), to be a spring of burgeoning life. Now, a century after his death, Hopkins no longer "seems the stranger." His "hoard" of words is no longer "unheard, / Heard unheeded" ("To seem the stranger"). Neither "banned" by heaven nor "thwarted" by hell, his poems have long since taken their rightful place in the great tradition to which they so frequently alluded.

Notes and References

Preface

1. Robert Lowell, "Hopkins' Sanctity," in *Gerard Manley Hopkins, By the Kenyon Critics* (New York, 1944), p. 93.

Chapter One

1. Francis Galton, *Hereditary Genius* (New York: Appleton, 1870), pp. 1, 228–29.
2. Launcelot Sieveking, *The Eye of the Beholder* (London: Hulton, 1957), p. 276.
3. See Jerome Bump, "Manual Photography: Hopkins, Ruskin, and Victorian Drawing," *Texas Quarterly* 16, no. 2 (1973): 90–116; for more illustrations of the drawings of Hopkins and his brother Arthur see R. K. R. Thornton, ed., *All My Eyes See: The Visual World of Gerard Manley Hopkins* (Sunderland, 1975).
4. G. F. Lahey, *Gerard Manley Hopkins* (London, 1930), p. 2.
5. *Pietas Metrica; Or, Nature Suggestive of God and Godliness. By the Brothers Theophilus and Theophylact* (London: Master, 1849), p. ix.
6. *The Journals and Papers of Gerard Manley Hopkins*, ed. H. House and G. Storey (London, 1959), p. 332; hereafter cited in the text as *J*.
7. *Further Letters of Gerard Manley Hopkins*, 2d ed., ed. C. C. Abbott (London, 1970), p. 240; hereafter cited as *F*.
8. This and other poems from this volume are reproduced in W. H. Gardner, *Gerard Manley Hopkins (1844–1889): A Study of Poetic Idiosyncrasy in Relation to Poetic Tradition* (London, 1966), 2:3–10.
9. *The Letters of Gerard Manley Hopkins to Robert Bridges*, ed. C. C. Abbott (London, 1970), p. 61; hereafter cited as *B*.
10. *Pietas Metrica*, pp. vii–viii.
11. *The Prelude*, bk. 6:313–14.
12. Baldassare Castiglione, *The Book of the Courtier*, trans. Sir Thomas Hoby (London: David Nutt, 1900), p. 92.
13. Henry Peacham, *The Compleat Gentleman*, ed. V. B. Heltzel (Ithaca: Cornell University Press, 1962), pp. 127–28.

14. Francis Fike, "Gerard Manley Hopkins' Interest in Painting after 1868," *Victorian Poetry* 8, no. 4 (1970): 317—a useful article written before comparisons of Gerard's and Arthur's sketches were made.

15. Lahey, p. 2.

16. John Eagles, *The Sketcher* (London: Blackwood, 1856), p. 97—for other connections between drawing and religion see pp. 146–47, 210.

17. Gardner, 1:13.

18. See *Journals,* pp. 112, 269; *Bridges,* pp. 81, 202, 206, 267; *The Correspondence of Gerard Manley Hopkins and Richard Watson Dixon,* ed. C. C. Abbott (London, 1970), pp. 3, 55, 61; hereafter cited as *D.*

19. Eagles, p. 169.

Chapter Two

1. See George Ford, *Keats and the Victorians* (New Haven: Yale University Press, 1944) and Jerome Bump, "Hopkins and Keats," *Victorian Poetry* 12, no. 1 (1974):33–43.

2. *The Letters of Matthew Arnold to Arthur Hugh Clough,* ed. H. F. Lowry (London: Oxford University Press, 1932), p. 63.

3. Ibid., p. 97.

4. *The Works of John Ruskin,* ed. E. T. Cook and A. Wedderburn (London: George Allen, 1903–12), 35:311; hereafter cited parenthetically in the text as in (35:311).

5. Henry Ladd, *The Victorian Morality of Art* (New York: Long and Smith, 1932), pp. 149, 159.

6. See Bump, "Manual Photography," p. 101.

7. John Nicoll, *The Pre-Raphaelites* (London: Dutton, 1970), p. 98.

8. Ibid., p. 125.

9. E. D. H. Johnson, ed. *The Poetry of Earth* (New York: Atheneum, 1974), pp. vii, ix.

10. Compare *Journals,* pp. 142–44, 165, 199, 201 with Philip Gosse's *A Year at the Shore* in E. D. H. Johnson, pp. 274, 277, 280.

11. Compare *Journals,* p. 228, for example, with Knapp or Waterton in E. D. H. Johnson, pp. 199–241.

12. See *The Diaries of John Ruskin,* ed. Joan Evans and J. H. Whitehouse (Oxford: Clarendon Press, 1956–59), 1:58–59 and *Kilvert's Diary,* ed. William Plomer (London: J. Cape, 1938), 1:308–9.

13. Ruskin, *Works,* 4:164–73; 7:22; 10:203; 15:119; for more on Ruskin's influence see Francis Fike, "The influence of John Ruskin upon the aesthetic theory and practice of Gerard Manley Hopkins" (Ph.D. diss., Stanford University, 1963).

14. *Journals,* p. 60; Walter Bagehot, "Wordsworth, Tennyson, and Browning; or Pure, Ornate, and Grotesque Art in English Poetry," in *Literary Studies* (London: Longmans, 1911), 2:319, 327; J. C. Shairp, "Wordsworth: The Man and the Poet," *North British Review* 81 (1863): 31–33.

15. *Journals,* pp. 244–48; see Jerome Bump, "Hopkins, Millais, and Modernity," *Hopkins Quarterly* 2, no. 1 (1975):5–19.

16. C. R. S. Harris, *Duns Scotus* (Oxford: Clarendon Press, 1928), 2:16–17, 24; Efrem Bettoni, *Duns Scotus,* trans. B. Bonansea (Washington: Catholic University of America Press, 1961), pp. 54–56, 58, 62–63.

17. Duns Scotus, *Philosophical Writings,* trans. A. Wolter (Edinburgh: Nelson, 1962), pp. 32–33, 28, 19.

18. *The Sermons and Devotional Writings of Gerard Manley Hopkins,* ed. Christopher Devlin (London, 1967), p. 290; hereafter cited as *S.*

19. John Keating, *The Wreck of the Deutschland: An Essay and Commentary* (Kent, 1963), p. 62.

20. David Downes, "Hopkins and Thomism," *Victorian Poetry* 3 (1965): 270–72.

21. Bettoni, pp. 64, 122–23.

Chapter Three

1. Matthew Arnold, "Preface," in *Essays in Criticism,* 1st ser. (Boston: Ticknor and Fields, 1865), p. xv.

2. See Jerome Bump, "Hopkins, Pater, and Medievalism," *Victorian Newsletter* 50 (1976):10–15, and "Art and Religion: Hopkins and Savonarola," *Thought* 50 (1975):135–36.

3. For the impact of her presence on Swinburne see Georges Lafourcade, *La Jeunesse de Swinburne* (London: Oxford University Press, 1928), 1:174–76.

4. Oscar Kuhns, *Dante and English Poets from Chaucer to Tennyson* (New York: Holt, 1904), p. 182; for a similar interpretation of Dante's love for Beatrice see James Russell Lowell's response to Maria Rossetti's book on Dante in *Among My Books* (Boston: Houghton Mifflin, 1904), pp. 85, 95, 105.

5. Christina Rossetti, "Dante, the Poet Illustrated out of the Poem," *Century Magazine* 27, no. 4 (February 1884):566–73.

6. Geoffrey Hartman, "Introduction" in *Hopkins, A Collection of Critical Essays,* ed. Geoffrey Hartman (Englewood Cliffs, 1966), p. 13.

7. Cited by Rayner Unwin, "Keats and Pre-Raphaelitism," *English* 8, no. 47 (1951):233.

8. Campion Ms. D. V., "On the true idea and excellence of sculpture," p. 4; even Arthur Hallam, the defender of Tennyson's early Keatsian poetry, called for a "marriage of religion with literature" (*The Writings of Arthur Hallam*, ed. T. H. Vail Matter [New York: Modern Language Association, 1943], p. 234).

9. Bodley Mss. Engl. poet. d. 149, 150.

10. For more on these and related paintings see Susan P. Casteras, "Virgin Vows: The Early Victorian Artists' Portrayal of Nuns and Novices," *Victorian Studies* 24, no. 2 (1981):157–84.

11. Campion Ms. D. VI., "How far may a common tendency be traced in all pre-Socratic philosophy?" p. 9; Campion Ms. D. XI., "Connection of the Cyrenaic Philosophy with the Cyrenaic Morals," p. 7; "The Position of Plato to the Greek World," *Journals*, p. 116.

12. D. M. Stuart, *Christina Rossetti*, English Association Pamphlet, no. 78 (London: H. Milford, Oxford University Press, 1931), p. 5.

13. Walter Houghton, *The Victorian Frame of Mind* (New Haven: Yale University Press, 1957), p. 65.

14. Alexis Rio, *The Poetry of Christian Art* (London: T. Bosworth, 1854), p. 240. For more on Hopkins and Savonarola see note 2.

15. Walter Pater, "Winckelmann," *Westminster Review*, n.s. 31 (1867): 106; for more on Hopkins and Pater see David Downes, *Victorian Portraits: Hopkins and Pater* (New York, 1965), and note 2.

16. Rio, p. 255.

17. Walter Pater, "Poems by William Morris," *Westminster Review* 90, n.s. 34 (1868):303.

18. Walter Pater, "Dante Gabriel Rossetti," in *Appreciations* (London: Macmillan, 1910), p. 212.

19. See Jerome Bump, "Hopkins, Christina Rossetti, and Pre-Raphaelitism," *Victorian Newsletter* 57 (1980):2–3.

20. Pater, *Appreciations*, pp. 212–13.

Chapter Four

1. "Let me be to Thee as the circling bird," l. 9.

2. For this poem as a dramatic monologue see Florence K. Riddle, "Hopkins' Dramatic Monologues," *Hopkins Quarterly* 2, no. 2 (1975): 64, and Elsie Phare, *The Poetry of Gerard Manley Hopkins* (Cambridge, 1933), p. 66. Hopkins's first version of his Dorothea poem, "For a Picture of St. Dorothea," no. 10 in *Poems*, was composed in 1864 and will be designated as version I. His second version, "Lines for a Picture of St. Dorothea: Dorothea and Theophilus," no. 25 in *Poems*, is undated, and will be

designated as version II. His third version, "St. Dorothea (Lines for a Picture)," which is appendix A in *Poems*, will be designated as version III.

3. See Virginia Surtees, *The Paintings and Drawings of Dante Gabriel Rossetti* (Oxford: Clarendon Press, 1971), p. 12; William Sharp, *Dante Gabriel Rossetti, A Record and Study* (London: Macmillan, 1882), p. 270; *The Poetical Works of Christina Georgina Rossetti*, ed. William Michael Rossetti (London: Macmillan, 1928), pp. 216–17; *The Swinburne Letters*, ed. Cecil Lang (New Haven: Yale University Press, 1959), pp. 1, 38; K. L. Goodwin, "An Unfinished Tale from *The Earthly Paradise*," *Victorian Poetry* 13, nos. 3 and 4 (1975):91–102.

4. *Further Letters*, p. 214; *Journals*, p. 31; one of Hopkins's contemporaries even suggested that painting was more Hopkins's "natural bent" than poetry or religion: *The Austral Edition of the Selected Works of Marcus Clarke*, ed. Hamilton MacKinnon (Melbourne: Ferguson and Mitchell, 1890), p. 308.

5. Campion Ms. D. VI., "Is the difference between *apriori* and *aposteriori* truth one of degree only or of kind," pp. 2–3.

6. Philip Collins, *Reading Aloud, A Victorian Metier* (Lincoln: Tennyson Research Centre, 1972), pp. 10, 27. For a personal account see M. V. Hughes, *A London Child of the 1870's* (London: Oxford University Press, 1977), pp. 75–76, 109–10.

7. Ms. University of Texas at Austin; reprinted in *Hopkins Research Bulletin* 4 (1973):6–12.

8. Jean H. Hagstrum, *The Sister Arts: The Tradition of Literary Pictorialism from Dryden to Gray* (Chicago: University of Chicago Press, 1958), p. 29.

9. *Keble's Lectures on Poetry*, trans. E. Francis (Oxford: Clarendon Press, 1912), 1:47–48.

10. M. H. Abrams, *The Mirror and the Lamp* (New York: W. W. Norton, 1958), pp. 50–51, 91–94; John Hollander, *Vision and Resonance, Two Senses of Poetic Form* (New York: Oxford University Press, 1975), pp. 23–24. See especially Wordsworth's "Ode on the Power of Sound," Shelley's "Ode to a Skylark," and the endings of Keats's Autumn and Nightingale Odes.

11. Hollander, pp. 12–13, 21.

12. Walter Pater, *Plato and Platonism* (London: Macmillan, 1912), p. 70.

13. See L. M. Findlay, "Aspects of Analogy: The Changing Role of the Sister Arts Tradition in Victorian Criticism," *English Studies in Canada* 3, no. 1 (1977):52; William Wordsworth, *The Prelude*, 14:59–62 (1850).

14. Longinus, *On the Sublime*, trans. B. Einarson (Chicago: Packard, 1945), p. 68; Newman, *Idea of a University*, 9th ed. (New York: Longman, Green, 1889), p. 139.

15. See Gerald L. Bruns, *Modern Poetry and the Idea of Language* (New Haven: Yale University Press, 1974), p. 93.

16. Anna Jameson, *Sacred and Legendary Art* (London: Longman, 1848), 1:62.

17. Walter Ong, *The Presence of the Word* (New York: Simon and Schuster, 1970).

18. "Hopkins' Paradigms of Language," *Victorian Newsletter*, no. 59 (1981), 17–21.

19. See James Leggio, "Hopkins and Alchemy," *Renascence* 29 (1977): 115–30.

20. Philip Wheelwright, *Metaphor and Reality* (1962; reprint, Bloomington: Indiana University Press, 1971), p. 192.

21. *Further Letters*, p. 98; for other examples of Pusey's influence see pp. 28, 30, 93–94, 221, and *Journals*, pp. 16, 60, 71, 137, 299n., 339n., 350n. For the context of their relationship see Alison G. Sulloway, *Gerard Manley Hopkins and the Victorian Temper* (London, 1972), pp. 11, 15, 19–20, 55–58.

22. For Hopkins's familiarity with Keble see *Journals*, p. 60 and *Dixon*, p. 99. There was a copy of *The Christian Year* in the Hopkins family library.

23. See Herbert Sussman, *Fact into Figure: Typology in Carlyle, Ruskin, and the Pre-Raphaelite Brotherhood* (Columbus: Ohio State University Press, 1979); George Landow, *Victorian Types, Victorian Shadows* (Boston: Routledge, Kegan Paul, 1980); and *William Holman Hunt and Typological Symbolism* (New Haven: Yale University Press, 1979); and G. B. Tennyson, *Victorian Devotional Poetry: The Tractarian Mode* (Cambridge: Harvard University Press, 1980).

24. John Henry Cardinal Newman, *Apologia Pro Vita Sua*, ed. David J. DeLaura (New York: W. W. Norton, 1968), p. 21, n.

25. John Keble, "On the Mysticism Attributed to the Early Fathers of the Church," no. 89 in *Tracts for the Times, By Members of the University of Oxford* (London: Rivington, 1840), 6:166.

26. Newman, *Apologia*, pp. 27–28; see G. B. Tennyson, "The Sacramental Imagination," in *Nature and the Victorian Imagination*, ed. U. C. Knoepflmacher and G. B. Tennyson (Berkeley: University of California Press, 1977), pp. 370–90; and G. B. Tennyson, *Victorian Devotional Poetry: The Tractarian Mode*.

27. See William York Tindall, *The Literary Symbol* (Bloomington: Indiana University Press, 1955), pp. 31–44.

28. *Sermons,* p. 129; Ian Fletcher, "Some Types and Emblems in Victorian Poetry," *Listener* 77 (1967):679–81; Joseph E. Duncan, *The Revival of Metaphysical Poetry* (Minneapolis: University of Minnesota Press, 1959), p. 90.

29. T. S. Eliot, "Tradition and the Individual Talent," in *Selected Prose of T. S. Eliot,* ed. F. Kermode (New York: Harcourt, Brace, Jovanovich, 1975), p. 38.

30. Yvor Winters, "The Poetry of Gerard Manley Hopkins," *Hudson Review* 2 (1949):61–89; Donald Davie, "Hopkins, The Decadent Critic," *Cambridge Journal* 4 (1951):732; F. R. Leavis, *The Common Pursuit* (London: Chatto & Windus, 1952), pp. 51–52; T. J. Kelly, "Gerard Manley Hopkins," *Critical Review* 11 (1968):53; C. X. Ringrose, "F. R. Leavis and Yvor Winters on G. M. Hopkins," *English Studies* 55 (1974):32–42.

31. T. S. Eliot, "Deux Attitudes Mystiques, Dante et Donne," *Le Roseau d'Or* 14 (1927):150–51.

32. See Jerome Bump, "Hopkins' Imagery and Medievalist Poetics," *Victorian Poetry* 15, no. 2 (1977):109.

33. E. B. Pusey, "Lectures on Types and Prophecies of the Old Testament," Ms. Pusey House, Oxford, pp. 14, 19.

34. Though onomatopoetic theories of etymology are less popular now, linguistics still offers support for Hopkins's assumption of a connection between phonic and semantic harmony. Roman Jakobson, for instance, uses Hopkins's poetry to illustrate how "equivalence in sound, projected into the sequence as its constitutive principle, inevitably involves semantic equivalence," "Linguistics and Poetics" in *Essays on the Language of Literature,* ed. S. Chatman and S. R. Levin (Boston: Houghton Mifflin, 1967), p. 314; D. I. Masson discusses Hopkins's extremely high "bond density" in "Thematic Analysis of Sounds in Poetry" in the same volume, p. 55.

35. Pusey, "Lectures on Types," p. 23.

36. Keble, "Tract 89," p. 45; see Sussman, pp. 7–9, 35–41, 137–39.

37. Pusey, "Lectures on Types," p. 107.

38. *Keble's Lectures on Poetry,* 2:481.

39. Pusey, "Lectures on Types," pp. 5–6.

40. *Pietas Metrica,* pp. viii–ix.

Chapter Five

1. Bridges's note to the poem, omitted in later editions. All the stanza numbers are provided in parentheses. I underline the title of this long

poem following Hopkins's example and that of the Milward anthology cited below.

2. J. Hillis Miller, "The Linguistic Moment in 'The Wreck of the Deutschland,' " in *The New Criticism and After,* ed. Thomas D. Young (Charlottesville: University of Virginia Press, 1976), p. 48.

3. "Note F," *Further Letters,* p. 441 (an account from the *Illustrated London News,* December 18, 1875); "Appendix," in *Immortal Diamond,* ed. Norman Weyand (London, 1949), pp. 360, 368 (accounts from the *Times,* December 8–11, 13, 1875).

4. *Further Letters,* p. 440; *Immortal Diamond,* pp. 361–63.

5. *Immortal Diamond,* p. 358.

6. See Paul L. Mariani, " 'O Christ, Christ, Come Quickly!,' Lexical Plenitude and Primal Cry at the Heart of *The Wreck*"; Marcella M. Holloway, " 'The Rarest-Veined Unraveller,' Hopkins as Best Guide to *The Wreck*"; and Kunio Shimane, "Speech Framed to be Heard, The Function and Value of Sound Effects in *The Wreck*"; all in *Readings of the Wreck,* ed. Peter Milward (Chicago, 1976), pp. 32–41, 86–99, 142–53; and Frans Josef van Beeck, "Hopkins' Cor Ad Cor," *The Month* 136, no. 1299 (1975): 340–45.

7. *The Poems of Gerard Manley Hopkins,* ed. W. H. Gardner and N. H. MacKenzie (London, 1970), pp. 45, 49; hereafter cited as *P.*

8. See Collins, p. 25.

9. *Immortal Diamond,* p. 368.

10. George Landow, "Iconography and Point of View in Painting and Literature: The Example of Shipwreck," *Studies in Iconography* 3 (1977): 89.

11. Robert Aitken, *The Teaching of the Types* (Oxford: Shrimpton, 1854), p. 4; *Journals,* p. 60.

12. *Keble's Lectures on Poetry,* 2:482. See also Pusey, p. 24; Newman, Tract 73; Isaac Williams, Tracts 80 and 87.

13. G. B. Tennyson, "The Sacramental Imagination," pp. 373–74; see also his "Tractarian Aesthetics: Analogy and Reserve in Keble and Newman," *Victorian Newsletter* 55 (1979):8–10.

14. "Centenary Celebrations of *The Wreck of the Deutschland,*" *Hopkins Quarterly* 4, no. 2 (1977):70–71, 77–80.

15. Elizabeth Schneider, *The Dragon in the Gate: Studies in the Poetry of Gerard M. Hopkins* (Berkeley, 1968), p. 37. The apparent absence of unity in the poem is also discussed by W. H. Gardner in *Gerard Manley Hopkins,* 2:192; by Todd K. Bender in *Gerard Manley Hopkins, The Classical Background and Critical Reception of His Work* (Baltimore: Johns Hopkins University Press, 1966), p. 83; and by Wendell Stacy Johnson in *Gerard Manley Hopkins, the Poet as Victorian* (Ithaca, 1968), p. 74. The problem

of "the discrepancy between the heightened emotion and its represented cause" is defined by Phare, pp. 70, 109, and by Yvor Winters in *The Function of Criticism* (Denver: Swallow, 1957), pp. 101–57.

16. W. S. Johnson, p. 43.

17. In *The Central Self* (London: Athlone, 1968) Patricia Ball cites *The Wreck* as an example of the "egotistical" romantic convention of self coalescing with object (p. 244) but in her *The Science of Aspects* (London: Athlone, 1971) she also considers Hopkins as a relatively objective poet (pp. 133 ff.). Louis Martz invokes the conventions of meditative poems in *The Poetry of Meditation* (New Haven: Yale University Press, 1962), pp. 321–26. Bender suggests the relevance of Pindar's poetic methods, pp. 71–96. Many critics, including Pick, McNamee, Downes, and Heuser, have emphasized parallels between the poem and *The Spiritual Exercises of St. Ignatius*. W. S. Johnson has suggested that the nervous self-revelation in *The Wreck* makes it a Victorian version of religious poetry (p. 24); Alison Sulloway regards it as a Victorian apocalypse (pp. 158–96).

18. Immanual Kant, "Critik der Urtheilskraft," in *Sammtliche Werke,* ed. Gedan et al. (Leipzig, 1906), 2:93–113.

19. F. R. Leavis, *New Bearings in English Poetry* (London: Chatto and Windus, 1954), p. 176.

20. " 'The Wreck of the Deutschland' and the Dynamic Sublime," *ELH* 41, no. 1 (1974):110–15.

21. Thomas Gray, *Letters,* ed. D. C. Tovey (London: G. Bell and Sons, 1900), 1:45; see Samuel Holt Monk, *The Sublime* (Ann Arbor: University of Michigan Press, 1960), p. 211.

22. *The Autobiography of Charles Darwin,* ed. Francis Darwin (New York: Dover, 1958), p. 65.

23. See Keating, p. 24.

24. See Robert Boyle, "Hopkins' Use of 'Fancy,' " *Victorian Poetry* 10, no. 1 (1972):17–29.

25. See Dante, *Paradiso,* 19:61–64 and Ernst Robert Curtius, *European Literature and the Latin Middle Ages,* trans. W. Trask (New York: Pantheon, 1953), pp. 407–13, 159–62.

26. Kant, p. 93; A. P. I. Samuels, *The Early Life, Correspondence, and Writings of Edmund Burke* (Cambridge: Cambridge University Press, 1923), p. 84; Monk, p. 87.

27. See J. Hillis Miller, *The Disappearance of God* (New York: Schocken, 1965), p. 319, and John Ferns, " 'The Wreck of the Deutschland': Voice and Structure," *Victorian Poetry* 9, no. 4 (1971):383–94.

28. W. S. Johnson, p. 57.

29. Edmund Burke, *A Philosophical Enquiry into our Ideas of the Sublime and the Beautiful,* ed. J. T. Boulton (London: Routledge, 1958), p. 63; see Monk, p. 94.

30. Thomas Carlyle, *Sartor Resartus* (New York: Odyssey, 1937), p. 188; see Landow, " 'Swim or Drown,' Carlyle's World of Shipwrecks, Castaways, and Stranded Voyagers," *Studies in English Literature* 15, no. 4 (1975):641–55.

31. See Alan Heuser, *The Shaping Vision of Gerard Manley Hopkins* (New York, 1968), p. 44.

32. Ms. University of Texas at Austin; reprinted in Jerome Bump, "Providence, 'The Wreck of the Deutschland,' and a New Hopkins Letter," *Renascence* 31, no. 4 (1979):195–97.

33. Mary Adorita, "Wings that Spell," *MLN* 70, no. 5 (1955):345–47.

34. This conventional phrasing of the concept of providence was used by Leo XIII, among others, Pope at the time this letter was written, in his encyclical, *Libertas Praestantissimum*: E. J. Carney, "Theology of the Providence of God," in *New Catholic Encyclopedia* (New York: McGraw-Hill, 1967), 11:917–19.

35. Even such an ardent admirer as W. H. Gardner regards stanzas 22–23 as an "amazing 'metaphysical' digression" reminiscent of "Donne and Crashaw" (1:63).

36. Kim Malville, *A Feather for Daedalus: Studies in Science and Myth* (Menlo Park: Cummings, 1975), p. 142; see also Fritjof Capra, *The Tao of Physics* (New York: Bantam, 1977), pp. 31, 80, 133, 177, 230.

Chapter Six

1. Herbert Marshal McLuhan, "The Analogical Mirrors," in *Gerard Manley Hopkins: The Windhover,* ed. John Pick (Columbus, 1969), p. 24.

2. See Abrams, pp. 239–41.

3. M. L. Grossman and J. Hamlet, *Birds of Prey of the World* (New York: C. N. Potter, 1964), p. 407.

4. Paul Mariani, *A Commentary on the Complete Poems of Gerard Manley Hopkins* (Ithaca, 1970), p. 111.

5. Ibid., p. 112; see also David J. DeLaura, "Hopkins and Carlyle: My Hero, My Chevalier," *Hopkins Quarterly* 2, no. 2 (1975):67–76.

6. Grossman and Hamlet, p. 79.

7. Michael Sprinker, *'A Counterpoint of Dissonance'; The Aesthetics and Poetry of Gerard Manley Hopkins* (Baltimore, 1980), pp. 12–13.

8. A. C. Charity, *Events and their Afterlife* (Cambridge: Cambridge University Press, 1966), p. 168.

9. See D. W. Robertson, *A Preface to Chaucer* (Princeton: Princeton University Press, 1962), pp. 301–2; Claude Tresmontant in William E. Lynch, *Christ and Apollo* (New York: Sheed and Ward, 1960), pp. 219–20; and Georges Poulet, *Studies in Human Time,* trans. E. Coleman (Baltimore: Johns Hopkins University Press, 1956), pp. 6–7.

10. Henry de Lubac, *Exégèse Médiévale,* vol. 4 (Paris: Aubier, 1964), pp. 172–77.

11. John Chydenius, *The Theory of Medieval Symbolism* (Helsingfors: Societas Scientiarum Fennica, 1960), pp. 19, 29.

12. See Sulloway, *Gerard Manley Hopkins and the Victorian Temper,* pp. 158–95. For a parallel with Wordsworth see M. H. Abrams, *Natural Supernaturalism: Tradition and Revolution in Romantic Literature* (New York: W. W. Norton, 1971).

13. McLuhan, p. 23.

14. Chydenius, pp. 13, 15.

15. Stephen Manning, "Scriptural Exegesis and the Literary Critic," in *Typology and Early American Literature,* ed. Sacvan Bercovitch (Amherst: University of Massachusetts Press, 1972), p. 64.

16. *The Spiritual Exercises of St. Ignatius,* trans. A. Mottola (New York: Doubleday, 1964), p. 104.

17. Ford Madox Hueffer [Ford], *The Pre-Raphaelite Brotherhood* (London: Duckworth, 1907), p. 164.

18. See Miller, *The Disappearance of God,* pp. 298–305.

19. Henry D. Thoreau, *Walden and Civil Disobedience,* ed. Owen Thomas (New York: W. W. Norton, 1966), p. 57.

20. Ibid., pp. 87, 166.

21. See Jerome Bump, "Hopkins, the Humanities and the Environment," *Georgia Review* 28, no. 2 (1974):238–39.

22. Aldous Huxley, *Literature and Science* (New York: Harper and Row, 1963), pp. 53–54.

23. Robert Langbaum, *The Modern Spirit* (New York: Oxford University Press, 1970), pp. 109, 102–3.

24. See Jerome Bump, "Science, Religion, and Personification in Poetry," *Cahiers Victoriens & Edouardiens,* no. 7 (1978):123–37; and Max Black, *Models and Metaphors* (Ithaca: Cornell University Press, 1962).

25. See Sigurd Burkhardt, "Poetry and the Language of Communion," in *Hopkins,* ed. Hartman, pp. 160–67, and Jerome Bump, "Stevens and Lawrence: The Poetry of Nature and the Spirit of the Age," *Southern Review* 18, no. 1 (1982):44–61.

26. See "Preface," note 1.

Chapter Seven

1. Gardner, 2:330.

2. Siegfried Wenzel, *The Sin of Sloth: Acedia in Medieval Thought and Literature* (Chapel Hill: University of North Carolina Press, 1967), pp. 158–59. My account of *acedia* relies primarily on Wenzel and Reinhard Kuhn, *The Demon of Noontide, Ennui in Western Literature* (Princeton: Princeton University Press, 1976).

3. Yvor Winters, "Gerard Manley Hopkins" in Hartman, pp. 41, 38, 46.

4. Sister Mary Humiliata, "Hopkins and the Prometheus Myth," *PMLA* 70, no. 1 (1955):58.

5. T. S. Eliot, "Tradition and the Individual Talent," p. 38.

6. Ibid., p. 43.

7. Francis Fike, "The Problem of Motivation in 'No Worst, There is None,' " *Hopkins Quarterly* 2, no. 4 (1976):175–76.

8. Winters, p. 40.

9. See David Downes, *Gerard Manley Hopkins: A Study of His Ignatian Spirit* (New York, 1959), pp. 115–16.

10. A. Alvarez, *The Savage God* (New York: Bantam, 1972), p. 197.

11. See notes on typology above, especially Landow, Sussman, and G. B. Tennyson, as well as Michael Wheeler, *The Art of Allusion in Victorian Fiction* (London: Macmillan, 1979) and Jane Vogel, *Allegory in Dickens* (Tuscaloosa: University of Alabama University Press, 1977).

12. Gardner, 1:175–79, and Peter Milward, *A Commentary on the Sonnets of G. M. Hopkins* (London, 1970), pp. 109–13, 148–50.

13. Maria Rossetti, *A Shadow of Dante* (Port Washington: Kennikat, 1969), p. 62.

14. *Bridges,* p. 225; *Journals,* pp. 9, 279; *Further Letters,* pp. 257, 359, 296.

15. *The Divine Comedy of Dante Alighieri,* trans. and ed. John D. Sinclair (New York: Oxford University Press, 1979), 1:129–30; all references to Dante are to this edition.

16. Sinclair, 1:56.

17. "Those who proceed intensely in purgating their sins" (*Sermons,* p. 205); on the application of "Purgative Way" and other mystical terms to Hopkins's poetry see Downes, *Gerard Manley Hopkins,* pp. 131–46, and Robert J. Andreach, *Studies in Structure* (New York: Fordham University Press, 1964), pp. 3–38.

18. The birth imagery in "No worst" was first suggested to me by Carolyn Pruett.

19. Charity, p. 202.

20. *Confessions of St. Augustine,* trans. E. B. Pusey (New York: Modern Library, 1949), p. 59.

21. Cited by Kuhn, p. 119.

22. Charity, pp. 244–45.

23. Eliot, "Tradition and the Individual Talent," p. 39.

24. Ibid., p. 38.

25. Avrom Fleishman, *Virginia Woolf: A Critical Reading* (Baltimore: Johns Hopkins University Press, 1975), pp. x–xi.

26. E. E. Kellett, *Literary Quotation and Allusion* (Cambridge: W. Heffer and Sons, 1933), pp. 26–28.

27. Bump, "Hopkins' Imagery and Medievalist Poetics," pp. 106–9.

28. Maria Rossetti, p. 119; *Paradiso,* 2:19–21, 31–33.

29. Pater, *Plato and Platonism,* p. 282.

Selected Bibliography

PRIMARY SOURCES

All My Eyes See: The Visual World of Gerard Manley Hopkins. Edited by R. K. R. Thornton. Sunderland: Coelfrith Press, 1975. Reproduces Hopkins's drawings, along with relevant photographs and paintings; also includes essays on Hopkins and the visual arts.

Correspondence of Gerard Manley Hopkins and Richard Watson Dixon. Edited with notes and an introduction by Claude Colleer Abbott. London: Oxford University Press, 1970.

Further Letters of Gerard Manley Hopkins. 2d ed. Edited with notes and an introduction by Claude Colleer Abbott. London: Oxford University Press, 1970. Includes letters to his mother, to A. W. M. Baillie, and the correspondence with Patmore.

The Journals and Papers of Gerard Manley Hopkins. Edited with notes by Humphry House and Graham Storey. London: Oxford University Press, 1966. Includes diaries, journal, some undergraduate essays, the lecture notes on rhetoric, and a listing of the unpublished manuscripts and their locations.

The Letters of Gerard Manley Hopkins to Robert Bridges. Edited with notes and an introduction by Claude Colleer Abbott. London: Oxford University Press, 1970.

The Poems of Gerard Manley Hopkins. 4th ed. corr. Edited with notes and an introduction by W. H. Gardner and N. H. MacKenzie. London: Oxford University Press, 1970.

The Sermons and Devotional Writings of Gerard Manley Hopkins. Edited with notes and an introduction by Christopher Devlin. London: Oxford University Press, 1967.

SECONDARY SOURCES

1. Bibliographies

Bump, Jerome. "Catalogue of the Hopkins Collection in the Humanities Research Center of the University of Texas." *Hopkins Quarterly* 5, no. 4 (1979): 141–50.

Dunne, Tom. *Gerard Manley Hopkins, A Comprehensive Bibliography.* Oxford: Clarendon Press, 1976. Most comprehensive bibliography to date but terminates 1969–1970. Needs to be supplemented by Schultz and Giles for 1967–1977. For 1978 to the present see the annual bibliographies in the *Hopkins Quarterly* and the sections on Hopkins in the annual bibliographies in *PMLA* and *Victorian Studies*.

Giles, Richard F. "A Hopkins Bibliography: 1974–1977." *The Hopkins Quarterly* 5, no. 3 (1978): 87–122.

Schultz, Susan I. "A Chronological Bibliography of Hopkins Criticism," 1967–1974." *Hopkins Quarterly* 3, no. 4 (1977): 157–83.

Seelhammer, Ruth. *Hopkins Collected at Gonzaga.* Chicago: Loyola University Press, 1970. Describes the extensive collection of secondary sources, as of 1970, in the Crosby Library of Gonzaga University, Spokane, Washington.

2. Concordances

Dilligan, Robert J., and Bender, Todd K. *A Concordance to the English Poetry of Gerard Manley Hopkins.* Madison: University of Wisconsin Press, 1970.

3. Biographies

Bergonzi, Bernard. *Gerard Manley Hopkins.* New York: Macmillan, 1977. An introductory critical biography (Hopkins's poems as they reflect his experience of life) with a final evaluation.

Kitchen, Paddy. *Gerard Manley Hopkins.* New York: Atheneum, 1979. A fairly detailed but somewhat speculative biography.

Lahey, G. F. *Gerard Manley Hopkins.* London: Oxford University Press, 1930. The first biography. Now superseded but accurate in some respects and still useful.

Pick, John, *Gerard Manley Hopkins: Priest and Poet.* 2d ed. New York: Oxford University Press, 1966. A pioneering critical biography relating Hopkins's art to his religion.

Ruggles, Eleanor. *Gerard Manley Hopkins: A Life.* New York: Norton, 1944. An early biography blending fact and fiction.

Thomas, Alfred. *Hopkins the Jesuit: The Years of Training.* London: Oxford University Press, 1969. Very thorough and detailed, but limited to Hopkins's Jesuit training.

4. Commentaries

Keating, John E. " 'The Wreck of the Deutschland': An Essay and Commentary." *Kent State University Bulletin* 51, no. 1 (1963). Excellent essay and line-by-line commentary.

MacKenzie, Norman H. *A Reader's Guide to Gerard Manley Hopkins.* Ithaca: Cornell University Press, 1981. A poem-by-poem commentary with notes, cross-references to other criticism, and bibliography.

Mariani, Paul L. *A Commentary on the Complete Poems of Gerard Manley Hopkins.* Ithaca: Cornell University Press, 1970. A thorough, poem-by-poem analysis.

Martin, Philip M. *Mastery and Mercy: A Study of Two Religious Poems.* London: Oxford University Press, 1957. Brief introduction to Hopkins and commentaries on *The Wreck of the Deutschland* and T. S. Eliot's "Ash Wednesday."

McChesney, Donald. *A Hopkins Commentary: An Explanatory Commentary On the Main Poems.* London: University of London Press, 1968. A line-by-line introduction to the major poems.

Milward, Peter. *A Commentary on G. M. Hopkins' "The Wreck of the Deutschland."* Tokyo: Hokuseido Press, 1968. A useful word-by-word explication.

―――. *A Commentary on the Sonnets of G. M. Hopkins.* London: Hurst, 1970. A useful line-by-line commentary on the sonnets of 1877–1889.

Walliser, Stephen. *"That Nature is a Heraclitean Fire and of the Comfort of the Resurrection": A Case Study in G. M. Hopkins' Poetry.* Berne: Francke, 1977. Line-by-line interpretation of this poem and extended criticism of it.

5. Book-Length Criticism and Interpretation

Boyle, Robert. *Metaphor in Hopkins.* Chapel Hill: University of North Carolina Press, 1960. Analysis of eight significant themes and images in Hopkins's mature poetry.

Cotter, James Finn. *Inscape: The Christology and Poetry of Gerard Manley Hopkins.* Pittsburgh: University of Pittsburgh Press, 1972. Relates Hopkins's poetry and thought to the Christian tradition.

Downes, David A. *Gerard Manley Hopkins: A Study of His Ignatian Spirit.* New York: Bookman, 1959. A good introduction to the role of Christian theology and meditative prayer (especially Ignatian) in Hopkins's life and art.

―――. *Victorian Portraits: Hopkins and Pater.* New York: Bookman, 1965. Discusses the relation between Hopkins, Pater, and romanticism.

Fulweiler, Howard. *Letters from the Darkling Plain: Language and the Grounds of Knowledge in the Poetry of Arnold and Hopkins.* Columbia: University of Missouri Press, 1972. The relation between language and theology in Hopkins.

Gardner, W. H. *Gerard Manley Hopkins (1844–1889): A Study of Poetic Idiosyncrasy in Relation to Poetic Tradition.* 2 Vols. 1949. Reprint. London: Oxford University Press, 1966. This great pioneering work remains the most thorough and comprehensive account of Hopkins's poetry.

Heuser, Alan. *The Shaping Vision of Gerard Manley Hopkins.* London: Oxford University Press, 1958. A concise account of Hopkins's creative vision from 1860 to 1889.

Johnson, Wendell Stacy. *Gerard Manley Hopkins: The Poet as Victorian.* Ithaca: Cornell University Press, 1968. Focuses on the Victorian concern with self and nature in four major poems.

MacKenzie, Norman. *Hopkins.* Edinburgh: Oliver and Boyd, 1968. A good introduction.

Miller, J. Hillis. "Gerard Manley Hopkins." In *The Disappearance of God: Five Nineteenth-Century Writers.* 1963. Reprint. New York: Schocken, 1965. Pp. 270–359. Brilliant, influential, and concise summary of Hopkins's art.

Milroy, James. *The Language of Gerard Manley Hopkins.* London: Andre Deutsch, 1977. Extensive analysis of Hopkins's diction, with a commentary on words used in rare, special or nonstandard senses in Hopkins's poetry.

Peters, W. A. M. *Gerard Manley Hopkins: A Critical Essay Towards an Understanding of His Poetry.* London: Oxford University Press, 1948. A good discussion of Hopkins's diction, especially "inscape" and "instress."

Phare, Elsie. *The Poetry of Gerard Manley Hopkins: A Survey and Commentary.* Cambridge: Cambridge University Press, 1933. Still useful for comparisons with other poets, especially Crashaw and Wordsworth.

Ritz, Jean-Georges. *Le Poète Gérard Manley Hopkins, S.J., 1844–1889: L'Homme et L'Oeuvre.* Paris: Didier, 1963. Very thorough account with a detailed chronology of Hopkins's life and art.

Robinson, John. *In Extremity: A Study of Gerard Manley Hopkins.* Cambridge: Cambridge University Press, 1978. Good on the sixties and the eighties, uneven on Hopkins's religion, *The Wreck of the Deutschland,* and "The Windhover."

Schneider, Elizabeth W. *The Dragon in the Gate: Studies in the Poetry of G. M. Hopkins.* Berkeley: University of California Press, 1968. Especially good on style and metrics.

Sherwood, H. C. *The Poetry of Gerard Manley Hopkins.* Oxford: Blackwell, 1969. A good short introduction.

Sprinker, Michael. *"A Counterpoint of Dissonance": The Aesthetics and Poetry of Gerard Manley Hopkins.* Baltimore: Johns Hopkins University Press, 1980. A "poststructuralist" and "deconstructionist" reading of Hopkins as a "sort of 'Victorian Mallarmé.' "

Storey, Graham. *A Preface to Hopkins.* London: Longman, 1981. A succinct, illustrated introduction.

Sulloway, Alison G. *Gerard Manley Hopkins and the Victorian Temper.* London: Routledge and Kegan Paul, 1972. A good account of Hopkins as a Victorian, especially the religious controversies at Oxford, the apocalyptic mood, the influence of Ruskin, and the ideal of being a gentleman.

Thornton, R. K. R. *Gerard Manley Hopkins: The Poems.* London: Edward Arnold, 1973. A concise, insightful introduction.

Walhout, Donald. *Send My Roots Rain: A Study of Religious Experience in the Poetry of Gerard Manley Hopkins.* Athens: Ohio University Press, 1981. Excellent analysis of the stages of Hopkins's spiritual development.

6. Collections of Essays

Bottrall, Margaret, ed. *Gerard Manley Hopkins' Poems: A Casebook.* London: Macmillan, 1975. Short selections from a century of criticism, including Richards, Empson, Read, and Eliot.

Gerard Manley Hopkins, By the Kenyon Critics. New York: New Directions, 1945. A good early collection, including Warren, Miles, Lowell, and Leavis.

Hartman, Geoffrey H. ed. *Hopkins: A Collection of Critical Essays.* Englewood Cliffs: Prentice-Hall, 1966. Many classic selections, including Leavis, Winters, Bridges, McLuhan, Miller, Hartman, Ong, and Burkhardt.

Milward, Peter, ed. *Readings of "The Wreck": Essays in Commemoration of the Centenary of G. M. Hopkins' "The Wreck of the Deutschland."* Chicago: Loyola University Press, 1976. An excellent set of essays commissioned for this occasion.

Pick, John, ed. *Gerard Manley Hopkins: "The Windhover."* Columbus: Merrill, 1969. Excellent selection of criticism on the poem, including Richards, Empson, McLuhan, Winters, Grigson.

Scott, Carolyn and James, eds. *Gerard Manley Hopkins*. St. Louis: Herder, 1975. Essays by Miller, Downing, McNamee, Templeman, Stobie, and Mellown.

Weyand, Norman, ed. *Immortal Diamond: Studies in Gerard Manley Hopkins*. London: Sheed and Ward, 1949. Essays by members of the Society of Jesus, including Boyle, Noon, and Ong, and Schoder's "Glossary of Difficult Words in Hopkins' Poems."

Index